UNVEILING JESUS
Beholding Him in His Amazing Grace

ParresiaMinistries.com

UNVEILING JESUS
Beholding Him In His Amazing Grace

by
Tricia Gunn

ParresiaMinistries.com

ParresiaMinistries.com

Unveiling Jesus

Beholding Him in His Amazing Grace

Copyright © 2014 Patricia Gunn

ISBN: 9781545583791

Unveiling Jesus LLC

parresia@parresiaministries.com

Produced in the United States of America.

ENDORSEMENTS

I love the title of this book! *Unveiling Jesus* is exactly what Tricia does in this life changing book. The person of Christ and what He accomplished through His finished work is clearly presented and brilliantly expressed. I believe Tricia Gunn will soon become one of the most listened to women in the Body of Christ. I pray that to happen because what she has to say is utterly transformational. Please read this profound presentation of truth that will leave you wanting more from this exceptional teacher!

Clark Whitten
Founder of Grace Church, Orlando, FL , and author of Pure Grace

I am utterly convinced that the cure for the world's woes is a revelation of Jesus Christ. This is why Tricia Gunn's book, *Unveiling Jesus*, is so important. This Biblically-based book will bring freedom and joy to many, including those who have been burdened by expectations and fear. Like a bottle of the finest perfume, this book emanates the sweet fragrance of Jesus. It will leave you resting in the arms of the One who really has done it all.

Paul Ellis
Author of Letters From Jesus; website EscapeToReality.org

Unveiling Jesus is an amazing study that reveals the provision of God for the needs of humanity. It is the story of God's incredible grace that draws us, transforms us and equips us for abundant, victorious life! You won't be disappointed!

Barry Bennett
Dean of Instructors, Charis Bible College, Woodland Park, Colorado

Unveiling Jesus is a classic on grace - from A to Z. It has the full spectrum of what the Bible teaches about grace. After the Bible, it is the best book on grace I have ever read.

Rob Rufus
Pastor of City Church International, Hong Kong

Unveiling Jesus is a banqueting feast inviting the reader to partake of the Lavish Grace of God. Tricia is an outstanding communicator with an effortless style, unveiling truth in such a way as to draw the reader on a journey of discovery and encounters of the extravagance of God's Love, Grace, and eternal plan for them and releasing them through revelation from the treadmill of performance Christianity.

This book brings clarity and gives you a solid foundation to have confidence before God. If you want more of God, this book is for you. If you need clarity on the truths of Grace, this book is for you. If you have labored under guilt and condemnation and disapproval then, YES, this book is for you! Lastly, if you have already been intro-duced to Grace and want to grow deeper in this revelation, this book is for you.

Tricia, thank you for devoting your gift to God to benefit count-less people and bring them into the Freedom Christ paid for. Thank for standing in the midst of many voices and hearing and obeying The One Voice to Unveil this magnificent Message.

Your friend, Glenda Rufus
Wife, Mother, Grandmother
Pastors with her husband, Rob Rufus, at City Church International Hong Kong

Unveiling Jesus is a book uniquely born out of Tricia's heart and experience; yet it demonstrates sound hermeneutic coupled with life-changing insight. There isn't a more important subject today for the church and for the world. Read it now, then read it again. Grace is spreading to more and more people causing everyone it touches to respond with great joy – and God is delighted. (2 Corinthians 4:15)

Bill Snell
President of Missionary Ventures

I have known Tricia for several years and we have, and continue to minister together. I can honestly say that she is one of the most solid grace ministers around, as well as an amazing friend. *Unveiling Jesus* is a life-changing book that will help people receive a solid foundation in grace through the precious Scriptures. Tricia has an amazing way of communicating the Undiluted True Gospel that makes it easy to understand and receive. She lays out all of the Scriptures in such a clear and precise way so all can benefit from understanding our Identity in Christ and experience Jesus in a deeper way.

Unveiling Jesus is perfect for personal study or a Bible Study with a group of people. I have and continue to refer many people to this powerful book and have heard testimonies about how it has caused them to effortlessly fall deeper in love with Jesus as they receive the finished work of the cross and the amazing love that is available to us all and never wavers through Jesus Christ. The truth in this book will help people to experience freedom, especially those who may be struggling with depression, addictions, condemnation and shame, anxiety or past trauma. I highly recommend *Unveiling Jesus*.

Nichole Marbach
Founder, Nichole Marbach Ministries, Author of Hold On to Hope

I believe *Unveiling Jesus* should be required reading for pastors and leaders. A revelation and accurate understanding of grace is necessary to be able to receive God's love and then express that love to hurting people and see them delivered from the power of the dark-ness! It is rare to find a book that is very down to earth and easy to understand, yet filled with sound doctrine that is supported by Scrip-ture. Tricia's passion for the true Gospel of Grace is felt throughout her book. Catch the revelation; catch the passion; and see Jesus for Who He really is!

Mark Machen
Pastor of Life of Faith Church, Birmingham, AL

Tricia makes the Word of God so easy to understand. Line upon line, precept upon precept, and faith to faith. As you read this book, freedom will come to your life because it does just what the title says, it unveils Jesus in His Amazing Grace. Every week I teach inmates from this book. In addition to my weekly study, every night they take this book and have bible studies in their cells. I have seen remarkable changes in their outlooks. From rejection to acceptance, and from feeling un-loved to loved as they gain an understanding of God's unconditional love towards them. I highly recommend this book. It and my Bible go with me wherever I go.

T. R. Harper
Jail Ministry

Through the scriptures unpacked in *Unveiling Jesus*, The Father has sweetly wooed me to release my tightly clenched life and to free-fall into grace. When I finally cast all my weight onto the cross, my life burst into color and dazzling freedom. His spirit began to open my eyes to a living walk with Christ, and ministry became unstoppable. I found myself singing all day about His love and effortlessly sharing the good news everywhere — from the grocery line, to my darling husband and children at home. As He continues to deepen my trust and adoration, even life in a storm has become a beautiful adventure, like clenching the feathers on the back of a soaring eagle. *Unveiling Jesus* has touched my heart deeply. It is nestled among my prized possessions, the lace and pearls of my wedding, because through it I have found that Jesus is my greatest treasure.

Mandii Erwin
Franklin, TN

As I read *Unveiling Jesus*, it's like the sails of my soul open up and I breathe in sync with the Spirit. My appetite for the Word and revelation of my intimacy with Jesus—because of Jesus—springs up as I enjoy each page of this book. Tricia's teaching style, deep understanding of the Father's heart and love of the Word overflows on each page. Grace flows from every sentence in this book.

Leah Waggoner
Parresia Team Member

What you hold in your hands is a gift that I cannot wait for you to open! After 36 years of being a believer, I had learned a lot and assumed I had heard it all when this gift so graciously came to me. I did not even know that I wanted it. As Tricia's message gently un-folded and became revelation for me, everything in the gospel made sense, and it was as if I had been born again once again after all of these years. This message of the finished work of Jesus has changed my family as well. The way we talk, the way we relate, our passions, our motivations, our love, our future, and the way we read the Bible have been transformed by the beautiful message of God's deep love and grace, the gift of his son Jesus. We will never be the same. And we will never tire of it. Enjoy the gift!

Heather Downey
Panel Member of A Real View of the Grace Life

WARNING: DO NOT READ THIS BOOK IF YOU DON'T WANT YOUR LIFE TO BE RADICALLY CHANGED! I am forever grateful for the message in *Unveiling Jesus* that God has given Tricia. I am blown away by her desire to study the scriptures and the revelation that He has given her. It is powerful and contagious. It is miraculous, healing, loving and full of grace. This book is a "must read" – and this revelation is a "must get"!

Laura Vogtle
Birmingham, AL

The magnitude of God's grace and love is something that is impossible to put into words. Once you have experienced how freeing it is to live in grace, you can't fathom falling back in living to please God by your works. When our mom, Tricia, had an amazing grace encounter from God, it not only changed her life, but it changed our whole family's life. This book is an excellent representation of our family's journey of learning about God's grace and how it really can change your life!

Martha Ellen Gunn, Ann Claire Bishop, Frances Gunn, Elizabeth Gunn, Neil Gunn
Tricia's amazing kids

Following is a sampling of the comments of those impacted by the *Unveiling Jesus* video Bible study series:

"My experience thru Unveiling Jesus left me exploding with the love of God. As Tricia tells God's story, I heard my own story thru His heart beat. Healing and freedom flowed in my life as I gazed at Jesus." Leah

"This study has unlocked the mystery and beauty of Jesus in a way I have never seen Him. It has allowed me to understand more clearly the new creation I am and not someone I need to become. There is so much freedom and excitement to share the simplicity of this beautiful mystery with others." Debbie

"Have you ever heard someone proclaim 'this message will change your life' only to be let down time and time again? The gospel of grace is the only message that lives up to the promise of true transformation. Get ready to be transformed!" Connie

"It is powerful and contagious. It is miraculous, healing, loving and full of grace." Laura

"I have never experienced such freedom! Understanding the truths outlined, all scripturally based, tear down the barriers and fill you with a pure awakening of all that He is and all that you are, be-cause of what He has done — the finished work of the cross, and His deep love for you." Sarah

"I have only just started in this wonderful journey with Jesus. Learning to rest in what He has already done for me has forever changed my life. I am so grateful!" Lorrie

DEDICATION

Unveiling Jesus is dedicated to the memory of my mother, Martha Ann Kenny Bland. Thank you, Jesus, for giving me a Mama who taught me about You.

ACKNOWLEDGMENTS

The journey of *Unveiling Jesus* has been one I will cherish forever. I am forever grateful to my Lord Jesus for opening my eyes to His love. There really aren't words to tell the story of how He has changed me and how He has revealed Himself to me, but this book is the beginning of a lifetime of attempting to articulate what I am discovering about my Lord and what it means to be a new creation in Him.

I thank God for my husband Mark, my knight in shining armor, who has encouraged me, protected me, listened to me, and supported me with his unconditional love and partnership throughout the last few years of ardent Bible study and personal transformation. Our wonderful children have been on this journey with us, and nothing brings more joy to a mother's heart than to watch each one grow in amazing grace.

My heart also rejoices in the fellowship of friends around me who have unabashedly embraced undiluted grace. The only thing better than having a revelation of God's grace is having people around you see the same thing. We are having a blast together!

Lastly, I want to acknowledge Bill and Von Jenkins who have partnered with Mark and me to share *Unveiling Jesus* with as many people as we can. They have been the best friends in the world. I've never known a couple so unified and focused on the Gospel of the grace of our Lord Jesus Christ going forth across the world. Together we have big vision for Jesus to be unveiled to the nations. May *Unveiling Jesus* be an instrument that God uses in this revolution of grace!

Tricia Gunn

TABLE OF CONTENTS

Unveiling Jesus is a verse by verse study of the pure gospel of Christ, leaving one forever changed and more in love with their Savior than ever before. It is an amazing journey of love, identity, and freedom in Christ.

I became a believer as a child and grew up attending church on a regular basis. I have lived a blessed life, with a wonderful husband and family. As a wife, mother, and grandmother, I have had very few worries, and have known happiness most of my days.

About five years ago something began to change. The change was subtle, but I began to feel as if I did not love Jesus like I should. Having grown up in church, I knew the commandment "love the Lord your God with all your heart and all your soul and with all your might." It wasn't a question of whether or not I loved Jesus. God had been so good to me — why didn't I love him more?

Through the years I had heard many testimonies of people who had been delivered from addictions or who were going through personal tragedies in their lives. Through the process they cried out to God, and God in His faithfulness met them right at their point of need. The result always seemed to be just a sweet, pure relationship with Jesus.

I longed for that same kind of relationship with Jesus. Yet for me, there was no apparent outward driving force causing me to get to know my Savior in this way. I wanted to know Him more, but I felt almost passive by comparison. Looking back now, I can almost see Jesus smiling. While self-effort couldn't create the drive to love Him more, He through the Holy Spirit was slowly but surely opening my eyes to see Him more clearly and draw me to Himself.

I looked at the many times in Scripture that Jesus said, "I say nothing unless I first hear My heavenly Father say it. I do nothing unless I first see My Father do it." Wow! What a picture of unity — Jesus and the Father — totally one, totally unified. I began asking, "Lord, is it possible for me to know You like that? If it is, please show me."

As I cried out to the Lord, I began to have a better understanding of just what Jesus really accomplished for me when He died on the cross. In the Scriptures I saw clearly the many exchanges of the cross.

- Jesus died — that I might have abundant and eternal life.
- Jesus bruised — that I might be healed.
- Jesus was punished — that I might be forgiven.
- Jesus became poor — that I might walk in abundance.
- Jesus was rejected — that I might be accepted.
- Jesus was shamed — that I might walk in glory.

But the scripture that touched my heart the most was found in 2 Corinthians 5:21: "God made Jesus who knew no sin to become sin for us, that we might become the righteousness of God in Him."

- Jesus became sin — that I might be made righteous.

It was an exchange, a gift from God. All I had to do was believe that He had taken my sin upon Himself, all my sin: past, present, and future. He gave me a gift — His perfect and holy righteousness. It was a gift, not dependent on my behavior or my actions, but on His behavior and His actions. As I pondered all these things and wondered if it could really be true, Jesus seemed to wrap me in His arms of love. In the months that followed, each night as I climbed in bed, tears of joy would stream down my face.

The story of Jesus being baptized in the River Jordan became personal. As Jesus came up out of the water, God the Father said: "This is my Son, whom I love, and in Him I'm well pleased." As I thought about this familiar account, it took on new meaning. It was almost as if I heard the Father say, "Von, you are my daughter (identity), whom I love (acceptance), and because you are in Me, in you I am well pleased (approval)."

As the revelation of how much Jesus loved me unfolded within, everything changed. The questions I had struggled with for five years vanished in a moment. I realized the gospel is all about Jesus: how much He loves me, how much He accepts me, and how He has placed me in Him and in Him I now have full approval. He has forgiven me of all my sins and made me righteous. He became sin with my sinfulness and I became righteous with His righteousness.

Now I find myself thinking about Him all the time with effortless love. The Bible says in 2 Corinthians 3:18 that if we behold Him, He will change us into His image from glory to glory. All we do is "behold Jesus." That's so easy when we understand how much He loves us!

Unveiling Jesus is a must read. The truths from this book will leave you beholding Him, and you will see God's grace in action in your life. It tells the story of God's amazing plan of redemption. The gospel is the power of God unto salvation for all who believe. I believe *Unveiling Jesus* will help you know and experience the pure gospel of Jesus Christ in a way you have never known.

Von Jenkins

INTRODUCTION

One encounter with Jesus, our wonderful Lord, can change everything. It did for me! Just as the blind man said following his encounter with Jesus, I too can say: I was blind and now I see ... and what I have seen I can never un-see for my spiritual eyes now see with greater clarity than ever before.

My Testimony

Several years ago, I was "successful" in ministry according to anyone's standards of measurement. I wrote Bible studies on deliverance and prayer and led conferences that thousands of people participated in. The numbers were good, the momentum was strong, and there was no reason to doubt that the future would be bright. At least that's how it appeared. Yet, with the prospect of such a promising future how and why had I become so discontented?

I was frustrated ... stirred to the point of almost exploding ... so miserable and burnt out ... struggling with my thoughts and desperate for the joy of my salvation to return ... Fasting, praying, worshipping, serving God and the church more and more, trying to fix myself...

And then someone shared a song with me entitled, "Not Guilty Anymore" by Aaron Keyes. The first time I listened to it, something amazing began to happen: my heart began to soften as the truth captured in the song washed over me. Some of the phrases from the song that touched me so deeply said:

It doesn't matter what you've done;
It doesn't matter where you're coming from;
Doesn't matter where you've been;
Hear me tell you I forgive.

You're not guilty anymore,
You're not filthy anymore,
I love you, mercy is yours,
You're not broken anymore.
Can you believe that this is true?
Grace abundant I am giving you.[1]

The lyrics of the song went on with a similar theme to remind me that I am spotless, holy, faultless, whole, righteous, blameless, pardoned, and His forever. I listened to that song hundreds of times over the coming months. No exaggeration, I listened to the song in the car. I listened to it at home. I sang it from the top of my lungs everyday. It was so much a part of all my daily activities that I made everyone else listen to it, too. In fact, it became the theme song of my ministry during that season. I played it at every prayer meeting, every planning meeting, every training meeting, at the conference. But the song was mostly for me. My hard heart was breaking. All my own efforts to "fix myself" were beginning to crumble as I began to understand who I was in Christ.

As weeks turned into months, my heart became more pliable and I was encouraged by what was happening in my life. I was starting to feel alive again spiritually, not realizing that all of this was only preparation for what was ahead.

A Life-Changing Encounter

Then … a few months later, it happened: an encounter with the Lord like I had never had. I was on the beach walking and praying after listening to a message called, "Let's Put the Amazing Back into Grace." Someone had shared the CD with me before I left for my vacation. Normally I wouldn't even have listened to this message — people were always giving me stuff to listen to or read and I never "had time," but God had another plan and this time I listened. The message was on grace, and I had never heard the clarity of the Gospel taught like this before. So much of what I heard in that message was what we would say in church, and it was terminology I had used my entire life as a Christian. Yes, the words were familiar but the message was different … very different.

At that time in my Christian life I was in the habit of praying what was called the "Tabernacle Prayer Format." It's a method of praying where we would symbolically start at the "gate" and end up in the "holy of holies." There we could experience the presence of the Lord. It was "seven steps to the presence of God" and was patterned after the Tabernacle system of priestly sacrifices in the Old Testament. The prayer format included lots of confession of sins and asking for forgiveness, and praying things like, "Search me and know my heart, Lord. Let me know if there is any wicked way in me." After listening to the message on grace, my eyes were beginning to open to this marvelous revelation on the Gospel, and somehow I felt tension in my prayer format. Were there seven steps to the presence of God? I asked the Lord, "Where is the moment of encounter with the Spirit of Grace in my prayer format?" I was getting very close to the encounter with Jesus that I had been waiting for my entire forty-five years of life.

I could sense the presence of the Lord walking with me on the beach, and I heard Him say, "Start at the brazen altar." Eager to obey, I did that. I saw my sin being punished in the body of Jesus. I saw the enormity of His sacrifice and the absoluteness of God's forgiveness. I was touched more deeply than ever before as I let this truth penetrate my heart. After years of teaching others, I was finally getting it myself! I said, "Lord, is this it? Is this the encounter with Grace?" I was a blank slate, and it was as if I was starting all over.

He said, "No, the brazen altar is My mercy. I took the punishment that you deserved. Go on to the laver." The laver in the Old Testament tabernacle was a large bowl, lined with mirrors and filled with water that stood outside the entrance to a tent, which was comprised of two parts, the Holy Place and the Holy of Holies. So the priest would have to wash in the laver before he could take one more step towards the presence of the Lord.

I started my routine "approach-the-laver" prayer: "Search me and know my heart and let me know if there is any wicked way in me..." However, it seemed inappropriate to pray that way because I had just seen the Lamb of God take away my sins at the brazen altar. The Lord said, "STOP praying that, and just look down in the bowl." I stopped and looked down and was blown away. It was the most pivotal moment of my entire life — and continues to be even to this day! I felt like I was born again at that moment! The joy of my salvation returned in an instant! As I looked down through the water into the mirrors of the laver, I saw what Jesus saw: perfected, blameless beauty. It was glorious. And then I was speechless. "But Lord, (and I motioned back to the brazen altar) but Lord! Look at all my sin! This can't be!" He smiled at me.

I looked at Him and I said, "I don't deserve this. This can't be right! This is the most unfair thing I have ever seen!" All of a sudden my first love returned, and I exclaimed, "I love You, Lord. I love You! I will do ANYTHING for You. I want to live for You forever." His response: "Tricia, I just want you to rest." All of the pressure I had felt disappeared. All the heavy burdens fell off, and I felt so free that it seemed almost like I could fly. For me at last there was no more "HAVE to" … no more duty-bound obligations. The need for man's approval, all the exhaustion, the do-do-do mentality, the need to please the Lord all dropped off of my shoulders. With that freedom came the realization that He was pleased with me and had been all along. Nothing else mattered to me at that moment except His love, His acceptance, and His approval.

On the beach that day, Jesus gave me revelation of the great New Covenant reality: by His blood all my sin has been removed. All of my condemnation was nailed to the cross. Now I was like Him, raised and seated in heavenly places. I had known the theological facts, but I encountered the Person of Grace, and my spiritual eyes were opened. In that glorious moment my life changed forever.

Every day since then has been a more amazing day than the one before. Each day has been full of joy explosions on the inside — even when I have messed up, even when I have had trials, even when I have been hurt by others. Ever since that day, I have been hidden in the secure, peaceful wings of my Father. I am under Grace. I am not perfect in my behavior, but I can say this: I am learning what it means to love Jesus with all my heart, all my mind, all my soul, and all my strength as I experience His love for me. However, I am no longer laboring to convince Him or anyone else of that. I love Him that way because I now know that He loved me that way when He took all my sins away and died in my place, and He continues to love me that way every second of every day. I am in a forever season of gratefulness.

Now I know there is only ONE step to the presence of God: the cross of Jesus Christ.

The veil has been torn, and I've entered into God's presence. Now I'm inside ... forever.

> *Yet now he has reconciled you to himself through the death of Christ in his physical body. As a result, he has brought you into his own presence, and you are holy and blameless as you stand before him without a single fault. But you must continue to believe this truth and stand firmly in it. Don't drift away from the assurance you received when you heard the Good News. (Colossians 1:22-23, NLT)*

This is a passage of scripture that I have read countless times over the past few years because it so clearly states what Christ has done for us. Paul wrote this statement to the Colossians to combat dangerous heresies that were becoming popular in the community of Colosse. One of those heresies denied the deity of Christ. Another heresy was the mixing of law with faith for salvation. Paul wanted the believers to know that Jesus Christ, although God, became a man with flesh and blood so that He could die our death and raise us up in Him. Having finished the work for our redemption, we can say we are in His presence NOW. We are blameless and holy NOW. We are without a single fault NOW. Paul pleaded with the Colossian church to stand firm in this truth because the truth sets us free!

A Revelation of Grace

Since this revelation of God's grace began to unfold in my life, I've learned to rest in His timing of the process of discovering His great love for me. There seemed to be so much un-doing that needed to take place from decades of believing a mixed up gospel. I had lost the assurance I had received when I first believed.

For me the revelation of grace was such a paradigm shift, I felt like I needed to relearn almost everything I'd ever been taught. It seemed like everything I knew was from the perspective of an unfinished work. My spirit "got it," but my mind had to be renewed to it. This takes time.

Just so you know, I'm not a theologian. I'm a wife and a mom. I've raised five wonderful children and have been married to the love of my life for twenty-nine years at the time of this writing. My family is the greatest evidence of God's grace in my life, and I wouldn't trade the value of family and real life experiences of God's love and grace for anything that might give me greater credentials in the eyes of man. Out of brokenness and desperation I was immersed in God's grace.

Over the past few years, God has provided time and space for me delve into the scriptures for hours a day to learn about and get to know this amazing Person of Jesus Christ in a way I had never known Him before. He is my Best Friend. No one compares.

I have listened to many teachers of the pure Gospel of grace during this time of immersion in the scriptures. I have many mentors, some whom I have had the privilege of knowing and some whom I have never met, all of whose revelation of God's word have changed my life. They have sown seeds of the truth of God's grace and watered them. These seeds of grace have weathered the storms of hardship and persecution, establishing deep roots of grace in my heart. I can never go back.

We need teachers. It's a God-given gift for the body of Christ, and I thank God for all of them. They have led me on this treasure hunt where I have found one priceless gem after another. In this process, God has given me nuggets of wisdom and revelation in the secret place of His presence that have given me inexpressible joy explosions on the inside and have been so fresh and tailor-made to me that they seemed brand new. However, there is nothing new under the sun. The truth has always been there. I just didn't see it.

Having said that, always search the scriptures out for yourself, and never let any human teacher or preacher take the place of the Holy Spirit.

But the anointing which you have received from Him abides in you, and you do not need that anyone teach you; but as the same anointing teaches you concerning all things, and is true, and is not a lie, and just as it has taught you, you will abide in Him. (1 John 2:27)

While we read books (even this one!), listen to sermons, and attend Bible studies, we need to know that every believer has the indwelling presence and voice of the Holy Spirit. He will guide us into all truth, and if we listen, we will know truth and it will set us free.

My prayer for you as you make your journey through **Unveiling Jesus** is one that the apostle Peter prayed for believers who were dispersed throughout the ancient world of his time:

Grace [the unmerited favor of God] and peace [completeness, soundness, welfare, safety, health, and prosperity] be multiplied to you in the knowledge of God and of Jesus our Lord. (2 Peter 1:2, brackets added for emphasis)

The word "knowledge" in the original language of the New Testament scriptures is the Greek word "epignosis"[2] which means FULL knowledge. It means "a greater participation by the 'knower' in the object 'known,' thus more powerfully influencing him." The fuller the knowledge we have of our Lord Jesus Christ, the more the grace and peace of God will influence us and flow in our lives.

May you experience joy explosions as you get to know our Jesus more and more. I encourage you to rest and allow grace adequate time to grow in your heart. I pray that this study will plant and water seeds that will burst and bring forth the fruit of the Spirit of grace in your life. May grace and truth be exponentially multiplied to you in the intimate knowledge of our Lord Jesus Christ.

CHAPTER ONE

A Revelation of Jesus

Key scriptures:
1 Peter 1:13, Romans 1:16-17, 2 Corinthians 5:21, Titus 2:11-12

Preparing for the Journey

Unveiling Jesus is a series of life-changing nuggets of truth – some small, some large. In the beginning chapters of the book several scripture passages are expounded upon to open our eyes to the pure Gospel of grace, to convey the contrast between religion and grace, to impart understanding regarding the issue of sin, to reveal the role of the Holy Spirit in the life of the believer, and to present the heart of God towards all of us. I think of these beginning nuggets as the "appetizer."

From there the teaching moves more towards the "entrée" with a verse by verse flow of scripture with thorough reflection of the truths outlined, expressions of personal application, and lots of stories. We'll look at the Garden of Eden, the two trees in the garden, the fall of man, and how all of that relates to us today. Next, we'll travel verse by verse through Romans 5, 6, 7, and into chapter 8 following the Apostle Paul's brilliant explanation of federal headship, superabounding grace, union with Christ, and freedom from condemnation. This will lead to an in-depth discussion of the contrast between the Old Covenant of Law and the New Covenant of Grace in 2 Corinthians 3 and several Old Testament passages. Next, we'll study Abraham and what it means that he's the "father of our faith" and how the righteousness of faith is the only way to qualify for salvation and blessing. Then we'll delve into several passages in Galatians where we find Paul's strongest rebukes in the epistles in which he lambasts the mixing of religion with grace and then his teaching on the sonship that we enjoy through grace as opposed to the slavery that results from self-effort. After that we'll gain insights into the eternal value of the blood of Jesus and the significance of the finished work of the cross by journeying through key passages in the book of Hebrews.

The study concludes with "dessert," my favorite part of the meal! I will share the sweet truths of rest, faith, joy, and peace that have marked my life as I have grown in grace. I cannot read these chapters myself without weeping over how much God loves each of us and how much His amazing grace has radically changed my life and those around me. It's my desire that you, dear reader, might experience the same joyful ecstasy and indescribable rest as you behold the Master, Jesus, in the light of His glory and grace. Let's begin the journey!

G.R.A.C.E.

Grace is one of those words that people love making into an acrostic, such as "God's Riches At Christ's Expense" or "God's Redemption At Calvary Expressed." I like those, but when I think of grace, I think of something like a funnel of God's goodness flowing from heaven. I brainstormed and came up with this one:

Gushing
Rivers of
Abundance
Ceaselessly
Emanating from God's throne.

God's throne is called the "throne of grace,"[3] and the river of life flows from His throne to us.[4] Life flows to us because of God's grace — if it weren't for His grace, we would not even be alive! By Jesus, the manifestation of Grace, everything was created. Everything was created by Him, through Him, and for Him; and in Him everything is held together.[5] Jesus lives after the power of an endless life, and that is the life He has given to us by His grace.[6] Jesus told the woman at the well that she would never be thirsty if she drank the living water He was offering.[7] Jesus said that once the Holy Spirit came into the hearts of believers, rivers of living water would flow from our innermost being.[8] All of this speaks of a continuous flow of life. Jesus came to give us abundant God-life, the kind that never ends and never ebbs.

Is your life marked by "gushing rivers of abundance ceaselessly emanating from God's throne?" You might be like I was. I knew the scriptures about grace and abundant life, but there seemed to be something obstructing God's grace in my life. Honestly, I thought it was my sin or the devil; therefore, in order to find the abundant life I was seeking, I focused on those two things and tried to defeat them. In reality, neither my sin nor the devil were blocking God's amazing grace or causing God to withhold His grace from me. His grace is always flowing. My problem was blindness to the truth. I needed an unveiling so my spiritual eyes could behold the immeasurable expanse of God's amazing grace.

The Unveiling

The apostle Peter wrote two letters, which we know as 1 Peter and 2 Peter, to the Christians who had been scattered abroad from Jerusalem because of persecution throughout the country. In Peter's first letter he wrote to encourage them saying,

In this you greatly rejoice, though now for a little while, if need be, you have been grieved by various trials, that the genuineness of your faith, being much more precious than gold that perishes, though it is tested by fire, may be found to praise, honor, and glory at the revelation of Jesus Christ, whom having not seen you love. Though now you do not see Him, yet believing, you rejoice with joy inexpressible and full of glory... (1 Peter 1:6-8)

He then spoke of the Old Testament prophets who prophesied of the GRACE that would come to them and to us today. Those prophets inquired diligently and searched into the timing and the manner in which God would send the Messiah. The Spirit of God had given them some foreknowledge of the sufferings of Christ and the glories to follow, but they wanted to know more. Can you relate, dear reader? Discovering more and more about Jesus is like a treasure hunt that never ends! The more we know Him, the more we know ourselves because our lives are hidden in Him.

Angels even desire to look into this grace because they are merely spectators of this great salvation, but not participants of it. God gave His only begotten Son for human beings who could have cared less about Him, but who were created in His image to bear His glory. Peter went on to say,

Therefore gird up the loins of your mind,... (1 Peter 1:13)

In those days the men wore robes that came down to their feet. The "girdle" was their belt that would hold up their robes, but also it was the place where they would hang their money pouch, their sword, and a short dagger. To "gird up the loins" was a common saying in ancient times denoting readiness for action and watchfulness for enemies.[9] Peter was using the analogy of pulling up long robes that would impede them from running forward. However, Peter was not referring to physical girding. He was talking about removing anything from our minds that might impede our progress or put us in a vulnerable position for attack, things like fear or worry.

"Loins" speak of the part of the body that includes the reproductive system. What Peter was saying is that seeds planted in the mind will reproduce so we need to tighten it up like we are putting on a girdle! He's telling us "Don't let your thoughts go astray." Why? Because our thoughts reproduce. Thoughts of fear or doubt or lust or envy will reproduce if we don't gird up the loins of our mind.

The verb "gird up" is in the Greek aorist tense. This verb tense speaks of a one time action never to be repeated.[10] The Holy Spirit was saying through Peter that the NORMAL state of mind for the believer is one where we have put out of the way once for all anything that would thwart the freedom to think good thoughts, to be positive, to be carefree, to think well of others, and to be at peace. Peter said, "Gird up the loins of your mind" and —

...be sober, and rest your hope fully upon the grace that is to be brought to you at the revelation of Jesus Christ;... (1 Peter 1:13, cont.)

We're to be sober, calm and collected in our spirit,[11] and to completely rest all of our hope — all of our joyful, confident expectation of good in our future — upon one thing and one thing only: GRACE, the unmerited favor of God given to us through Jesus Christ.

As you read this verse, it might seem that the scripture is telling us that this grace will be brought in the future, but the verb sometimes translated "to be brought" isn't in the future tense in the original Greek manuscript. The verb tense is the present passive participle,[12] which means it should be literally worded "is being brought to you."

- Present means it's happening now.
- Passive means you're the recipient.
- Participle tells you how it's happening — on-going — grace is BEING brought!

The word "revelation" is the Greek word "apokalypsis."[13] In Greek dictionaries it is defined as the "unveiling of something hidden, so that it may be seen for what it is."[14] An unveiling of what? Or WHO? JESUS CHRIST!

Let's look at this verse in Young's Literal translation of the Bible:

Wherefore having girded up the loins of your mind, being sober, hope perfectly upon the grace that is being brought to you in the revelation of Jesus Christ. (1 Peter 1:13, Young's Literal Translation)[15]

Grace IS BEING brought to us NOW IN the unveiling of Jesus! This is the purpose of ***Unveiling Jesus***. May you experience "gushing rivers of abundance ceaselessly emanating from God's throne" as the we expound upon and examine the scriptures concerning Jesus Christ.

The Gospel

In Paul's letter to the Romans, he made a very radical statement.

For I am not ashamed of the gospel of Christ, for it is the power of God to salvation for everyone who believes, for the Jew first and also for the Greek. (Romans 1:16)

The word translated "gospel" is a Greek word that was rarely used in the culture of that day. It meant news that was almost too good to be true. There just wasn't a use for such a superlative term in the fallen world and the extreme legalism of that time. This word was "a technical term for news of victory"[16] in the ancient world. Paul used the word "gospel" to describe what Jesus had done, and this was highly offensive to the Jews who were trying to impose the law on the mostly Gentile church at Rome.

The Apostle Paul said he wasn't ashamed. Obviously he had been accused of being shameful for what he believed. It's so simple: our efforts have no power to save us, and our efforts have no power to keep us saved. That certainly was a scandalous idea to embrace in the religious system of Paul's day. What he was saying is that the POWER of God, "dynamis"[17] in the Greek, from which we get the word dynamite, is in the Good News. In my life as a Christian I have been taught many things about how to "get the power of God working" in my life. Paul said I can speak in the tongues of men and angels, have the gift of prophecy, understand all the mysteries of knowledge, have the faith to move mountains, feed the poor, and give my life for Jesus, but all of that work and investment will profit me NOTHING without one vital and priceless thing: receiving the unconditional love of God as demonstrated when He gave His only begotten Son for us.[18] Neither tongues nor prophecy nor faith nor generosity nor martyrdom is the power of God. The Gospel of grace is the power of God for our complete salvation: our wholeness, healing, provision, deliverance, and redemption, now and forever.

What is the Good News? I'll tell you what the Good News is NOT. The Good News is NOT that you hear about Jesus; you believe in Jesus; you love Jesus; you serve Jesus; and you die for Jesus. That's not the Gospel. It's not even close to the Gospel.

The Gospel is that Jesus knew YOU; Jesus loved YOU; Jesus came as YOU; Jesus died as YOU; Jesus rose as YOU so you can be as He is in perfect union with God. That's the Gospel. Jesus served you. He came down, stooped down, and made you one with Him.

The Gospel which says that the blood of Jesus paid our debt and made us righteous before God is the power for our salvation. We are saved when we believe by faith that His blood has washed all of our sins away, and we now have HIS righteousness.

The word translated "salvation" is the Greek word "soteria"[19] from the verb "sozo" which involves much more than our get-out-of-hell-free-card. The Gospel is also the power of God to heal, to rescue, to preserve, and to deliver us from every demonic force. Jesus is our all in all. His blood has paid the debt for our sins and put us in a position to receive all of heaven's goodness. We are co-heirs with Jesus and heirs of God![20]

Grace Sufficient for All

Grace tells us that when we fall flat on our face in our failures and sins, Jesus' perfect performance on our behalf gives us the freedom to stand back up, brush ourselves off, look to Him, say thank you, and keep on moving forward. The church is not for perfectly behaved people. The throne of God is the throne of GRACE. Our only criterion to receiving grace is realizing that we couldn't do anything to earn it!

This amazing grace flows for those who believe that they are righteous by faith:

> *For in it the righteousness of God is revealed from faith to faith; as it is written, "The just shall live by faith." (Romans 1:17)*

This verse is not referring to our own righteousness. The Good News of the Gospel is that we have been given the free gift of Christ's righteousness. Righteous means right standing. To believe we are in right standing all day every minute of every day takes faith! Why does it have to be by faith? Because every day we get up, wash our face, brush our teeth, look in the mirror, and see anything but a righteous person. Our actions and thoughts will tell us that we are not righteous and try to condemn us. That's when we need to believe we are righteous from "faith to faith."

As you therefore have received Christ Jesus the Lord, so walk in Him... (Colossians 2:6)

We received Christ by grace through faith, and that's how we live it out every day until we go to heaven.

For by grace you have been saved through faith, and that not of yourselves; it is the gift of God, not of works, lest anyone should boast. (Ephesians 2:8-9)

Paul tells us that the righteousness of God must be "revealed." That's why we need the Spirit of wisdom and revelation. Paul prayed for the Ephesians:

...making mention of you in my prayers: that the God of our Lord Jesus Christ, the Father of glory, may give to you the spirit of wisdom and revelation in the knowledge of Him... (Ephesians 1:16-17)

Grace doesn't make sense to the natural mind. All we understand is deductive reasoning which says, "Do good, get good. Do bad, get bad." Every religion including Buddhism, Hinduism, Judaism, and Islam believes that. It's the same thing as karma. Every religion believes that we should get the good we have earned and the bad we deserve. It's only by the revelation of the Holy Spirit that we can understand grace because grace tells us that we get the good we could never earn, and we never have to get the bad we deserve. It's scandalous. It's not fair...especially if we consider that Jesus who never sinned became sin for us so that we could never have our sins counted against us in heaven, and especially when we consider living under an open heaven even though we haven't behaved perfectly.

Just Believe

The righteousness of God is a gift that must be received. It must be BELIEVED to be received. This word "believe" in Romans 1:16 is the Greek word "pisteuo,"[21] and it means rely on, be persuaded, put your confidence and trust in HIS righteousness.

In John 6 we see a question that gives the simplicity of the Gospel. The disciples had just seen Jesus feed the five thousand. They thought, "Wow, this guy is the real deal. We're in!" They asked Him an excellent question, the question that we all have asked in one way or another:

"What shall we do, that we may work the works of God?" (John 6:28)

Isn't that what every Christian wants to know? Everyone knows they haven't lived up to God's holy standards so they ask their leaders and pastors, "What do I have to do to do the works that God requires of me?" Often the answer will be "DO this and then DO that, and then DO another thing for God....and perhaps He will be pleased with your efforts."

However, here was Jesus' answer:

"This is the work of God, that you BELIEVE in Him whom He sent."
(John 6:29, emphasis added)

Our job is just to believe. We're not to seek to attain or earn right standing with God. Just believe. Nothing in true Christianity is earned. Everything is accessed through simple faith in the finished work of the cross of Jesus Christ.

The Great Exchange

The greatest exchange in all history took place on the cross of Calvary. Jesus became sin at the cross apart from any sinful actions, and when we receive the free gift of righteousness, we become righteous apart from anything good that we have done. He took our sin. We receive His righteousness. He never committed a single sin, and we never did anything righteous that was worthy to qualify us.

Who committed no sin, nor was deceit found in His mouth. (1 Peter 2:22)

Jesus became a curse for us because He received our sin.[22] Today we receive His righteousness, and God treats us as His very own children, completely forgiven and as perfectly holy as our elder Brother Jesus.

For He made Him who knew no sin to be sin for us, that we might become the righteousness of God in Him. (2 Corinthians 5:21)

This reminds me of a dream that a friend of mine had where she was standing before Jesus in a white shirt. She was very uncomfortable wearing white in His presence and knew that underneath she was dirty, so she unbuttoned the shirt to remove it only to find another white shirt underneath. Now she was even more uncomfortable, so she quickly took off that shirt as well, but once again there was another white shirt under that one. She kept trying to get rid of the white shirts, but there was no end to them! She was white to the core! She was clean and worthy to be in the presence of His holiness. It was His robe of righteousness she was wearing, and it wasn't a robe that just covered sin. It was a robe that removed it!

If Jesus took away our sin, where did it go? It was transferred to Him! He became our sin that we might become His righteousness. Jesus went into the grave with our sin and rose again with out it!

And you know that He was manifested to take away our sins, and in Him there is no sin. (1 John 3:5)

I know what you're thinking: "But I still sin!" Yes, but that's only when our mind is set on this world and our flesh, and this temporary natural realm is the focus rather than the eternal invisible one.[23]

The mind set on the flesh is death, but the mind set on the Spirit is life and peace. (Romans 8:6, NASB)

Jesus Christ is the plumb line of our lives. Ask yourself, "Does this apply to Jesus?" If the answer is yes, then it applies to you. "Does that apply to Jesus?" If the answer is no, then it doesn't apply to you. It is a very simple thing, but in our heads, we want to do something to be righteous. However, if we do ANYTHING to be righteous, then we are saying, "Jesus, that's great! Thanks for dying for me on the cross! But it's not enough. For me to be righteous in Your sight and for You to be happy with me and bless me...

It's Your cross PLUS me reading the Bible.
It's Your cross PLUS me loving others.
It's Your cross PLUS me attending prayer meetings.

It's Your cross PLUS me fasting.
It's Your cross PLUS me eating right.
It's Your cross PLUS me serving others.
It's Your cross PLUS me giving ten percent of my income.
It's Your cross PLUS me behaving perfectly."

No! Jesus said, "It is finished!"[24]

For he who has entered His rest has himself also ceased from his works as God did from His. (Hebrews 4:10)

What does it mean that the work is finished? It's a spiritual truth that will change your life if you understand it. When our eyes are opened to what Jesus has done for us, we will do all those good things listed above out of the overflow of a heart of gratitude and not out of a sense of duty or obligation. We won't HAVE to. We'll WANT to!

There are more than a thousand imperatives in the epistles written to the church, but until we understand grace, they will be a burden, and not a joy! We must understand grace first!

Grace has become a hot "topic" in the church today. (Incidentally, Grace isn't a topic, He's a Person and His name is Jesus.) With all the buzz concerning grace, there have been lots of definitions thrown around. We don't need to redefine grace because if we do, it's just another form of works, and a little leaven leavens the whole loaf.[25]

Grace is simply the unmerited favor of God.[26] Grace is not the ability to do good. If we believe that grace is the ability, then we will fall under condemnation and say to ourselves, "What's wrong with me? I don't have grace to DO that, so I must be lazy...or rebellious... or not praying enough..." That's just another form of works.

Here's how Paul described grace:

And if by grace, then it is no longer of works; otherwise grace is no longer grace. But if it is of works, it is no longer grace; otherwise work is no longer work. (Romans 11:6)

Grace and works are the opposite of each other. We either work for God's blessing and earn it, or we simply receive His unmerited favor.

Grace Instructs Us

What is the "main idea" or theme of the Bible? What do we think the Bible is all about? Is it to tell us how to be better people? If that's true, then why do we need to be better people? Is it so we can be acceptable to God? Is the Bible just good instruction or is it Good News? Yes, the Bible has some very good instruction, but if we think the purpose of the Bible is to tell us how to be better Christians and what will happen to us if we don't follow those instructions, we put ourselves in bondage again to the legalistic system of religion. We will wear ourselves out and miss the whole point of the Bible! God's word is the revelation of the amazing grace of Jesus Christ, the extravagant love of our heavenly Father, and the intimate friendship of the Holy Spirit!

You might ask the question: what about behaving right? Don't we need the law so we will know how to behave ourselves? Some advocate that we are saved by grace in the New Covenant, but we still need the law of the Old Covenant as a reminder of what God expects of us. However, what they don't realize is that this very law that they think will keep them from sinning actually throws wood on the fire of fleshly desires!

...the strength of sin is the law... (1 Corinthians 15:56)

That word "strength" is the same word translated "power" in Romans 1:16 where it says the Gospel is the "power" of salvation. Again, it's the Greek word "dynamis"[27] from which we get our word dynamite. The dynamite power of sin is in our efforts to keep the rule, the resolution, or the law. The more we try, the worse it gets.

I want to submit to you that if the strength of sin is the law, then it makes sense that the strength of holy living is grace!

For the grace of God has appeared, bringing salvation to all men, instructing us to deny ungodliness... (Titus 2:11-12)

Grace "has appeared" because Grace is a Person! Grace is actually our mentor to instruct us to deny ungodliness. The law will not lift a finger to help us live holy lives, but the more we know about the amazing grace of our Lord Jesus Christ, the more we will shine forth His image in godliness.

CHAPTER TWO

Grace and Truth
vs. Religion

Key scriptures:
John 1:14, 16-17; Romans 3:19-20; John 8:4-12; 1 John 1:7

A few years ago after my eyes were gloriously opened to amazing grace, I began to teach everything I was learning in Bible studies and on a daily blog, and the response was tremendous. Grace was spreading like wildfire and joy was erupting everywhere I went! However, a concerned pastor met with me and advised me that I should teach on other topics besides grace so that I would be "balanced" in my teaching. He asked me why I didn't teach on parenting or finances. He spent a considerable portion of our discussion trying to convince me to teach on the wrath of God. He was genuinely trying to help me. As I was listening to him, I prayed, "Lord, how do I respond to this?" I just sat in silence for most of the discussion because there seemed to be no opening to share this revelation of the simplicity of the Gospel. You see, grace isn't a topic! Grace is Jesus. Grace is everything. Grace is the foundation for every teaching and every subject! I didn't feel led to argue with this pastor, so I just said, "Well, grace is what the Lord has told me to teach."

A Balance of Grace and Truth

We hear about the need to "balance grace and truth." This phrase implies that grace and truth are polar opposites on either side of a see-saw, and we need to make sure we keep them balanced. In other words, truth is synonymous with law, and we need the law to make sure we don't sin because grace doesn't do anything to keep us from sinning. That sounds reasonable, doesn't it? If we completely remove the law, people will just go crazy and do whatever they want. We need the law as a reminder of what we should and shouldn't do. Right? Actually, no! As we will see, that goes completely against the scriptures, and in my opinion, that kind of thinking is why so many Christians are suffering.

What the "balance" folks are saying is that truth is about obeying God's commands, and grace is about not getting punished when you don't embrace God's commands through obedience. In some instances truth is when we feel compelled to share our insight and tell someone something they need to hear, but don't want to hear it; and grace is letting them off the hook and not telling them what they need to hear.

What Is Truth?

Truth has nothing to do with obeying commandments or delivering rebukes. The word "truth" actually means "the reality lying at the basis of an appearance; the manifested, the veritable essence of a matter."[28]

It's what IS behind that which is seen.

In Jesus we have grace (the unmerited favor of God) and we have truth (the reality lying at the basis of an appearance; the manifested). In Jesus we have the reality of who God really is.

He is the image of the invisible God, the firstborn over all creation. (Colossians 1:15)

And He [Jesus] is the radiance of His glory [the Father] and the exact representation of His nature. (Hebrews 1:3, brackets added for emphasis)

The Word became flesh and dwelt among us, and we beheld His glory, the glory as of the only begotten of the Father, full of GRACE AND TRUTH... And of His fullness we have all received, and grace for grace. For the law was given through Moses, but GRACE AND TRUTH came through Jesus Christ. (John 1:14, 16-17, emphasis added)

Grace and truth are one. They are inseparable. You can't have one without the other. Grace and truth are on the one side and law is on the other. However, as we will discover as we study several passages of scripture that rightly divide the word of truth, no balance is needed. Jesus has fulfilled the law, and the Father has removed the record of all our law breaking.[29]

Grace and truth came through Jesus Christ who came to establish a New Covenant with better promises. The cross changed EVERYTHING. Absolutely everything!! The old has gone, the new has come. It's time to take off our Old Covenant lenses and see life through the reality of the finished work of the cross ... or perhaps some of us need to simply wipe the Old Covenant scratches off of our New Covenant lenses.

Two Covenants

In the Bible there are several covenants that God made with man or on behalf of man. All of them can be categorized into to two basic covenants:

Two covenants: law and grace.

Two deals cut: one with the people; one with God's Son.

One kills; one gives life.

One is all about man's lack of faithfulness; one is all about Jesus' faithfulness.

One shines the light on sin; one shines the light on the perfection of God's Son.

One was given to bring out man's sin; one was given to make man holy.

One condemns; one justifies.

One brings sin consciousness; one brings Jesus consciousness.

One covers sin; one takes it away!

As believers we do believe that the Mosaic law was given by God for a purpose. The law is holy, just, and good, but it cannot make us holy, just, and good. The purpose of the law is to point out sin, not to remove it. It's to make everyone guilty. It's to bring sinners to repentance, but the law is useless to believers. The law diagnoses our condition as sinner before we are saved, but it cannot cure the condition. Only the blood of Jesus Christ can give us the righteousness that God desires, and if we do ANYTHING to obtain or maintain righteousness through working for it, it's religion. Worthless to God. Filthy rags.

> *Now we know that whatever the law says, it says to those who are under the law, that every mouth may be stopped, and all the world may become guilty before God. Therefore by the deeds of the law no flesh will be justified in His sight, for by the law is the KNOWLEDGE of sin. (Romans 3:19-20, emphasis added)*

There is nothing wrong with the law. It's a mirror that showed us we were not much to look at before Christ. However, it's not the mirror's fault. It only shows or reveals sin. The law showed us that we were dirty and in need of a bath. Some people try to use the mirror of the law to clean the dirt off only to find that it doesn't work. The law can't cleanse us. It only shows the need for cleansing, and it only brings a consciousness of sins.

In Hebrews we read that if the Old Covenant law had worked, we should have no more consciousness of sins:

> *For then would they [the blood sacrifices of the law] not have ceased to be offered? For the worshipers, once purified, would have had no more consciousness of sins. (Hebrews 10:2, brackets added for emphasis)*

The sacrificing of animals in the Old Testament was the "work" that covered the sins of the people, but the blood of animals never cleansed the consciences of the worshippers because it never worked to purify them. The result was that they still had the consciousness of sins. Today, because the blood of Jesus has purified us, we should have no more consciousness of sins.

Under the New Covenant we have this wonderful promise:

I will be merciful to their unrighteousness, and their sins and their lawless deeds I will remember no more. (Hebrews 8:12)

Why should we spend time mulling over our sins when God said that He won't remember them? Think about what it means for God to remember sins: when He remembers them, He punishes the sinner. But hallelujah...

Behold, the Lamb of God who takes away the sin of the world! (John 1:29)

When God looks at us today, He does not see sin between us and Him. It's been taken away!

For Christ is the end of the law for righteousness to everyone who believes. (Romans 10:4)

The Greek word for sin is "harmartia."[30] This word means to miss the mark and fall short as when an archer pulls back his bow, aims the arrow to try to hit the bullseye and fails. With this example in mind, the law says we must hit the bull's eye every time or we are condemned. Jesus came and took away our "missing of the mark."

Jesus ever lives to intercede for us.[31] His intercession is His work of redemption through His blood. Every single beating, every brutal scourging, and every drop of blood shed was an arrow perfectly meeting the mark for us, and now we are completely and perfectly redeemed from missing the mark!

However, for those of us who still attempt to hit the bull's eye for ourselves, depending upon our own ability, it's nothing more than self-righteousness.

The Mixture

Today nobody in the church preaches pure law. What they preach is a mixture, and it goes something like this:

"Try to be as kind and loving and patient and faithful and disciplined as you can, but if you fail, remember that God still loves you.

Now get back up and do better. Here are seven steps to help you. Come back and report on your progress next week." After you fail and come back, you hear, "God still loves you and He WILL forgive you if you ask Him to. Now get back up and try again. Here's a book to read and a conference to attend and a Bible study to join and a few more folks to keep you accountable..."

It's the ministry of defeat and condemnation!

Are you so foolish? Having begun in the Spirit, are you now being made perfect by the flesh? (Galatians 3:3)

The "flesh" is referring to our self-efforts to be made perfect before God. Wherever there is the very deadly cocktail of law and grace, we will operate in the flesh, and there are a few things it will produce:

- Hidden sin (It's there! You just can't see it!)
- Self-righteousness (People striving to "get right" with God.)
- Pride and arrogance
- Burn-out
- Competition and comparison
- Loss of love
- Patch-work theology (Messages that take a little of the old, out of context, and mix it with the new, out of context)
- Feelings of rejection from people and from God

However, at the same time because of the mixing of the law with grace, in the church we have been hearing and even saying wonderful things such as the following:

- Jesus came to shine a light in our darkness, not on our mistakes.
- Jesus came to set you free, not to make you sorry.
- Jesus came to say that He's enough, not that we aren't good enough.
- Jesus knows you and loves you anyway.
- Jesus didn't come to make bad people good; He came to make dead people live!

- Jesus came to remove sin, not to expose it. (The problem was that we thought Jesus was removing our sins progressively, one sin at a time as we confessed them!)
- Religion is spelled "do", Christianity is spelled "done."

Our spirits cry, "YES! That's the truth!" But what do we mean?

How radical is grace after all?

Why doesn't our experience line up with those glorious statements? It's because of the mixture of law and grace. It's religion.

A Look at Religion

Religion is the same thing as self-righteousness: it's man's pursuit to make himself right before God. Religion operates through guilt and fear. Dependency on guilt is what keeps religion alive and well, like a drug dealer giving an addict a small dose of the drug to keep him coming back for more. Even those who teach the Gospel often mix it with guilt without even realizing it. The result is a feeling in people that they aren't quite right with God. It's as if there is a carrot on the end of the stick that says, "Just do one more thing for God, and He'll be pleased with you."

We all think we are against religion. We love to think of ourselves as pure grace and no law. We say we hate legalism. Here's a litmus test of pure grace: if there is burn-out, there is guilt. If there is competition, there is condemnation. If there is jealousy, there is shame. If there is hidden sin, there is law. If there is fear of man, there is insecurity, dishonesty, idolatry, control, manipulation, and a focus on perception at the expense of reality. If there are fears of ANY kind, there is law. If there are doubts, there is a misunderstanding of the goodness of God. This is not pure grace.

If you have experienced these things, you have taken on works that God didn't design you for, or others have put ill-fitting burdens on you out of their need to fulfill their agenda. You accepted because you sincerely believed that it would make you closer to God, and you'd be "a team player" in God's kingdom. It all starts very subtly and sounds very spiritual, but if we buy into any form of works-based religion, control will sneak in to steal our liberty in Christ. How can we know if we are staying in a place of freedom from religion?

You can tell when you are under grace, living in freedom everyday, because you will have certain qualities about you. For example, you have:

nothing to hide,
nothing to prove,
nothing to gain,
nothing to lose,
no one to convince,
no one to impress.

You don't need followers. You don't need man's approval. You are marked with joy and peace and security. You are free to serve and free to love. You don't need a position or a title. You are free to succeed because you are free to fail. And the biggest one is this: YOU ARE FREE TO HEAR THE VOICE OF GOD FOR YOURSELF! The Gospel of grace transforms religious robots into eagles who soar without any of the constraints of the law.

The Woman Caught in Adultery

There is no more beautiful story of the amazing grace of Jesus than the account of the woman caught in adultery. The story began as Jesus was confronted by the Pharisees who threw this adulteress at Him in the temple courtyard. They used the occasion to test Him as to whether or not He would obey the law.

> *"Teacher, this woman was caught in adultery, in the very act. Now Moses, in the law, commanded us that such should be stoned. But what do You say?" This they said, testing Him, that they might have something of which to accuse Him. (John 8:4-6)*

If Jesus responded, "Don't stone her," they would accuse Him of breaking the Mosaic law. If He said, "Stone her," they could ask what happened to all His teachings on grace? For instance, when He told Nicodemus that anyone who believed in Him would not be condemned.[32] So they thought they had Him cornered. Imagine trying to corner God...

But Jesus stooped down and wrote on the ground with His finger, as though He did not hear. So when they continued asking Him, He raised Himself up and said to them, "He who is without sin among you, let him throw a stone at her first." And again He stooped down and wrote on the ground. (John 8:6-8)

The ground of the place where Jesus was teaching in the courtyard of the temple was made of stones, not dirt. He wrote with His finger on stone. Perhaps there was dust that He ran His finger through to draw a picture or write something, but I believe the main point is that He was writing with His finger on stone. Where is the first place in the scriptures that we see a finger writing on stone? It was God writing the Ten Commandments.[33] So by writing on stone, Jesus is saying, "I am the Author of the law! Since you're so bound and determined to use the law against this woman, let's see how you measure up to it!" Then He stood up and demonstrated the purpose of the law when He said: "He that is without sin, cast the first stone." Only Jesus could have brought the law to it's intended standard while keeping the purity of it.

Then those who heard it, being convicted by their conscience, went out one by one, beginning with the oldest even to the last. And Jesus was left alone, and the woman standing in the midst. When Jesus had raised Himself up and saw no one but the woman, He said to her, "Woman, where are those accusers of yours? Has no one condemned you?" (John 8:9 10)

Jesus, the only sinless One was the only One who stayed by her side. There is only one Person who could have thrown a stone at her, for He was sinless but He wouldn't do it. The Pharisees would have happily thrown their stones, but their consciences wouldn't allow them to do so for they were NOT sinless.

Notice that even though Jesus is God and the Author of the Ten Commandments, He didn't remind her of the commandment, "Thou shall not commit adultery."

Jesus was preoccupied with her freedom from condemnation, not her sin!

She said, "No one, Lord." And Jesus said to her, "Neither do I condemn you; go and sin no more." (John 8:11)

Think about our wonderful Jesus. He was the only One to defend this sinner. Are we defending sinners? Or are we condemning them? The message of the Gospel is this: there is no condemnation for those who are in Christ.[34] Why? Because Jesus took our condemnation. The power for this woman to "go and sin no more" was in the truth that Jesus did not condemn her.

Often the church today gives the opposite message: "If you will just stop sinning, we won't condemn you." However, if people know there is no condemnation, no reproach, no shame, and no judgment from God when they fail, they will go and sin no more!

Walking in the Light

The following verse in John 8 is profound:

Then Jesus spoke to them again, saying, "I am the light of the world. He who follows Me shall not walk in darkness, but have the light of life." (John 8:12)

The story of the woman caught in adultery is the context of that familiar verse!

Before the cross, He implored people to follow Him to the cross where He would die their death, and then they would enter into His resurrection life. Since the cross, He implores every person to believe that we have been reconciled to God through the cross, so that we receive the free gift of righteousness. Today we don't need to be afraid of His light because when we enter that light in the new birth, we enter Christ Himself. That light does not expose our sin. It reveals the perfection of Christ's blood in taking our sin away.

In this verse we find the phrase "shall not walk in darkness..." Today for the believer who is in Christ, it is impossible to walk in darkness ever again. We still sin, but we will never be in darkness again.

Let's look at 1 John 1:7 for more clarity on this truth.

But if we walk in the light as He is in the light, we have fellowship with one another, and the blood of Jesus Christ His Son cleanses us from all sin. (1 John 1:7)

This scripture says, "If we walk in the light..." If we have a performance or works mindset and we see a phrase like this, we will automatically assume it is talking about behavior. This phrase is not referring to how we walk. It's referring to where we walk. To say it is talking about behavior would not make sense. It would mean "if we behave ourselves like Jesus behaves Himself ('as He is'), the blood of Jesus cleanses us from all sin." Why would we need the blood of Jesus to cleanse us if we were perfect?

If it were true that we were only in the light when we behaved, and then we were in the dark when we misbehaved, then we would switch back and forth from the light to the dark many times a day! The only way to stay in the light would be to never sin.

This scripture is talking about the realm we are in as a believer, not the way we are performing. We are in the light because we have been cleansed from all our sin.

> *...giving thanks to the Father who has qualified us to be partakers of the inheritance of the saints in the light. He has delivered us from the power of darkness and conveyed us into the kingdom of the Son of His love, in whom we have redemption through His blood, the forgiveness of sins. (Colossians 1:12-14)*

> *But you are a chosen generation, a royal priesthood, a holy nation, His own special people, that you may proclaim the praises of Him who called you out of darkness into His marvelous light; who once were not a people but are now the people of God, who had not obtained mercy but now have obtained mercy. (1 Peter 2:9-10)*

If you are a believer, you are in the LIGHT, and you walk where God is because you are in Christ, and He is in us.

The word "cleanses"[35] in this verse is in the present active indicative verb tense in the original Greek. Present tense means that the blood is effective right now, forever keeping us in the light. Wow! This is because our spirits are in Christ, completely holy and protected. The blood of Jesus has forever separated us from sin.

That's incredibly Good News!

CHAPTER THREE

Not Counting
Our Sins Against Us

Key scriptures:
Matthew 8:2-3; Romans 8:6-9; Romans 4:6-8; Isaiah 53:4-6, 12; Isaiah 54:8-10, 14, 17; John 16:8-11

When my son was a little boy, I walked in on him watching a television program that would fall in the category of what we referred to as a "bad show." It was "teenager" show where the kids were disrespectful, and the adults were portrayed as fools. As I approached my son, the screen flickered, and it was obvious that he had changed the channel. The remote control was gripped tightly in his guilty palm. Instead of giving him the riot act that he was expecting, I took him in my arms and set him on my lap. He seemed uncomfortable at first. What he really wanted to do was bolt!

I said, "Son, did you know that God forgave you for watching that show? And He has already forgiven you for every bad show you'll ever watch in your entire life? Did you know that there is nothing you could ever do that would make God mad at you or not love you? That's what Jesus did for you and me when He died on the cross and took our sins away." All of a sudden he started weeping. I was a little surprised at his reaction and I asked him, "What's the matter? Does that upset you?"

With big crocodile tears running down his red cheeks, he said, "No, mom. I'm not upset. Jesus just loves me so much!!"

After hugging him for a minute or two, and telling him more about the love of Jesus for us, I thought I'd ask him a question, "Does this make you want to go and watch a bad show?"

His answer: "No, I don't want to anymore."

Like my son wanting to bolt through the door when I caught him red-handed watching that program, the natural result of guilt is the feeling that we should run from God. Is it possible that God would want us to "climb in His lap" even when we sin?

The Cleansing of the Leper

In the Old Testament there were many "types" and "shadows" of truths that would be revealed in the New Testament. A "type" or "shadow" in the Bible is a prophetic symbol.

The highly contagious skin disease known as leprosy in the Old Testament was a type of sin. Just as sin put Adam and Eve outside the garden of Eden, lepers were ostracized people who had to live outside the camp or face stoning. Not only were they "unclean," anyone who touched them would also become "unclean." Even their families could not be near them. Before they came anywhere near people, they had to cry, "Unclean!" to warn the people so they could flee.[36] Can you imagine the shame anyone stricken with leprosy must have endured?

Think of it: Jesus came and touched each of us with His love and grace and cleansed us from the "leprosy" of sin!

In Matthew 8 we see the beautiful story of Jesus touching a leper and healing him. Jesus was coming down the mountain after preaching the Sermon on the Mount, and the leper stopped Him and worshipped Him.

And behold, a leper came and worshiped Him saying, "Lord, if You are willing, You can make me clean." (Matthew 8:2)

First, notice the word "if." The leper knew that there was only one thing needed for his cleansing from leprosy: the willingness of Jesus to heal him. He knew that Jesus had the power to heal him, but he doubted whether Jesus would use His power for him. Many of us have that mindset when we come to God.

Notice that the man said, "You can make me clean" instead of "You can heal me." Why? Because he was using the Old Testament terminology in the law. The law can only bring shame and condemnation. "Unclean" is a word that we associate with shame, guilt, or being stained or dirty.

Jesus then answered the man's question, and the verb tense tells us that He forever and perpetually answers that same question for us today because of who HE IS:

Then Jesus put out His hand and touched him, saying, "I am willing; be cleansed." Immediately his leprosy was cleansed. (Matthew 8:3)

"I am willing" is Jesus' nature. He is always willing to cleanse and heal anyone who comes to Him! Jesus did what the law forbade: He touched a leper. Think about what happened in this account. According to the law, Jesus should have become unclean by touching the leper. However, when Jesus touches someone, their uncleanness does not touch Him, yet His cleanness transforms them! Under law, uncleanness spread to all who touched the unclean. Under grace, righteousness spreads to all who come in contact with the Righteous One, Jesus Christ.

Though your sins are as scarlet, they will be as white as snow! (Isaiah 1:18)

Many Christians think that they were only partially bad when they were saved. They believe Jesus just came to fix the part of them that was messed up. A lot of us think that we weren't too bad before we were saved — that there are others who are much worse than we were! However, the scriptures say that we all fell short of God's glory and deserved death.[37] The law says if we broke one law, we broke them all:

> *For whoever shall keep the whole law, and yet stumble in one point, he is guilty of all. (James 2:10)*

God Demonstrated His Love

At one time every single one of us was a "leper," a sinner, darkened in our understanding, and alienated from the life of God.

> *For when we were still without strength, in due time Christ died for the ungodly. For scarcely for a righteous man will one die; yet perhaps for a good man someone would even dare to die. But God demonstrates His own love toward us, in that while we were still sinners, Christ died for us. Much more then, having now been justified by His blood, we shall be saved from wrath through Him. (Romans 5:6-9)*

The scandal of the Gospel is that Jesus died for the ungodly! All of the wrath of God against all sin was poured out on the spotless Lamb of God, and because of that our Father will never, ever be angry with us! Here's how The Message translation describes this truth:

> *Now that we are set right with God by means of this sacrificial death, the consummate blood sacrifice, there is no longer a question of being at odds with God in any way. (Romans 5:9, The Message)*

Today Jesus Christ is seated at the Father's right hand, having cleansed us of our sins completely.

> *When He had by Himself purged our sins, sat down at the right hand of the Majesty on high. (Hebrews 1:3)*

Not a single sin that we have committed or will commit was left unpunished. Do you know what this means? Not one single, solitary sin remains in us! This means that God is not counting our sins against us!

God Is Not Counting Our Sins Against Us

A long time ago before Jesus entered time and history to remove our sins at the cross as far as the east is from the west, David prophesied of the era we are in today, and he envied us!

> *...just as David also describes the blessedness of the man to whom God imputes righteousness apart from works. "Blessed are those whose lawless deeds are forgiven, And whose sins are covered; Blessed is the man to whom the LORD shall not impute sin." (Romans 4:6-8)*

In this passage David described two distinct blessed conditions for the person for whom God is not counting his sins against him. The first blessed condition is that our sins are forgiven. He's got you covered because He covered the charges against you! The first blessed condition tells us that our debt for sin has been paid.

The second blessed condition says "Blessed is the man to whom the Lord shall not impute sin." This means that all of the record of our debt of sin has been wiped out. It's as if we never sinned. God does not count our sins against us because the record of our sins does not exist in heaven! It's been taken away!

You might ask the question, "But don't we still sin?" Yes, obviously we do because we are still human beings. This passage does not say we are blessed because we don't sin. It says we are blessed because when we do sin, God does not count our sins against us! God can not count our sins against us because they were counted against Jesus. Sin cannot go unpunished, so all of the punishment that we deserved fell on Jesus so that we would be redeemed.

He Became a Curse For Us

Galatians 3:13 tells us that Jesus became a curse for us when He became sin on the cross. He didn't have to ask for the curse to come on Him; He became the curse that we deserved because He became our sin. The curse was simply attracted to our sin on Him.

The curse of the law is described in Deuteronomy 28:15-68. Read it some time and see what evil fell upon Jesus for our sakes. When you do, I believe you'll love Him all the more! Here's just a taste of the horror that He took for you and me:

[The curse of sickness] Extraordinary plagues—great and prolonged plagues—and serious and prolonged sicknesses. Moreover He will bring back on you all the diseases of Egypt, of which you were afraid, and they shall cling to you. Also every sickness and every plague. (Deuteronomy 28:59-61)

[Curses on Marriage] You shall betroth a wife, but another man shall lie with her. (Deuteronomy 28:30)

[The curse of rebellious children] Your sons and your daughters shall be given to another people, and your eyes shall look and fail with longing for them all day long; and there shall be no strength in your hand...You shall beget sons and daughters, but they shall not be yours; for they shall go into captivity. (Deuteronomy 28:32, 41)

[The curse of poverty] You shall carry much seed out to the field but gather little in, for the locust shall consume it. You shall plant vineyards and tend them, but you shall neither drink of the wine nor gather the grapes; for the worms shall eat them. You shall have olive trees throughout all your territory, but you shall not anoint yourself with the oil; for your olives shall drop off. (Deuteronomy 28:38-40)

We should take great comfort in knowing that God is our Healer and Deliverer and Sustainer of all life. Why? Because the full force of the entire curse of the law fell on Jesus. That's why we are redeemed from the curse and should never receive any of the effects of it. Don't you think that Jesus should get what He paid for?

Surely He has borne our griefs and carried our sorrows; yet we esteemed Him stricken, smitten by God, and afflicted. But He was wounded for our transgressions, He was bruised for our iniquities; the chastisement for our peace was upon Him, and by His stripes we are healed. All we like sheep have gone astray; we have turned, every one, to his own way; and the Lord has laid on Him the iniquity of us all... He bore the sin of many, and made intercession for the transgressors. (Isaiah 53:4-6, 12)

God's Not Mad

In the context of that detailed description of Jesus' work on our behalf in Isaiah 53 above, in the very next chapter of Isaiah God swore that because of that great act of intercession, He will never be angry with us again.

With a little wrath I hid My face from you for a moment; But with everlasting kindness I will have mercy on you," Says the LORD, your Redeemer. For this is like the waters of Noah to Me; for as I have sworn that the waters of Noah would no longer cover the earth, so have I sworn that I would not be angry with you, nor rebuke you. (Isaiah 54:8-9)

The "waters of Noah" were the waters of God's judgment. Here is that last part of that passage in the New Living Translation:

I swear that I will never again be angry and punish you. (Isaiah 54:9, NLT)

Why will He never be angry with us or punish us? Because Jesus took the waters of judgment for us! If you read somewhere or hear that God is angry with you, please know that it is not true. The accuser of the brethren, satan, wants you to believe that.

We all know about the symbol of the rainbow as God's promise that He would never destroy the earth again by means of a flood, but the rainbow is also a symbol of the promise that Christ has taken the floods of judgment for us, and He has promised He will never be angry with us or punish us! In heaven right now, there is a rainbow around the throne of grace where the King of kings is seated at the right hand of God.[38] When you imagine Jesus in heaven, I want you to see this rainbow all around Him and all around yourself because you are in Him! Envision this with your spiritual eyes any time you think God is angry with you!

The word "angry" in Isaiah 54:9 is "qatsaph"[39] in Hebrew, the original language of the Old Testament, and it means "to be displeased, to be furious." God is not displeased with us because God is not displeased with the perfect work of His Son, Jesus! This word "qatsaph", as with all words for anger, is not used in reference to God being angry with His covenant people until AFTER the law was given at the foot of Mount Sinai in the book of Exodus.

Paul says,

...the law brings about wrath... (Romans 4:15)

Why does the law bring wrath? Because under law if a person doesn't measure up, he will suffer wrath! Under grace, we focus on His love for us and the great demonstration of that love that while we were still sinners Christ died for us.

God's Enduring Covenant

When bad things happen to us or when we do bad things, we need to hang on to this truth that God is not mad at us. God has made an enduring covenant with us and wants us to rest in His presence and in His love. He will never be angry with us — not because we are good, but because the work of His Son on our behalf is perfect and finished!

Isaiah 54, which gives us this promise, is one of the most awesome chapters of promise in the scriptures:

"For the mountains shall depart And the hills be removed, But My kindness shall not depart from you, Nor shall My covenant of peace be removed," Says the LORD, who has mercy on you... In righteousness you shall be established; you shall be far from oppression, for you shall not fear; And from terror, for it shall not come near you... No weapon formed against you shall prosper, And every tongue which rises against you in judgment You shall condemn. This is the heritage of the servants of the LORD, And their righteousness is from Me," Says the LORD. (Isaiah 54:10, 14, 17)

When the prophet Isaiah speaks of being established in righteousness, he is not referring to our righteousness. He is referring to God's righteousness. "Established" means stable, fixed, and settled.[40] We could never be stable in our own righteousness. Jesus has interceded for us with ONE great act of intercession! We are blessed, protected, healthy, and provided for because He is our righteousness! God wants us stable, fixed, and settled in Christ's righteousness!

The Conviction of the Holy Spirit

Alright. If God is not angry with us, then what does the Holy Spirit convict us of? Isn't His job to tell us that God is not pleased with us? We talk about the Holy Spirit convicting us of our sins, but what does the Bible say? And what sins will the Holy Spirit convict of?

Before Jesus went to the cross, He prophesied about the coming of the Holy Spirit when He said,

> *And when He has come, He will convict the world of sin, and of righteousness, and of judgment: of sin, because they do not believe in Me; of righteousness, because I go to My Father and you see Me no more; of judgment, because the ruler of this world is judged. (John 16:8-11)*

The Holy Spirit convicts of three things: sin, righteousness, and judgment. It's vital that we understand WHOM He is convicting of WHAT. The word in the Greek for "convict"[41] means to convince. It denotes the idea of convincing of a verdict in a court of law. What are we being convicted of? Just so there would be no misunderstanding, Jesus clarified it:

"Of sin, because THEY do not believe in Me." This is talking about unbelievers, and unbelief is the sin. There is only one sin that the Holy Spirit convicts of, and it's the sin of unbelief in Jesus Christ. Unbelievers are convicted as in a court of law as sinners because of one thing: unbelief. How can we say such a strong statement? It's because when the Father sent the Son to receive our sin and condemnation,

> *God was in Christ reconciling the world to Himself, not imputing their trespasses to them. (2 Corinthians 5:19)*

Every other sin was completely obliterated at the cross and forgiven, paid for. God was reconciling the world, not just the church, to Himself in the body of Jesus. God is not counting men's sins against them! Do you understand why He is not counting men's sins against them? Again, it's because all of our sins were counted against Jesus, our sacrificial Lamb, at the cross. If God were to count men's sins against them it would be the crime of double jeopardy: punishing the same sin twice. That would be unjust!

See the heart of God in sending His beloved Son, Jesus:

> *For God so loved THE WORLD that He gave His only begotten Son, that whoever believes in Him should not perish but have everlasting life.*

For God did not send His Son into the world to condemn the world, but that the world through Him might be saved. (John 3:16-17, emphasis added)

And if anyone sins, we have an Advocate with the Father, Jesus Christ the righteous. And He Himself is the propitiation for our sins, and not for ours only but also for THE WHOLE WORLD. (1 John 2:1-2, emphasis added)

"Behold! The Lamb of God who takes away the sin of THE WORLD!" (John 1:29, emphasis added)

He took away the sins of the whole world!

Sadly, people will remain lost even though God is not counting their sins against them! There is only one sin that Jesus didn't die for: the sin of unbelief, and this is the sin that the Holy Spirit convicts the world of. He convicts them — convinces them in their conscience — that they are sinners in need of a Savior because they do not believe. It's the sin of rejecting Jesus Christ.

There are only two types of people, dead or alive. Because Jesus took away the sins of the world and the free gift of righteousness is offered to all without discrimination, the way we are to view people is according to the Spirit, not according to the flesh. What should our desire for them be? To fix them or to see them according to the will and love of the Father for them? Imagine how things would change if we stopped viewing people according to their behavior and saw them with the loving eyes of God.

Paul describes the condition of the unbeliever in Ephesians,

...having their understanding darkened, being alienated from the life of God, because of the ignorance that is in them, because of the blindness of their heart... (Ephesians 4:18)

Are they alive in Christ or alienated from the life of God? Sometimes we can't know for sure so we treat everyone with love, and we treat no one with condemnation. The way we view people is important because we are here for a purpose. God didn't just beam us up to heaven when we were born again. We were left in these mortal bodies to connect us to this earth for the purpose of reconciling people to God.

> *Therefore, from now on, we regard no one according to the flesh. Even though we have known Christ according to the flesh, yet now we know Him thus no longer. Therefore, if anyone is in Christ, he is a new creation; old things have passed away; behold, all things have become new. Now all things are of God, who has reconciled us to Himself through Jesus Christ, and has given us the ministry of reconciliation, God was in Christ reconciling the world to Himself, not imputing their trespasses to them, and has committed to us the word of reconciliation. Now then, we are ambassadors for Christ, as though God were pleading through us: we implore you on Christ's behalf, be reconciled to God. For He made Him who knew no sin to be sin for us, that we might become the righteousness of God in Him. (2 Corinthians 5:16-21)*

Paul said that God was pleading through us! What is the message that we are to tell the world? It's that through Christ, God has reconciled the world to Himself by becoming our sin and giving us His righteousness, and God is not counting their sins against them! This is the Good News!

The greatest tragedy is that Jesus shed His precious blood, died, rose again, and is seated in heaven today having purged our sins, and yet many do not believe it! We have the choice to receive the gift of righteousness or reject it. Rejecting Jesus as the Messiah who saved us from our sin is the only sin that will be judged at the end of time. It's rejecting the witness of the Holy Spirit who was sent to testify of Jesus. That is the sin the Holy Spirit convicts the unbeliever of.

What does He convict the BELIEVER of?

"Of righteousness, because I go to My Father and YOU see Me no more." He was speaking to His disciples. This is talking about the believers today. For the believer, He convicts (convinces as in a court of law) YOU of righteousness because "you (not THEY) see Me no more." Jesus was prophesying of the coming New Covenant reality of the indwelling presence of the Holy Spirit for believers. The Holy Spirit is in the believer's life to convict us of righteousness. What is Jesus doing at the Father's right hand? He ever lives to make intercession for us with His work for us. His nail pierced hands and

[handwritten margin notes: "It is NOT ok to judge someone for sinning. IT IS ok to say what is a sin. is why we can still call sin 'sin.' THAT"]

His blood mediate for us, declaring that we are righteous, acquitted, and deserving of our inheritance and every blessing in Christ. Jesus is the anchor for our souls, and the Holy Spirit is here to remind us of that truth. The Holy Spirit is helping us to overcome our unbelief. He is our Advocate who reminds us that we are the righteousness of God. He is helping us to see that the accuser, the devil, has been condemned and triumphed over at the cross. He is the Comforter, and He guides us into all truth. You might ask how are we going to change our behavior if the Holy Spirit isn't pointing out our sins. Our new nature in Christ will know when we're not walking in consistency with the nature of God, and the Spirit of God operating in our new nature will lead us into godliness. Grace leads to righteous living.

Whom does He convict of judgment?

"And of judgment, because the ruler of this world is judged." It is not believers who are being judged. It's the devil who has been judged. The Holy Spirit reminds us of the victory we have over the devil because we are righteous through the blood of Jesus.

We need to have full assurance that it is not the Spirit's desire to remind us of sins. An unworthy conscience will tell us that we cannot enjoy His presence. We need to take those thoughts captive because they come against the knowledge of God![42] It's not our obedience that puts us in a position to approach God. It's the obedience of Jesus Christ, even to the point of death.[43] Never fear that God is angry with you or that He would ever leave you.[44] He will never leave you nor forsake you.[45] He will abide with you forever.[46]

Does Sin Matter To God?

We have been declared innocent in the courtroom of heaven, and the Holy Spirit is here to remind us that we have been made righteous. However, this doesn't mean the Holy Spirit isn't there to help us when temptation comes. He loves us and wants to protect us and others from being hurt by our sinning. He will never condone sinning because He knows it is distracting and destructive for us. How could He just stand by and say nothing when temptations come? Our new nature in Christ does not want to sin, and the Holy Spirit witnesses to that fact. In order for us to sin, we would have to go against our nature and suppress our true desire!

When we do sin, however, there is still no condemnation for those who are in Christ:

> *My little children, these things I write to you, so that you may not sin. And if anyone sins, we have an Advocate with the Father, Jesus Christ the righteous. (1 John 2:1)*

It seems that when we fall, God only wants us to see one thing: Jesus seated at the right hand of God! When we do that, we instantly feel loved, and we instantly get back in the flow of the Spirit!

Knowing we are righteous is the key to hearing the voice of the Holy Spirit. His constant song is "I love you. You are My cherished child." Never listen to a voice that brings condemnation, doubt, or fear. This is not the voice of the Holy Spirit! This is a good litmus test to use when thoughts come. Reject any thoughts that do not come with His peace. Even when the Lord corrects us, it is always with a sense of love and freedom, never with shame and guilt and fear.

We need to encourage others with the truth that we are still righteous when we fail. Think of it this way: what would the Holy Spirit say? We need to say those things to each other and lift each other up!!

CHAPTER FOUR **4**

The Love of God

Key Scriptures:
John 9:1-3; John 15:4-5; Luke 10:25-28; Luke 7:36-38, 47-48; 1 John 4:19

We can't have true, resilient, long-term peace in our lives in all circumstances until we have peace in our conscience. It's the peace that sustains all other peace. It's the peace that reassures us that no matter what — even if we face horrible consequences for our own sin in this world,

- GOD IS ON OUR SIDE!!!!
- God will see us through.
- God will make a way where there seems to be no way!

Fear of Punishment and Consequences

If there is any doubt that the cross has removed all of our sins — past present and future, we will doubt whether God has good in our future, and we will do something to cleanse the conscience to obtain good standing before God or to work our way back into the favor of man. This is self-righteousness. The motivation behind self-righteousness is fear of PUNISHMENT from God and fear of CONSEQUENCES from man.

If we don't have peace in our conscience, we will think God is responsible for the evil in our lives, and we will come to the conclusion that He is punishing us for our sin in some way. If we have a wrong conclusion about God, we will not flow in grace. We will think we are just reaping from Him what we deserve. How many people are walking around in this world living lives out of a sense that they are simply getting what they deserve?

- They mishandled their money, so they deserve to be poor.
- They committed adultery, so they deserve to lose their marriage.
- They were critical and demanding of their children, so they deserve to be estranged from them.
- They mistreated their bodies, so they deserve to be sick.
- They cheated at work, so they deserve to be fired.
- They were promiscuous in their youth, so they deserve to be barren.
- They were alcoholics, so they deserve to lose everything.
- They betrayed a friend, so they deserve to be friendless.
- They are ugly, grumpy, angry or just simply imperfect, so they deserve to be rejected.
- They turned their back on God, so they deserve for Him to turn His back on them.

Yes, there are consequences to our actions in this world, but the God of grace is seated on the throne of grace ready for us to come to the end of ourselves — to the end of the self-effort of the flesh — and throw ourselves at His mercy. He specializes in creating rivers in the desert and roadways in the wilderness.

Remember: we don't need grace if we have behaved perfectly. Grace is only for those who DON'T have it all together.

Most of us are more conscious of the flesh, conscious of satan, and conscious of sin than we are of the resurrected Christ and what He has accomplished. Why are we so sin conscious when Jesus has removed the sin barrier? The biggest obstacle in the church to living the abundant life that Jesus came to give us is unbelief in the finished work of the cross! It is causing people to WORK WORK WORK to fix their problems. And those in "ministry" are helping the problem right along. Typical "ministry" is actually quite sin-focused. The typical line of interrogation in ministry is the following:

- What did they do to get themselves in this trouble?

- What happened to them to cause them to be in this trouble?

- Are they in unforgiveness and thus unleashing tormentors and getting what they deserve?

- Or even worse: what demons are enforcing a curse on them? The devil loves that one because he gets the attention!

All of these are sin, self, and satan focused and cause introspection and unveiling of ugliness that will only bring us down and lead us to wrong conclusions about God. The natural reaction to sin consciousness is fear of punishment and feelings of shame. Then the natural, human consequences of sin will be misinterpreted as punishment from God. The goal of ministry should be to point the struggling, suffering one to the love of Jesus.

For the one who fears punishment, God's perfect love is not fully accomplishing it's purpose.[4] What is its purpose? First, it was to remove our sin and create us new in Christ — AS HE IS. Then, this demonstration of love should have cleansed our conscience so that we would draw near and enjoy His presence. Unless we remove the fear of punishment, we will not experience the perfect love of God!

The Blame Game

Have you ever wondered why bad things happen? A story found in John 9 goes right to where the "rubber meets the road" regarding the reason that bad things happen. Is it because God is punishing us for our sin? We know that there are natural consequences for foolish actions, but Jesus simply points out a truth in this story that reveals His primary focus when dealing with the problems that people face.

Now as Jesus passed by, He saw a man who was blind from birth. And His disciples asked Him, saying, "Rabbi, who sinned, this man or his parents, that he was born blind?" (John 9:1-2)

First of all, if the man was born blind, how would it be possible that HIS sin caused him to be blind? That makes no sense. It's just the illogical reasoning of religious thinking. Our focus when we are sin-conscious is always going to be blame oriented. Our preoccupation with sin distracts us from seeing the needs of people.

Jesus' answer is amazing. Let His answer teach us something about the mind of Christ and His way of seeing people because as believers we have been given the mind of Christ and the ability to see what He sees.[48]

Jesus answered, "Neither this man nor his parents sinned, but that the works of God should be revealed in him." (John 9:3)

That word "revealed" literally means "manifested."[49] His healing was the manifestation of God's glorious work in him, and his healing was the focus of Jesus' attention.

Because of all the training in the church, our default setting is to be conscious of sin, but we need to stop focusing on "Whose sin caused this problem?" Let's just begin asking, "Was this problem covered in Jesus' blood at the cross?" Blame games don't do anything to fix problems! Remember: needs exist to be met, and therefore, to manifest the glory of God!

Fruit

Christians love to talk about bearing the fruit of the Spirit. Shouldn't we be concerned about bearing fruit?

Have you ever tried to be patient? Have you ever done your best to love someone who seemed completely unlovable? Have you ever tried to be kind to someone when they were stepping on your last nerve? You were struggling to bear fruit.

However, trying to bear fruit doesn't work. Our very trying reveals our misunderstanding of how fruit comes forth. A fruit isn't focused on being a fruit. A fruit is born from its connection to the tree or the vine. The fruit of the Spirit — love, joy, peace, patience, kindness, goodness, faithfulness, gentleness, and self control — comes by abiding in the vine.[50] We're just the branches. We behold Jesus in His word and feast on His love for us, and we will love without even being conscious of it. We'll do random acts of kindness, and they will be random even to us! Self-discipline will be replaced with self-control. New Year's resolutions will be replaced with faithfulness that is so supernatural it's natural. Peace like a river will flow from God through us and splash onto others. And patience won't be an impossible feat, it will be a fruit. We abide in the vine — abide in God's love — and the fruit of the Spirit will be a result.

> *Abide in Me, and I in you. As the branch cannot bear fruit of itself, unless it abides in the vine, neither can you, unless you abide in Me. I am the vine, you are the branches. He who abides in Me, and I in him, bears much fruit; for without Me you can do nothing. (John 15:4-5)*

What does it mean to abide? It's the word "meno"[51] in the Greek and means "to remain as one, not to become another or different."

> *He who is joined to the Lord is one spirit with Him. (1 Corinthians 6:17)*

There is a joining to the Lord, a becoming one spirit with Him, that occurs when we are saved and the Spirit of God comes inside of us. We become the "temple of the Holy Spirit." While this is true, our character will still need improvement and maturing. There is an outflow of the new inward reality that comes from knowing and believing a certain foundational truth: we have been made righteous through the blood of Jesus. This is called fruit! But first we must know we are loved by him.

> *As the Father loved Me, I also have loved you; abide in My love. (John 15:9)*

> *We have known and believed the love that God has for us. God is love and he who abides in love abides in God and God in him. (1 John 4:16)*

The Love OF the Father

All of that sounds so heavenly and so encouraging, but what do we do about scriptures like the following verse in 1 John 2?

Do not love the world or the things in the world. (1 John 2:15)

What makes something "worldly"? What was John talking about in this verse? He goes on in this passage to define "worldly" and give the reason that people love the world.

If anyone loves the world, the love of the Father is not in him. For all that is in the world — the lust of the flesh, the lust of the eyes, and the pride of life — is not of the Father but is of the world. (1 John 2:15-16)

"Worldly" means of the lust of the flesh, the lust of the eyes, or the pride of life. In my former ministry, I taught heavily on this subject, dividing sin into these three categories. I spent considerable time diagnosing the disease of sin, and taught on the three gods behind each category of sin: Asherah, the god of lust; Mammon, the god of greed; and Baal, the god of pride. Sin was inspired by this three-headed monster, but all we knew to do was to try to cleanse ourselves and rebuke the demons behind these sins. The NUMBER ONE solution I pushed in order to overcome the love of the world was loving God MORE because I thought the number one problem was that people just didn't love God enough. I included myself in that reasoning. For years I thought God wasn't pleased with me because I couldn't love Him the way He wanted to be loved. It was logical to me that people would love the world less if they simply loved God more. But what really causes people to love the world? And what is the real solution?

If anyone loves the world, the love OF the Father is not in him. (1 John 2:15)

John says that people love the world because they don't know the love OF the Father. They don't know that God loves them! I used to believe and teach that people love the world because they don't have enough love FOR the Father, but what John was saying is the total opposite.

When we indulge in the lust of the flesh, the lust of the eyes, or the pride of life, it's because we don't know (or we've forgotten) how much God loves us, and we are filling our holes of insecurity with the things that the world offers. We don't believe that God loves us enough to bless every area of our lives, even those areas that seem hopeless.

The apostle Paul prayed for the Ephesians that they may know the love OF Christ – not the love FOR Christ. He prayed for them that they might comprehend the length, the depth, the breadth, and the height of it. The result: that they might be filled with all the fullness of God.

I pray that Christ may dwell in your hearts through faith; that you, being rooted and grounded in love, may be able to comprehend with all the saints what is the width and length and depth and height — to know the love of Christ which passes knowledge; that you may be filled with all the fullness of God. Now to Him who is able to do exceedingly abundantly above all that we ask or think, according to the power that works in us. (Ephesians 3:17-20)

In context, Paul is saying that God will give us exceedingly, abundantly, above all we can ask or think IF we know the love OF Jesus for us! Once we know and believe the love He has for us, all we have to do is think BIG, and He will exceed it! He promised!

The more we share the grace and love of God across the world, the less and less people will love the world and the lust of the flesh, the lust of the eyes, and the pride of life.

The Greatest Commandment

The perspective behind preaching love FOR God is the law. It's the greatest commandment under the law according to Jesus Himself as recorded in Luke 10:

And behold, a certain lawyer stood up and tested Him, saying, "Teacher, what shall I do to inherit eternal life?" He said to him, "What is written in the law? What is your reading of it?" So he answered and said, "'You shall love the Lord your God with all your heart, with all your soul, with all your strength, and with all your mind,' and 'your neighbor as yourself.'" And He said to him, "You have answered rightly; do this and you will live." (Luke 10:25-28)

This man who questioned Jesus was an expert in the law. Jesus answered in the purity of the law, but honestly, has anyone ever been able to do what Jesus Himself said was the key to eternal life? No! That's why God sent His Son, and in the final offering for sin the Trinity demonstrated loving us with all His heart, soul, strength, and mind!

A few years ago I had the opportunity to share the Gospel of God's grace with a large youth group. I poured out the scriptures regarding the cross and the love of Jesus for all of us. I taught them about how Jesus had made them perfect and removed their sins as far as the East is from the West. Tears were flowing all around the room as kids were receiving freedom from the performance-based religion that they had been under. Sadly, it seems that youth leaders feel more pressure to tell kids to stop sinning than to tell them who they are in Christ, not realizing that creating a sin consciousness goes against their very goal of making the kids behave. The strength of sin is the law![52]

In the teaching I shared Luke 10 and the story of the lawyer who questioned Jesus about eternal life. I told them that according to Jesus, under the law, the greatest commandment was to love God with all their hearts. I told the kids that they weren't under the law; they were under grace. I could feel the relief when I told them that what God really wanted was for them to receive His love and not TRY to love Him. We had a ministry time where kids came forward to be prayed for, and as is always the case when the pure Gospel is preached, bondages were broken, and many were set free.

Immediately after I taught and prayed for the kids, one of the youth ministers came up to the stage to close the meeting with an announcement that shocked me. He invited the kids to be a part of a new group called the "Front Line." This would be a leadership group that would show the other kids how much they loved God in an attempt to get the youth group to love God more and the world less. I was stunned. It was the complete opposite of what I had just taught. This leader paced back and forth across the stage with great passion, raising his voice: "Your job as a part of the Front Line is to come up to the front near the stage during the youth services and worship God like crazy! Get on fire for God! Raise your hands, jump up and down, and yell for Jesus. Be bold! If you don't have the courage to do that, you can't be on the team! If you can't lead, then don't even bother signing up. But if you want to be on the team, come up front now and sign up."

What do you think that type of display of self-righteousness will accomplish? It will cause the kids who already feel condemned and defeated to feel even less worthy of God's love as compared to those who are "on fire for God." Tragically, they will walk away and maybe never come back. This should not be!

Why not have the youth leadership spread out and find seats near the back of the auditorium where they can quietly befriend the new-comers and show them the love of God? Instead of telling people to love God, let's tell them that He loves them. After they receive His love, no one will have to tell them to love Him. They won't be able to help it!

Today because of the indwelling presence of the Lord in our heart, we can now love Him and others because He first loved us.

Behold what manner of love the Father has bestowed on us, that we should be called children of God! (1 John 3:1)

It's the love OF the Father that keeps us in peace and rest, not loving the world, but loving all of the people of the world with His love!

The Woman with the Alabaster Box

The story of Jesus that touches my heart more than any other story is the account of the woman with the alabaster box of perfume that she poured out on the feet of Jesus. Of all the women in the Bible, I relate to her the most because of her unabashed gratefulness to Jesus and her heart of love towards Him in response to His uncon-ditional love for her.

Now one of the Pharisees was requesting Him to dine with him, and He entered the Pharisee's house and reclined at the table. And there was a woman in the city who was a sinner; and when she learned that He was reclining at the table in the Pharisee's house, she brought an alabaster vial of perfume, and standing behind Him at His feet, weeping, she began to wet His feet with her tears, and kept wiping them with the hair of her head, and kissing His feet and anointing them with the perfume. (Luke 7:36-38, NASB)

This woman was probably a prostitute. In the culture of that day, the alabaster box of perfume was very expensive, possibly worth enough to live on for a year. The box was made of a beautiful species of marble, distinguished for its white, almost transparent, color.[53] The perfume oil it contained was very rare and of great value. This woman broke it and poured it on the Lord and worshipped Him with it. As a prostitute, we can imagine that she earned the money for this expensive alabaster box of perfume by selling herself in shame. All the shame of lying on her back night after night was removed because of Jesus' love for her. In response she poured her love on Him.

Jesus asked the Pharisee a question: which would love a creditor more — a debtor who had been forgiven a debt of five hundred denarii, or one who had been forgiven a debt of fifty denarii. Simon gave the obvious answer: the one who owed more. Jesus responded to him that he had answered correctly and then spoke of the affect of His forgiveness on this woman:

"...her sins, which are many, have been forgiven, for she loved much; but he who is forgiven little, loves little." Then He said to her, "Your sins have been forgiven." (Luke 7:47-48, NASB)

When we realize how much we have been forgiven, it doesn't make us want to sin more. When we know we are forgiven much, we will know that we are loved much, and we will sin less!

He who knows he is forgiven much, loves much.

This is real love—not that we loved God, but that he loved us and sent his Son as a sacrifice to take away our sins. (1 John 4:10, NLT)

We love, because He first loved us. (1 John 4:19, NASB)

CHAPTER 5IVE

Christ's Righteousness vs. Self-Righteousness

Key scriptures:
Acts 3:6, 12, 16; Genesis 1:26-28; Genesis 2:7-9, 16-17; Genesis 3:1-24; 1 John 1:9; Mark 11:12-14, 21-24

The more our spiritual eyes are opened to God's grace, the more we see the tension between what we see with our natural eyes and what we believe in our heart. We might ask, "If God is good, why am I not seeing good in my life?"

When my husband and I were newly-weds in the 1980's, we participated in a Bible study on the book of Job entitled, "Why Do Bad Things Happen To Good People?" The whole premise was that if people were obeying all the rules, giving to the poor, and attending church, then how could it be possible that bad things would happen to them? The answers that were offered to that question were so inconclusive that I do not remember them. The goal of the study was to make us feel better during hard times, but the only nugget I took away from that study was that Job got some really bad advice from his friends, and maybe we should just keep our problems to ourselves!

This creation is waiting for something. Things are not as they should be and if everyone were honest, they would admit it. Paul likened the feeling to a pregnant woman experiencing birth pains.[54] This barren creation is yearning for deliverance. This tension is not felt just between us and this world; it's a tension we feel in our own bodies. There's a sense that the deterioration that we experience is going against God's original intent.

We can lose heart when we focus on the outward. Paul said the outward man is perishing, but the inward man is being renewed each day by the transforming of our minds to the truth. The encouraging news is that the trouble of this life — the persecutions and the hardships — is accomplishing for us something awesome: an eternal weight of glory, an everlasting crown of authority. That's why we're to contemplate and give our attention to things that our natural eyes can't see.[55] We don't consider these outward bodies and these outward circumstances. We're to use our spiritual eyes to see what God sees.

This resurrection life you received from God is not a timid, grave-tending life. It's adventurously expectant, greeting God with a childlike "What's next, Papa?" God's Spirit touches our spirits and confirms who we really are. (Romans 8:15-16, The Message)

Do You Know What You Have?

When I look at the accounts of the displays of the supernatural power of God in the early church, a frustration with the state of the church today rises up in me and expresses itself with three words: "It's NOT okay!" It's not okay for sons and daughters of God to be treading water and waiting for the sweet by and by. It's not okay for the heirs of God to live this life in powerlessness while we sing, "When we all get to heaven what a day of rejoicing that will be." The Spirit of the resurrection dwells in us now![56] That power gives life to our mortal bodies, and that glory resides in us to be released!

Peter understood who he was in Christ. He was able to look into the eyes of a lame man, take him firmly by his hand, pull him to his feet, and release the healing power of God so much so that the man was leaping and dancing! Why? Because he knew what he had and he knew how to give it away.

"Silver and gold I do not have, but what I do have I give you. In the name of Jesus Christ of Nazareth, rise up and walk." (Acts 3:6)

Peter knew he was a son of God in the earth, crowned in the glory of Jesus Christ, and he revealed the glory of the Lord in the earth. The people were astonished at this power they saw demonstrated through the life of Peter. Here was his response to them:

"Men of Israel, why do you marvel at this? Or why look so intently at us, as though by our own power or godliness we had made this man walk?... And His name [Jesus], through faith in His name, has made this man strong, whom you see and know. Yes, the faith which comes THROUGH HIM has given him this perfect soundness in the presence of you all." (Acts 3:12, 16, emphasis added)

How can we live a life in the power and godliness and faith of Jesus Christ? Before we can answer that question, we need to answer another question: why aren't we already living that life? I believe that the best way to find the answer to that question is to go back to where it all started.

Crowned with Glory and Honor

Reader Study Reference, Genesis 1:26-28

What was God's original plan for mankind? Where did it all begin? What happened to mess things up? David wrote of God's original intent for man:

When I consider Your heavens, the work of Your fingers, the moon and the stars, which You have ordained, What is man that You are mindful of him, and the son of man that You visit him? For You have made him a little lower than the angels, and You have crowned him with glory and honor. You have made him to have dominion over the works of Your hands; You have put all things under his feet. (Psalm 8:3-6)

When God made Adam and Eve, He crowned them in glory and honor. This word "crown" is the Hebrew word "atar."[57] It isn't like the tiara that a king or queen wears. It means surrounding all over. "Honor" is the Hebrew word "hadar,"[58] and it means splendor, majesty, and beauty. When God made man, He created him kingly and majestic. God designed man to be encompassed all around in the splendor of His glory. "Glory" is the Hebrew word "kabowd,"[59] and it refers to God's abundance and riches and dignity. It's the manifestation of God in all His goodness. Man was created in the image of God to bear His glory. Man was crowned, literally surrounded, with the glory of God like a brilliant light. The word "glory" in Hebrew is also used to denote the heavy weight of authority. The word "kabowd" is derived from the word "kabad" which means "to be heavy."[60] A person with glory has authority, like in the idiom, "He carries a lot of weight around here." God spoke, and the world was created.[61] In the same way, whatever Adam said, it carried the weight of his authority.

> Then God said, "Let Us make man in Our image, according to Our likeness; let them have dominion over the fish of the sea, over the birds of the air, and over the cattle, over all the earth and over every creeping thing that creeps on the earth." So God created man in His own image; in the image of God He created him; male and female He created them. Then God blessed them, and God said to them, "Be fruitful and multiply; fill the earth and subdue it; have dominion over the fish of the sea, over the birds of the air, and over every living thing that moves on the earth." (Genesis 1:26-28)

The glory that surrounded Adam and Eve was not only the goodness of God and the weight of authority, it was also their protection. God gave them dominion over all the animals and everything on the earth. They could control everything by simply speaking and creation responded. Contrast that to today where even a microscopic bacteria has enough authority over man that it can kill him. What happened to the glory and honor that God originally intended for man? Tragically, they lost it, which we will see as we continue and the story of Adam and Eve unfolds.

Yahweh

Reader Study Reference, Genesis 2:7

Throughout Genesis 1, we see the name of God, the Hebrew word "Elohim," in the creation. "In the beginning God [Elohim]

..."[62] Elohim is a plural word for God because it is referring to the Father, Son, and Holy Spirit. Elohim is the Creator God.

In chapter 2 where we see passages referring to the creation of man, we have the introduction of the name, LORD GOD, or in Hebrew "Yahweh Elohim."[63]

> *And the LORD God formed man of the dust of the ground, and breathed into his nostrils the breath of life; and man became a living being. (Genesis 2:7)*

Yahweh (also called Jehovah[64]) is considered the most holy name of all the names of God, and even today the Jewish people will not pronounce it because they believe it is too sacred to utter. To say this word is considered blasphemous to Jewish people, and is looked upon as the worst kind of presumption. They call it the tetragrammaton[65] because it has four (tetra) Hebrew letters, Yud Hei Vav Hei. Instead of saying Yahweh, they will say "the name," or they use the name Adonai[66] which means "my Lord, master, owner." Yahweh is translated LORD in English with all caps in most English translations. However, when you find Lord (with just the L capitalized), it's not Yahweh, it's Adonai.

Yahweh is the LORD who was, who is, and who is to come. He is the great "I AM." Yahweh is the covenant-keeping God, the self-existing God, and the intimate God. He is the relational God. The reason we can say Yahweh is because the New Covenant in His blood has removed every barrier between us. The veil has been torn. We as believers in the New Covenant are in union with the covenant-keeping God of intimate relationship.

The Two Trees

Reader Study Reference, Genesis 2:8-9, 16-17

> *The Lord God planted a garden eastward in Eden, and there He put the man whom He had formed. And out of the ground the Lord God made every tree grow that is pleasant to the sight and good for food. The tree of life was also in the midst of the garden, and the tree of the knowledge of good and evil... And the Lord God commanded the man, saying, "Of every tree of the garden you may freely eat; but of the tree of the knowledge*

of good and evil you shall not eat, for in the day that you eat of it you shall surely die." (Genesis 2:8-9; 16-17)

God put the Tree of Life in the midst of the Garden. That word "midst" is the Hebrew word "tavek,"[67] and it means middle or center. The Tree of the Knowledge of Good and Evil is also mentioned, but without any description of its position. The Tree of Life was in the center of the world. The Tree of Life represents Jesus, and everything in this world is still peripheral to Him.

We often think of the Tree of Life as good, and the Tree of the Knowledge of Good and Evil as bad, but the Tree of the Knowledge of Good and Evil was not bad because everything that God created was good,[68] but this tree just wasn't good for man. The Tree of the Knowledge of Good and Evil was a foreshadowing of the law. Think of it this way:

- Tree of the Knowledge of Good and Evil/ law/ self-righteousness
- Tree of Life/ grace/ Jesus' righteousness

It is in the choice that God gave Adam that we see the amazing love of God. He did not create robots. Love is a choice, and God risked that man would make the wrong choice by creating us after His own kind. God chose to love us, and we choose to receive that love.

Every part of the fruit of the Tree of the Knowledge of Good and Evil was part of the fall of man, and therefore, NO part of that fruit could be part of the restoration. The forbidden fruit was "good and evil" — not just good, not just evil. Man cannot extract the good and leave the evil. He was supposed to leave it alone altogether. Partaking of this fruit brought spiritual and ultimately physical death.

The Great Deception

Reader Study Reference, Genesis 3:1-5

Let's look at Genesis 3 and the story of the fall of man and how it relates to the two trees in the garden.

Now the serpent was more cunning than any beast of the field which the Lord God had made. And he said to the woman, "Has God indeed said, 'You shall not eat of every tree of the garden'?" And the woman said to the serpent, "We may eat the fruit of the trees of the garden; but of the fruit of the tree which is in the midst of the garden, God has said, 'You shall not eat it, nor shall you touch it, lest you die.'" Then the serpent said to the woman, "You will not surely die. For God knows that in the day you eat of it your eyes will be opened, and you will be like God, knowing good and evil." (Genesis 3:1-5)

Both satan and Eve misquoted God and perverted what He said. The devil portrayed God as stingy when he claimed that God had said, "You shall not eat of every tree of the garden." God had actually said, "Of EVERY tree of the garden you may FREELY eat..." He only gave one boundary: do not eat from ONE tree. Eve also perverted what God has said when she described the Tree of the Knowledge of Good and Evil as being in the midst, "tavek," of the garden. The Tree of the Knowledge of Good and Evil wasn't the center of the world. The Tree of Life was, and still is, the center of the universe today.

These perversions of what God said were the beginning of the end of the innocence in the garden. Whenever truth is twisted, we will see freedom begin to slip away.

Eve's motive for eating the fruit of the knowledge of good and evil was to be like God. How could that be sin? Think about how that applies to us. Isn't that the goal of Christianity? Aren't we supposed to be moving towards being more righteous and holy and Christ-like? Actually, no. If we think that we can be MORE like Christ by our own righteousness, it is actually the sin of unbelief in His righteousness that was given as a gift. It's an insult to the cross of Jesus to think that we can make ourselves more godly by our own disciplines and self-efforts.

Adam and Eve were already made in the likeness of God's image. They bought into the lie that they had to do something to be like something that they already were! The greatest sin of mankind is trying to be like God independent of God by endeavoring to know good and evil and attempting to do our best to be good. That was the great satanic lie in the garden.

True Christianity is about receiving the gift of Christ's righteousness and walking by faith in that gift. It's not about aspiring to be more like Him. It's about believing that you have been transformed by the Holy Spirit in your spirit into complete holiness as a new creation in Him.

The Fruit of the Deadly Tree

Reader Study Reference, Genesis 3:6-11

Remember the account from 1 John 2:15 where the apostle John diagnosed the reason that people love the world? He said it's because the love OF the Father is not in them. The "world" is referring to the lust of the flesh, the lust of the eyes, and the pride of life. Do you know where the love of the world first crept in to the heart of man? It was in the Garden of Eden.

So when the woman saw that the tree was good for food, that it was pleasant to the eyes, and a tree desirable to make one wise, she took of its fruit and ate. She also gave to her husband with her, and he ate. (Genesis 3:6)

- "Good for food" — lust of the flesh
- "Pleasant to the eyes" — lust of the eyes
- "Desirable to make on wise" — pride of life

Adam and Eve bought into the lie that God would withhold something good from them. For a moment they turned away from the love OF God for them. Not believing the love of God for us will lead us to love the world, and the result will aways be shame. Our eyes will be shut to His love, but opened to something else entirely.

Then the eyes of both of them were opened, and they knew that they were naked; and they sewed fig leaves together and made themselves coverings. And they heard the sound of the Lord God walking in the garden in the cool of the day, and Adam and his wife hid themselves from the presence of the Lord God among the trees of the garden. Then the Lord God called to Adam and said to him, "Where are you?" So he said, "I heard Your voice in the garden, and I was afraid because I was naked; and I hid myself." And He said, "Who told you that you were naked? Have you eaten from the tree of which I commanded you that you should not eat?" (Genesis 3:7-11)

What were Adam and Eve's eyes opened to? The devil had told them that their eyes would be opened to being more like God; but tragically, their eyes were opened to their nakedness. All this time they had been without physical covering. Their covering was the far superior covering of the glory of God. When they ate the fruit of that tree, the all encompassing light of the glory of God left them, and their eyes were opened to their shame.

Consciousness of their sin produced condemnation which produced self-righteousness – fig leaves! When they were conscious of their sin, they hid from God. God said, "Adam, where are you?" And he came up with the great idea of covering himself with fig leaves. God never turned His back on Adam and Eve. God came looking for them. Even after they were banished from the garden, God continued to talk to man, but the intimacy of the garden that had existed between God and man was gone.

Adam and Eve had tried to be more like God by eating from the tree, but when they ate from the tree, they discovered how unlike God they actually were — they had lost their righteousness. They felt guilty and shameful and unworthy. This shows that they were created in the likeness of God, but not in the righteousness of God. They were created in their own righteousness. They were created without sin, perfect and righteous, but they didn't have God's eternal righteousness. That's why when they ate from the tree, they fell and abandoned the glory of God.

All have sinned and fall short of the glory of God. (Romans 3:23)

If they had been created in God's perfect righteousness, they would not have been able to fall. This is an important point. God's ultimate intent is that we become a NEW creation by receiving His perfect righteousness and relate to Him forever through that righteousness, which will keep us forever in Him throughout all eternity. Today our righteousness is not our own. It's Christ's righteousness[69]; therefore, it can never fail us. Our own righteousness would fall short of the glory of God on a daily basis, but His righteousness is a never-fading glory.

Today we can still "put on fig leaves," though, by attempting to be more righteous. We take a list of "to do's" to cleanse ourselves for the purpose of making ourselves "right with God" before we can "enter His presence." We go through the steps of confession and repentance and praying for forgiveness so that we will be ready to approach God's throne of grace. Yet this is an oxymoron! How can you make yourself deserving of God's grace? This whole scheme reveals a complete ignorance of what grace is! You can't earn grace. Grace is only for the undeserving!

Repentance, Confession, Forgiveness

What about confession, repentance, and asking for forgiveness? If we're not supposed to be sin conscious, what to we do with these spiritual exercises? Aren't we supposed to do those things? Yes, we are, but perhaps not in the way we have been taught.

Here are those three words and what they mean:

- **Confess** is the Greek word "homologeo"[70], and it means to say the same thing as another. As believers we are told in the scriptures to:

  ...draw near with a true heart in full assurance of faith, having our hearts sprinkled from an evil conscience and our bodies washed with pure water. Let us hold fast the CONFESSION of our hope without wavering, for He who promised is faithful. (Hebrews 10:22-23, emphasis added)

  What is the confession of our hope? It's that we are righteous through the blood of Jesus! If we are in Christ today, our confession is not that we are sinners, but that we are righteous. It doesn't mean we don't sin, but it means that when we do sin, it is not according to our new nature in Jesus!

- **Repent** is the Greek word "metanoeo"[71] and it simply means to change one's mind. It does not mean to change your behavior or even to be sorry and apologetic. It doesn't even mean to change your direction, although that could be the result of repentance. "Meta" means change, "noeo" means mind.[72]

When Jesus began His earthly ministry, He explained exactly the change of mind that the people needed:

Jesus came to Galilee, preaching the gospel of the kingdom of God, and saying, "The time is fulfilled, and the kingdom of God is at hand. RE-PENT, and believe in the gospel." (Mark 1:14-15, emphasis added)

The days of the law were coming to an end. Jesus said, "Believe in the Gospel." We need to believe the Good News that Jesus has come and washed us clean from our sins!

- **Forgiveness** is the Greek word "aphesis"[73], and it means "letting them (sins) go as if they had never been committed." God let go of our sins. He didn't hold them against us. When the bank forgives a debt, it means that the debt has been paid. The wages — the debt — of sin is death, and Jesus has paid our debt of death with His own blood! Our Creditor, God, has let go of the debt!

In Him we have redemption through His blood, the forgiveness of sins, according to the riches of His grace. (Ephesians 1:7)

We have been forgiven. Past tense. We are not forgiven as we go. We are not working towards being forgiven. We are not forgiven some time in the future. All of our sins — past, present, and future — were paid for at the cross. We are forgiven according to the riches of His grace, not according to anything we can muster through religious activities or re-defined ideas of repentance or confession. If we could ever measure the riches of His grace extended towards us, then we would comprehend how much we have been forgiven. Nothing in all of creation even touches the value of the payment of Christ's blood for our sins.

1 John 1:9

Before we move on, I want to cover one more point on this topic. Many Christians have the idea that we are to confess our sins to God on a daily or even hourly basis. The reasoning is that we want to stay "in fellowship" with God. 1 John 1:9 is a verse that many people have taken out of context and used to support the idea that believers need to confess their sins in order to be forgiven and stay right with God. Did you know that the phrase, "keep short accounts with God" is not in the Bible? Why? Because God is not keeping an account of our sins! If God is not counting our sins against us, why are we counting them?

> *If we confess our sins, He is faithful and just to forgive us our sins and to cleanse us from all unrighteousness. (1 John 1:9)*

Is this verse directed to the Christian who needs to confess his sins in order to be forgiven? But I thought that we only needed to believe in Jesus to be forgiven? What happens if I miss a sin and don't confess it? Dear reader, to believe this verse is written to believers would go directly against all of the scriptures that tell us that we are saved by grace through faith in Jesus! This scripture was written to the unbeliever, and we can see that clearly if we read it in context in 1 John 1.

Paul, the apostle of grace, who wrote most of the New Testament, never mentioned confession of sins one time! If confession of sins for the believer is so important as some say, then Paul short-changed us! You'd think he would have mentioned it at least once! In fact, 1 John 1:9, written by John, is the ONLY verse in ALL of the epistles that mentions the confession of sins to God, and it was not written to the believer. The unbeliever is convicted by the Holy Spirit that he is a sinner in need of a Savior, but once he accepts Jesus, he becomes a righteous saint in the light!

To clarify, I am not saying that we shouldn't talk to the Holy Spirit about our challenges with the flesh. I am not saying that we should deny that we have sinned. I am not saying that sin is ok. I'm not saying that we don't have godly sorrow over sin. All you have to do is look at the horror of the cross and the sufferings of Jesus on our behalf to see the evil of sin. We want to live lives that honor and exalt Jesus. We don't want to give a bad testimony to His name. But this murky gray area that says, "No, as believers we don't have to confess each sin in order to make it to heaven, but we should so that we'll be in fellowship with God, and if we don't, we won't be right with God" perpetuates a conscience in the body of Christ ridden with guilt and creates insecurity and fear in the relationship with the Lord that was intended for our enjoyment and pleasure.

If you feel guilty around someone, you will not have a good relationship with that person. If you fear someone, it's only a matter of time before you will hate them. Perfect love — the kind of love that God has for us — drives out fear. Fear involves punishment, but that was dealt with at the cross.

Back to Genesis ...

The Choice

What was the purpose of the Tree of the Knowledge of Good and Evil? I believe there are two purposes: one before they fell, the other after they fell.

Have you ever wondered why God put the tree there in the first place? The Tree of the Knowledge of Good and Evil was there to give man the choice to believe God or reject Him. Believing Him meant they would trust Him when He said that the forbidden fruit would kill them. Obeying His voice meant that they trusted Him. Not believing God is rejecting Him. Rejecting Him is rejecting His love because He is love. Love is a choice.

If God gave them the choice, they obviously had the ability to make the right choice, the choice to believe.

Adam and Eve did not choose the Tree of Life and never ate from the Tree of Life. We know they didn't eat from it AFTER they ate from the Tree of the Knowledge of Good and Evil because they were banned from the garden after they ate of that fruit. And we know that they didn't eat from the Tree of Life BEFORE they ate from the Tree of the Knowledge of Good and Evil because they would never have died. The Tree of Life gave eternal life.

What does all of this mean? God had truly given Adam and Eve the ability to choose. He did not take their hands and cause them to reach up and take the forbidden fruit. In fact, every human being since Adam and Eve was created with the ability to choose God or reject Him — to believe in Him or not. A person darkened in his understanding and alienated from the life of God has the ability to believe God or reject Him. Eternal life in Christ begins after we believe and receive salvation.

In Him, you also, AFTER listening to the message of truth, the gospel of your salvation—having also BELIEVED, you were sealed in Him with the Holy Spirit of promise. (Ephesians 1:13, NASB, emphasis added)

There are those who say that man has no ability to choose. They say this because they believe they are glorifying God. However, God is not glorified by something that's not true. This line of thinking implies a twisted image of God. In that doctrinal framework, God gives faith to some and withholds faith from others. God is the only one with the choice, and if He chooses you, He forces you choose Him. This makes God look like the captain of the Titanic who purposefully didn't provide enough life boats. We would lock that man up and throw away the key! The truth is God has provided enough life boats for everyone on the earth.

He Himself is the propitiation for our sins, and not for ours only but also for THE WHOLE WORLD. (1 John 2:2, emphasis added)

The Lord is not slack concerning His promise, as some count slackness, but is longsuffering toward us, not willing that any should perish but that all should come to repentance. (2 Peter 3:9)

For this is good and acceptable in the sight of God our Savior, who desires all men to be saved and to come to the knowledge of the truth. (1 Timothy 2:3-4, NASB)

On the other hand, in the same camp as those who adhere to this idea that man has no choice except the choice that God imposes on him are those who find it too distasteful that God would not provide enough life boats. So their solution to that dilemma is that God eventually causes everyone to choose Christ. This is the doctrine called Christian Universalism. Once again, no choice for man. If no one has a choice and everyone is eventually saved, then *why did Jesus need to die?* Think about it.

The result of the false idea that man has no choice has colossal implications when carried into the Christian life because it produces passivity in the body of Christ with a "whatever will be will be" attitude. With the mindset that our faith is inconsequential and man has no choice, God gets blamed for every evil in the world.

I believe the number one reason that so many have bought into the lie that man has no choice is because of pride. To believe that our faith matters would mean that God has given us responsibility, and we can't stay the victim. The bottom line is this: if we have choice, we can't remain as victims.

Before the fall, God put the Tree of the Knowledge of Good and Evil in the Garden of Eden to establish a principle: man had a choice.

So what about the purpose of the Tree of the Knowledge of Good and Evil AFTER the fall? After they ate the forbidden fruit, the Tree of the Knowledge of Good and Evil has had the same purpose as the law:

> *Therefore by the deeds of the law no flesh will be justified [made righteous] in His sight, for by the law is the knowledge of sin. (Romans 3:20, brackets added for emphasis)*

That tree revealed to mankind that relating to God through our own righteousness is impossible. There is only one way to relate to God, and that is through His gift of righteousness. Since Adam and Eve, mankind has been trying to relate to God through their own goodness and righteousness, yet it's only when we see how unrighteous that we truly are outside of Him that we are ready to receive His righteousness.

For us to use the very thing that was given to reveal unrighteousness to try to become more righteous (the law, the Tree of Knowledge) is just as effective as covering ourselves with fig leaves so God can't see our sin.

The Fruitless Fig Tree

Fig leaves are mentioned thousands of years later in the story of Jesus' encounter with a fruitless fig tree following His triumphal entry into Jerusalem. I believe this example can teach us much about man's efforts and self-righteousness. The account from Mark 11 first focuses on Jesus' entry into the city upon the back of a young colt as a welcoming crowd waved palm branches and shouted "Hosanna! Blessed is He who comes in the name of the Lord!" unaware that He was making His way to the cross. As the day grew late, He went out to Bethany to rest with His disciples. The next morning when Jesus and the disciples had come out from Bethany He was hungry, and He encountered the fig tree without fruit on it. He walked up to it, rebuked it, and cursed it.

Now the next day, when they had come out from Bethany, He was hungry. And seeing from afar a fig tree having leaves, He went to see if perhaps He would find something on it. When He came to it, He found nothing but leaves, for it was not the season for figs. In response Jesus said to it, "Let no one eat fruit from you ever again." And His disciples heard it. (Mark 11:12-14)

I can remember reading that story in the past and feeling sorry for the poor fig tree! Now I have a different understanding. Actually Jesus cursing the fig tree was a symbolic act. If we use the "law of first mention" of Bible interpretation to find out the roots and meaning of this symbolic act, we'll see that fig leaves are first seen in the Garden of Eden in the first act of self-righteousness. So Jesus was teaching His disciples about His view of self-righteousness in this story. He was cursing self-righteousness when He cursed the fig tree. He was saying in essence, "Never go back to the system of the law and self-righteousness again! Don't anyone ever eat from this deception ever again." I think it's interesting that "in response" to the tree's fruitlessness, Jesus cursed the tree. The lesson: Jesus is the answer to fruitless efforts to make ourselves righteous!

The next day we see that this tree had shriveled up from the roots and died.

"Rabbi, look! The fig tree which You cursed has withered away." So Jesus answered and said to them, "Have faith in God. For assuredly, I say to you, whoever says to this mountain, 'Be removed and be cast into the sea,' and does not doubt in his heart, but believes that those things he says will be done, he will have whatever he says. Therefore I say to you, whatever things you ask when you pray, believe that you receive them, and you will have them. (Mark 11:21-24)

If we remove the fig tree, then we can remove the mountain! Can you see what this passage is saying? If we remove all attempts to make ourselves righteous before God and trust that we are righteous through Christ, then our conscience will be free from guilt and unworthiness. If we believed we are worthy, we would have no hesitation receiving anything from God. Getting rid of self-righteousness is the key to living a miraculous faith-filled life.

The Devil Made Me Do It

Reader Study Reference, Genesis 3:12-13

> *Then the man said, "The woman whom You gave to be with me, she gave me of the tree, and I ate." And the Lord God said to the woman, "What is this you have done?" The woman said, "The serpent deceived me, and I ate." (Genesis 3:12-13)*

Did you notice that the man blamed the woman, and the woman blamed the devil? Here we see one of the results of the Tree of the Knowledge of Good and Evil: victimization. Victimization is a result of allowing the behavior of others to determine how we relate to God.

Recently someone who had experienced a great offense by someone close to her came to me for help. It was a big one, and she was angry with God for letting it happen. I told her that God was not responsible for another person's choices, but He cared deeply for her and understood her pain. I told her that God was there for her and would see her through the situation. I shared with her many things intended to comfort her, including my own experiences with extreme pain at the hands of others, and how God had seen me through by His grace. Her response was that God's empathy wasn't very comforting if it didn't change her circumstances. In the course of our discussions she said to me that this other person had destroyed her relationship and trust in God.

Is that possible? Can someone else ruin your relationship with God? How can that be? If that were possible, our relationship with the Lord would be on a pretty flimsy foundation! The truth is that nothing on the outside can change the reality on the inside. And if our relationship with the Lord and our peace relies on the behavior of others or any outside circumstances, then we are in a losing battle. We are promised that we will have trouble in this world.[74] We are also promised that He who is in us — the Tree of Life — is greater than he who is in the world.[75] We can feast at the banquet table of heaven in the presence of our enemies if our eyes see the spiritual reality.[76]

People often ask me to pray for peace for them. I used to go ahead and do what they asked even though it never felt quite right. Now I just won't do it. I'm not going to pray that God send a believer peace. If a person is a Christian, he has all the peace he'll ever need in his spirit already, and if I were to pray for peace to somehow plop on them from the outside, I would be saying that Jesus didn't tell the truth when He said He was leaving us with peace.[77] The Spirit of Peace lives on the inside. The well of the living waters that never runs dry f ows from our innermost being.[78]

If we believe we have no peace, we're going to look for peace from the outside, and we're going to be swung around by the tail by our circumstances.

For as he thinks in his heart, so is he. (Proverbs 23:7)

We're also going to think that someone else can steal our peace. If that were possible, they would have to somehow steal the Holy Spirit right out of our spirit! Dear reader, no one has the ability to steal our peace, but we have the ability to allow unbelief to cloud our eyes of faith.

When I pray for people, I usually just pray that God will open the eyes of their understanding to what already IS and for them to tap into it. If you are a believer, your spirit is as Jesus is: restful. Because of what Christ has done for us in removing our sins and making us one with Him, we can know that God is for us. If God is for us, who can be against us?

Several years ago I heard these words from the Holy Spirit, and I heeded them: "Tricia, you don't need to fight. You don't need to strive. You don't need to set people right. You don't need to defend your image. You don't need to set the record straight. Your peace is more important. Let go and let Me handle it."

Back to Genesis...

The Curse on Satan

Reader Study Reference, Genesis 3:14-15

Because of the fall of man, creation was cursed. Death entered where there had only been life. Enmity entered where there had only been harmony. The first curse was on satan.

> *So the Lord God said to the serpent: "Because you have done this, you are cursed more than all cattle, and more than every beast of the field; on your belly you shall go, and you shall eat dust. and you shall eat dust all the days of your life, and I will put enmity between you and the woman, and between your seed and her Seed; He shall bruise your head, and you shall bruise His heel." (Genesis 3:14-15)*

What is the "dust" that satan would eat? We'll see later in few verses when we get to verse 19...

The word "head" in "He shall bruise your head" speaks of authority. God promised that One would be born from the descendants of Eve (Jesus Christ) who would be wounded by satan while in the process of crushing satan's authority in the earth forever. "Bruise His heel" is referring to the cross. "Bruise your head" is referring to the resurrection. Jesus disarmed the devil and made a public spectacle of him![79]

Throughout biblical history we can see the devil's strategy to destroy the Redeemer or stop Him from being born. The devil attempted to stop God's plan of redemption from the beginning.

Satan was the one to put it into the heart of Cain to kill his brother in Genesis 4. Why? Inspiring Cain to murder Abel was his attempt to "bruise His heel" in order to kill Eve's Seed and stop God's plan to save His people from sin. The devil thought that Abel might be the Redeemer because he did not know God's timing of when the Messiah would be born.

Thousands of years later we see the Egyptian Pharaoh trying to suppress the growing Israelite population because God's people were growing greater and stronger and mightier than the Egyptians. Pharaoh commanded that every newborn Hebrew male was to be murdered.[80] Once again, we see satan attempting to stop the Seed.

About fifteen hundred years later, when our Savior was born and a myriad of angels filled the skies, satan knew that this could be his dreaded hour, and we see him on the rampage again. He did not know where the Baby was born, so he tried another clean sweep when he incited Herod to issue the decree to kill all the firstborn sons of the Hebrews.[81] Thank God for the angel who appeared to Joseph telling him to take the Baby to Egypt for protection.[82]

Throughout Jesus' life on earth, satan tried many times to kill Him by the hands of the Pharisees, but nothing could stop Jesus before His time. When Jesus hung on the cross and prayed, "My God, My God, why have You forsaken Me?"[83], satan figured he was finally triumphing over Jesus. When Jesus breathed His last, satan thought he had won the victory. However, he didn't realize that he had only "bruised his heal." In three days, Jesus would "bruise his head" forever.

Nothing could stop the Seed from being born. Nothing could stop the Seed from growing up as a human being in this world. Nothing could stop the Seed from giving up His life for us. Nothing could stop the Seed from being raised from the dead. Nothing could stop the Seed from bringing forth a new creation just like Himself.

Today there is a still a seed that satan tries to steal: the incorruptible seed of God's word in our hearts. Our part is just to believe that what God has said is true and to guard our hearts by rejecting satan's lies.

The Curse on Eve

Reader Study Reference, Genesis 3:16

In the next verse in Genesis 3, we see the curse that was placed upon the woman:

> *To the woman He said: "I will greatly multiply your sorrow and your conception; in pain you shall bring forth children; your desire shall be for your husband, and he shall rule over you." (Genesis 3:16)*

All the afflictions of women are wrapped up in that scripture, aren't they? But hallelujah:

Christ has redeemed us from the curse of the law, having become a curse for us (for it is written, "Cursed is everyone who hangs on a tree.") (Galatians 3:13)

If you are a woman, ask God what it means in your life that He has redeemed you from the curse on women and how it's possible to live the curse-free life in childbirth, motherhood, and marriage. God sent Jesus to give us the abundant supernatural life of peace and provision! Don't just accept the curse and listen to the world's assessments and solutions. God has something better in store for us because Jesus has reclaimed us and ransomed us from the curse by His precious blood!

The Curse on Adam

Reader Study Reference, Genesis 3:17-19

Then to Adam He said, "Because you have heeded the voice of your wife, and have eaten from the tree of which I commanded you, saying, 'You shall not eat of it': Cursed is the ground for your sake; in toil you shall eat of it all the days of your life. Both thorns and thistles it shall bring forth for you, and you shall eat the herb of the field." (Genesis 3:17-18)

After Adam sinned, the ground was cursed, and thorns and thistles came forth. The result was toil and hardship. Imagine Adam having lived in paradise with no pain and no toil, and then all of a sudden everything was difficult, and there was no way to find relief.

Today we can rejoice because Jesus took the toil, the travail, and the drudgery of this life when He wore the crown of thorns.[84] Jesus redeemed us from the curse of depression, heaviness, hopelessness, and fear. As the thorns were pressed into His brow and His blood trickled down His face, He paid for it all so that today He can crown us with the peace that passes understanding.

In the sweat of your face you shall eat bread till you return to the ground, for out of it you were taken;... (Genesis 3:19)

The sweat from Adam's face speaks of the stressful life, the hard life of human effort. Prior to the fall, there was no effort. Adam had dominion over everything in the earth, and food was free for the taking. However, after the fall, the ground was hard to till and sweat poured from his face.

Fast forward thousands of years to the Garden of Gethsemane the night Jesus was arrested. He shed His blood for the toil and stressful life that began in the Garden of Eden. Jesus poured blood from His face under the extreme pressure and agony of the looming condemnation and separation from His Father because of our sin.

And being in an agony He prayed more earnestly: and His sweat was as it were great drops of blood falling down to the ground. (Luke 22:44)

Jesus who hates sin because He loves the sinner, endured the agony and drank the cup for us. His love compelled Him to give His life for us. The sinless, pure One would be rejected, despised, stripped, spit upon, and condemned.

Jesus sweat drops of blood for us to redeem us from the curse of stress, pressure, and anxiety. Every drop of blood cries out "Peace, I am leaving you! Don't let your heart be troubled. Don't let it be afraid!"[85] Now we don't live under the curse that says, "By the sweat of your face we will eat bread." Today we can live the curse-free, sweat-free life of dependency on Jesus to provide our every need.

Don't you want to live like that? It's only a decision — a decision to live in the moment. It's only in the moment that grace flows. Don't worry about tomorrow. Tomorrow has enough worries of its own.[86]

And my God shall supply all your need according to His riches in glory by Christ Jesus. (Philippians 4:19)

The Lord is my shepherd; I shall not want. He makes me to lie down in green pastures; He leads me beside the still waters. (Psalm 23:1-2)

Dust

Reader Study Reference, Genesis 3:19

Now we come back to "dust." In Genesis 3:14 God told satan that he would eat dust all the days of his life. What is dust? In the Garden when God cursed Adam, He said this:

"...for dust you are, and to dust you shall return." (Genesis 3:19, cont.)

Dust is the flesh of man, and the flesh of man is the food of satan.[87] Flesh speaks of human self-effort. When we look to the flesh, we are looking to ourselves to redeem ourselves. We are striving to perfect ourselves, provide for ourselves, heal ourselves, deliver ourselves, and save ourselves by working in the sufficiency of our own strength. The food of satan is our fleshly perspective.

The mind set on the flesh is death, but the mind set on the Spirit is life and peace. (Romans 8:6, NASB)

The devil wants us to be conscious of the flesh, the sin in the flesh, all of our failures, and all of our weaknesses because he knows that when we are conscious of dust, it's death for us. How does satan get us to look at the flesh? He uses the weapon of the law which reminds us that we have fallen short. He shoots his fiery darts of doubt, fear, and condemnation by using the law against us. Jesus redeemed us from the curse of a fleshly perspective by giving us His own mind, the "mind of Christ," and sending the Holy Spirit to renew our minds to the truth.[88]

The First Shedding of Blood

Reader Study Reference, Genesis 3:20-21

And Adam called his wife's name Eve, because she was the mother of all living. Also for Adam and his wife the LORD God made tunics of skin, and clothed them. (Genesis 3:20-21)

When Adam and Eve sinned, they covered themselves with fig leaves. Man's answer to sin was insufficient. Why? Because no blood was shed.

Without the shedding of blood, there is no forgiveness of sins. (Hebrews 9:22)

So God clothed them with coats of animal skins. In other words, blood was shed to give them a covering for their sin. Prior to this first sacrifice of animals, no blood had been shed. God was the first one to kill animals, and this was the first time innocent blood was shed for the guilty.

Banished from the Garden

Reader Study Reference, Genesis 3:22-24

> *Then the LORD God said, 'Behold, the man has become like one of Us, to know good and evil. And now, lest he put out his hand and take also of the tree of life, and eat, and live forever'— therefore the LORD God sent him out of the garden of Eden to till the ground from which he was taken. So He drove out the man; and He placed cherubim at the east of the garden of Eden, and a flaming sword which turned every way, to guard the way to the Tree of Life. (Genesis 3:22-24)*

When God drove Adam and Eve out of the Garden of Eden, He stationed cherubim at the entrance to the garden with a flaming sword that turned every way forbidding entrance to the garden and access to the Tree of Life. God did this out of His mercy. If man had eaten from the Tree of Life in his sinful state, he would have forever remained in that sinful state and cut off from the life of God. Sin and God cannot meet, but because God loves us so much, He sent His Son that whoever believes in Him should not perish but have everlasting life.[89] This everlasting life is the fruit of the Tree of Life, Jesus Christ. Jesus came down from heaven so that we could be brought back to fellowship with God and the purpose for which we were created.

These cherubim guarding the Tree of Life can be seen many years later in the types and shadows of the ark of the covenant in the Tabernacle that God instructed Moses to construct as a chamber for His presence. In the Holy of Holies was a box containing the symbols of all man's failures to live up to His standards, to submit to His authority, and to trust His provision. The items representing these failures were the Ten Commandments, Aaron's rod, and manna. God covered man's sin with His mercy by placing a covering on the Ark, a golden seat called the Mercy Seat. Formed with one piece of gold with this seat were two angels that looked down on the seat. Each year the high priest would sprinkle the blood of an innocent lamb on the seat.[90] The angels would see the blood, and the sin of the people would be covered for another year. These angels were the guardians of God's righteousness just like the cherubim placed at the entrance of the Garden of Eden guarded the Tree of Life and Christ's righteousness.

Jesus Came Out To Take Us In

Fast forward thousands of years, and we see two angels in the empty tomb of our Savior: one at the head and one at the foot of where Jesus had laid.[91] Jesus, our Tree of Life, came out of heaven to die our death, and entered back into heaven to bring us back with Him.

The flaming sword of the cherubim at the entrance to the Garden of Eden was the sword of judgment. Jesus Christ, the Tree of Life came out through that sword of judgment to bring us back in with Him. The sword did not penetrate Him as He came out because of His sinless perfection. He came into our world as a human being, fully God and fully man, with only one purpose: to die for us. He lived a sinless life as a human being so that He could qualify as our Lamb of God. Our sin was transferred to Him, and then He went through the sword of judgment for us. That sword was the cross on which He was crucified. He endured until the end because of His undying love.

> *Remember that Jesus Christ, of the seed of David, was raised from the dead according to my gospel...For if we died with Him. We shall also live with Him. (2 Timothy 2:8,11)*

In a great mystery, which our brains cannot grasp, Jesus Christ took us with Him through the flaming sword into the presence of God, dying our death as our Substitute and protecting us from judgment. In our own righteousness we would never have passed the test. The sword of judgment would have condemned us all forever. However, as Jesus carried us through the judgment, we died with Him, and as we passed through to the other side, He formed a new sinless creation and raised us up together with Himself. Now we are free to eat from the Tree of Life and live.

CHAPTER SIX

Federal Headship

Key scriptures:
Romans 5:12, 18-19; Romans 3:26; Isaiah 53:2-3; Matthew 5:14-16

So many believers, who at one time experienced joy unspeakable in their newfound freedom in Christ and who understood the unconditional love of God when they simply believed that Jesus died and rose again to forgive them of their sins, today are no longer living under those sunny blue skies basking in the joy of their salvation. Instead, the skies are gray. The sun might shine for a little while, but then it goes back behind the clouds. They feel free today and in bondage tomorrow. Why? Because sometimes they feel like they are "right with God" and sometimes they don't.

How can we forever clear up this gray "getting right with God" mentality that many Christians are in bondage to and begin to live a life of freedom and power?

First Adam and Last Adam

Reader Study Reference, Romans 5:12-19

The truth of the New Covenant is not made complete until we understand the separating of the federal headship of first Adam from the federal headship of last Adam, Jesus Christ.[92] It is in the revelation of the absolute, black and white change in federal headship for the human race that we can truly grab hold of who we are in Christ and then see all of the supernatural, miraculous power of God released and manifested in the earth.

> *Therefore, just as through one man [Adam] sin entered the world, and death through sin, and thus death spread to all men, because all sinned—(Romans 5:12, brackets added for emphasis)*

This verse is saying that sin entered the human race through Adam, and because of his sin, the human race would die physically and every human being would be born in Adam's sin. God never intended for man to die. He created Adam and Eve's bodies to live forever, but when sin entered, their bodies began to decay, and they eventually died. Ever since the fall of man, the creation has been groaning and eagerly waiting to be set free from corruption, death, and decay.[93] The natural realm has been moving from order to disorder since Adam and Eve were banished from the Garden of Eden.

> *Therefore, as through one man's offense [Adam] judgment came to all men, resulting in condemnation, even so through one Man's righteous act [Jesus] the free gift came to all men, resulting in justification of life. For as by one man's disobedience [Adam] many were made sinners, so also by one Man's obedience [Jesus] many will be made righteous. (Romans 5:18-19, brackets added for emphasis)*

The first Adam was given dominion over the entire earth, yet he gave that authority away to satan when he fell. Now every single human being since Adam was born in Adam's sin and spiritually dead. The last Adam, Jesus Christ, came to forever remove the sin of first Adam and bring about a restoration and redemption that is far greater than what was lost in first Adam's sin.

Do We Have Two Natures?

We do not have two natures. We are either in Adam with a sin nature, or we are in Christ and partakers of the divine nature.[94] Think about what the word "nature" means. It has to do with origin and where we came from. Our nature speaks of who we are. The Spirit of God witnesses with our spirit that we are children of God.[95] When we walk in the Spirit, we are walking in our nature as sons and daughters of God. When we walk according to the flesh, we are not walking according to our nature. It's like when we tell kids, "Stop acting like animals!" It's because they aren't animals; they're people.

To say that a believer has two natures is to say that he has two origins, or two fathers. We once were of Adam. Now because of the new birth of the new creation, the scriptures clearly say that we are no longer of Adam's race, but of a new race of Christ who was raised from the dead. Two heads makes a freak. We don't have two daddies. We don't have two natures battling within us. It's crucial that we understand this because if we don't, then we will not get rooted and grounded in our true identity as a son or daughter of God. You're not from two worlds! You have been born again **FROM HEAVEN**, but you walk in this world. You are **IN** it, but not **OF** it.

The blood of everyone born since Adam has carried "the mystery of iniquity."[96] What God made in the Garden of Eden with Adam and Eve was not evil. The problem is not with the body, but with the power of sin or the "mystery of iniquity" that is in the human DNA from the eating of the Tree of the Knowledge of Good and Evil. Adam and Eve ate of it, took it in, it went into their system, and it was passed down to every generation of humans that has ever lived. We received it in our natural birth. We were all born with the power of sin in the flesh and under the law of sin and death. However, we as believers in Jesus Christ are no longer "sons of disobedience" in Adam in HIS disobedience, but sons of obedience in Christ in CHRIST'S obedience.[97]

There are only two races of human beings that God recognizes: those who are in first Adam and those who are in last Adam. It's one or the other. No one is in "no man's land." People aren't sinners because they sin. They are sinners because they were born in Adam's sin. Why? Because of governmental federal headship.

God Is Just

Romans 3:26 says that God is the "Just and the Justifier of the one who has faith in Jesus."

Whenever you see the words "just," "justifier," "justify," "justification," "righteous," or "righteousness," they all come from the same Greek stem, "dikai-."[98] God justifies, which means "acquit"[99], and the result is righteousness. When a person has been justified, he has been made righteous; literally, he has been completely cleared of all guilt.

Today when a sinner comes to God and confesses that He is a sinner, the Bible does not say that God is "merciful and loving" to cleanse him from unrighteousness, it says,

He is FAITHFUL and JUST to forgive us our sins and to cleanse us from all unrighteousness. (1 John 1:9, emphasis added)

How did He cleanse us from all unrighteousness? He removed the sin and conquered it! He condemned the sin so that we would never have to be condemned by it![100] Faithful, righteous, and just are judicial words of the courts. He is the Judge who has judged the work of His Son as "perfectly perfect, completely complete."[101]

Did you ever wonder what happened to all those people who believed in the coming Messiah before the cross? To show that He is a righteous God, our Father delayed the punishment of the sins of all the people of faith who lived before the cross.[102] He was being completely fair in this because He was looking forward to the time when Jesus would come and take away all of those sins. God passed over sin and allowed sin to be atoned for by the blood of animals for thousands of years. Prior to the cross, Old Testament believers were "on credit." Sin, whether it was Adam's sin nature that every human was born with or the individual sins that each person was liable for under the law, had not been paid for yet. Even so, the people received some of the benefits from what had not historically yet taken place (the cross).

It's like buying something on a credit card: we enjoy the purchased item even though we have not paid for it yet. Old Testament believers looked forward to what God would someday do, and believers today look back at what Christ has already done. God lives outside of time, but He chose to enter time on our behalf to save us!

The cross is the climax of all of the history of man. Everything points to Jesus and His amazing grace!

God was just in making us righteous. This means that He put His very character on the line when He declared us acquitted of all of our sins. If one sin was left unpunished, then God would not be just, and He would be a liar. God can't be just merciful and not righteous.

The wages of sin is death, but the gift of God is eternal life in Christ Jesus our Lord. (Romans 6:23)

Please don't think that grace makes sin light.

Sin makes you stay longer than you want to stay,
go further than you want to go, and
costs you more than you want to pay.

Yes, there are consequences to sin in this world. God hates sin because He loves us. He doesn't want us limping through this life suffering the consequences and condemnation of sin. As for the believer, it would be impossible for a person with the nature of Christ in his spirit to have absolutely no compunction whatsoever when he sins. In other words, whenever we sin, there is a tension between our new creation nature which is never inclined toward sin nor tempted to sin and the flesh where sin operates.

Are you sick and tired of living in that tension? The answer is take the focus off the sin and the flesh and put it on Jesus. The more we behold Jesus and the more steeped we are in His amazing grace, one day we will be able to look back and realize that those sinful tendencies that we used to struggle with have fallen off like dried leaves!

For God so loved the world... Love and mercy compelled the Trinity to send Jesus to earth, but the cross demonstrated God's justice. He is a righteous Judge who saw us with a problem: we were guilty as charged. He removed the problem so that we could live the abundant life in Him.

Mercy and truth have met together; righteousness and peace have kissed. (Psalm 85:10)

In the courtroom of all eternity, justice was served once and for all. Jesus cried,

"It is finished!" (John 19:30)

Every judgment of God fell on Jesus. Every curse, all the condemnation, all the poverty, all the sickness, all the separation from the life of the Father, and all the darkness fell upon Jesus for all our sins! It's wasn't for His sake that He endured the cross, it was for our sakes. It brought Him great joy for us to become a new creation in Him filled with HIS LIFE!

The Life of Jesus in Us

When we were born again, His uncreated life came on the inside of us. It's the life that God Himself lives by. It's the life that cannot die. It's the sin-free, curse-free life.

Whether we walk in it or not, Jesus has given us His own glory and honor. When Jesus walked the earth, He was THE example of a man crowned with glory and honor, and He was the image of what God wanted every man to be like.

When Jesus spoke to the fig tree, it died. When Jesus spoke to leprosy, it departed. Whenever He spoke, the creation responded because His words carried weight and authority. In the SAME exact way, our words carry weight and authority as well!

Christ's Honor

If you recall, Adam and Eve were crowned with glory and honor, but they forfeited that glory in the fall. The word for honor in the Hebrew is "hadar."[103] This word is also used in Isaiah 53 where it talks about Jesus on the cross.

He has no stately form or majesty ["hadar", honor] that we should look upon Him, nor appearance that we should be attracted to Him. He was despised and forsaken of men, a man of sorrows and acquainted with grief; and like one from whom men hide their face He was despised, and

we did not esteem Him. (Isaiah 53:2-3, NASB, brackets added for emphasis)

When Jesus hung on the cross, there was nothing about His appearance that would attract anyone to Him. There was no beauty in Jesus when He hung on the cross. His whole body was mangled. His face was hideous because they beat Him until He was marred more than any man.

His appearance was marred more than any man and His form more than the sons of men. (Isaiah 52:14, NASB)

A great exchange took place. He took our repelling defects and gave us His beauty for our ashes.[104] With open arms of compassion and love He willingly received our dishonor, and we received His honor in exchange. Now, at any point of the day on any day of the week, we are crowned in Christ's glory and honor.

Picture Jesus today:

[And He] has now entered into heaven and is at the right hand of God, with [all] angels and authorities and powers made subservient to Him. (1 Peter 2:22, Amplified Bible)

Those who receive the Lord Jesus Christ and His finished work are now crowned with that very glory and honor that crowns Him today at the right hand of the Father. So let's walk in it!

You are the light of the world. A city that is set on a hill cannot be hidden. Nor do they light a lamp and put it under a basket, but on a lampstand, and it gives light to all who are in the house. Let your light so shine before men, that they may see your good works and glorify your Father in heaven. (Matthew 5:14-16)

Arise, shine; for your light has come! And the glory of the Lord is risen upon you. (Isaiah 60:1)

This light is the glory of JESUS IN us and ON us!

Did you know that the only thing quicker than light is darkness? When light hits, darkness disappears! Light dispels darkness. Wherever we are, wherever our feet trod, whomever we come in contact with, we need to believe that the light within us overcomes the darkness in this world.

The Tree of Life

In the Garden of Eden, Adam and Eve ate the forbidden fruit of self-righteousness, and their eyes were opened to their nakedness. God asked them, "Who told you that you were naked?"[105] Whenever I read that question in Genesis 3, I sense the angst of God and the grieving of the Holy Spirit. God never intended for man to be self-sufficient or to be concerned with knowing good and evil. Love was all God wanted for mankind to know. Today, I believe He feels the same when His sons and daughters are enamored with the fruit that looks so good to their eyes, seems so pleasing to flesh, and desirable to give them wisdom, but in reality is the fruit of condemnation and death.

There is another tree that God wants mankind to eat from. It's the only tree that has the power to make us righteous. It's the Tree of Life. It is Jesus Christ. He is the Author of Life. Jesus is the Giver and Sustainer of Life. Jesus is the Bread of Life. All life comes from Him. Outside of Him, there is no life.

Jesus said of Himself:

Jesus said to him, "I am the way, the truth, and the life. No one comes to the Father except through Me. (John 14:6)

I have come that they may have life, and that they may have it more abundantly! (John 10:10)

The Bible starts out with a tree that brought curses and death, whose leaves could not offer a solution or healing. The Bible finishes with another tree that gives life, that breaks the curse, whose leaves are for the healing of the nations, and whose branches produce fruit all year round.

And he showed me a pure river of water of life, clear as crystal, proceeding from the throne of God and of the Lamb. In the middle of its street, and on either side of the river, was the tree of life [JESUS!!!], which bore twelve fruits, each tree yielding its fruit every month. The leaves of the tree were for the healing of the nations. (Revelation 22:1-5, brackets added for emphasis)

This fallen creation is anxiously longing for and eagerly awaiting the manifestation of the sons of God, those who reflect the glory of the firstborn of the new creation, the last Adam, Jesus Christ. This creation yearns for the life of Jesus Christ to be expressed through each one of us.

He who believes in Me, as the Scripture has said, out of his heart will flow rivers of living water." (John 7:38)

Right now we are seated in heavenly places in Christ on the throne with our spirits one with Him. The River flows out of Him, through us, and out of us to this world.

CHAPTER SEVEN

The Abundance of Grace

Key scriptures:
Romans 5:17-6:6, 2 Corinthians 10:4-5, Isaiah 61:1, Luke 4:16-18, 2 Kings 6:12-17, Ephesians 1:16-21

Many times in the New Testament we see the phrase "much more" regarding some aspect of the grace of God being poured out on us.[106] We see the "much more" regarding the value that we are to God as compared to the value of the rest of God's creation, "much more" regarding the work of Christ to bring salvation as compared to the disobedience of Adam in bringing us death, and "much more" regarding the eternal power of New Covenant as compared to the Old Covenant.

How much more will He clothe us...
How much more will He give us good things...
How much more will He give us the Holy Spirit...
How much more will He feed us...
How much more will we be saved from wrath...
How much more will we be saved by His life...
How much more the gift of righteousness abounds to many...

How much more the grace of God abounds to many...
How much more ministry of righteousness exceeds in glory...
How much more glorious is the ministry of the Spirit...
How much more is Jesus the guarantee of a better covenant...
How much more will the blood of Christ cleanse our conscience...

In this chapter we will look at Romans 5:17 through Romans 6:6 to discover how MUCH MORE the grace of God abounded through Christ's obedience than the judgment of sin brought condemnation through Adam's disobedience.

Two "Much Mores"

Reader Study Reference, Romans 5:17

By one man's offense many were made sinners and death entered the entire human race, but in Romans 5:17 we see two "much mores" that Christ's one righteous act has purchased for us that far surpasses the condemnation of sin and the tyranny of death brought by Adam's disobedience.

> *For if by the one man's offense death reigned through the one, much more those who receive abundance of grace and of the gift of righteousness will reign in life through the One, Jesus Christ. (Romans 5:17)*

Romans 5:17 tells us that we can reign in life through Jesus Christ. However, the experience of most Christians does not line up with this truth. Instead, the circumstances of many Christians are reigning OVER THEM! If you ask them how they are doing, they might say something like, "You wouldn't believe it if I told you" or "I'm under attack!" or "Well, under the circumstances, I'm alright..." Let that not be said of us! Let us be people who are not under UNDER anything, but reigning in life as overcomers through Jesus Christ!

If we are not reigning, we need to ask ourselves why. And what is reigning, generally speaking? Reigning is simply resting in the finished work of the cross of Jesus and in all the benefits of His resurrection! This doesn't mean we won't have any problems, but it means that we can be at rest in the middle of them, believing that God through Jesus has already provided everything we need! The Lamb was slain before the foundation of the world.[107]

Taking a closer look at Romans 5:17 will give us some clues and insight into reigning in life. Here are some of the phrases and their meanings from this verse:

- "those who receive": Receive is the Greek word "lambano"[108] and it means "to take, to lay hold of." It's an active verb. It's not just waiting on God to zap you. Also, it's in the Greek present active participle tense.[109] In other words, those who are continually receiving. Receiving what?

- "the abundance of grace": Not just a measure of unearned favor of God, but the abundance of it! Abundance is the Greek word "perisseia"[110] and it means "superabundantly, superfluously, gain, or profit."

- "the gift of righteousness": Gift is the word "dorea"[111] in the Greek and means a free gift. The word stresses its unmerited and undeserved character. The word "righteousness" literally means the "state of him who IS as he OUGHT to be, the condition acceptable to God."[112] The righteous have been cleared of all the record of their guilt before God, and Believer, you are AS YOU OUGHT TO BE! You are acceptable to God!

- "reign in life": Through receiving the free gift of righteousness, we reign in life. And this isn't talking about heaven one day. It's talking about now! The Amplified Bible says, "reign as kings in life." Reign is the word "basileuo"[113] which means to exercise kingly power. To reign in life means that we have authority. We exercise our kingly authority by taking captive any thought or fiery dart of the enemy, by using the power of our words, and by resting in Christ on the throne of heaven.

All the benefits of our resurrection life and all that God has for us must be received. There are two things that Romans 5:17 mentions that God has given to us: the abundance of grace and the gift of righteousness. These two things must be actively, aggressively, continually taken hold of to reign in this life.

Living in this fallen world, we are constantly in a tension with the accusation of the ruler of this world who tells us we are not righteous when we fail. Sadly, even those we go to for encouragement and counsel may give us bad doctrine that will cause us to doubt our righteousness in Christ and put us on a path of self-righteousness and defeat. Yet, the truth proclaims that we are under grace and perfectly righteous because of the blood of Jesus.

We never lose the abundance of grace and the gift of righteousness once we are born again, but our lives may not reflect this truth. When we believe the truth, it will set us free to receive the benefits of it. Even as we grow in the Lord, and His holiness is manifested in our lives, we will still sin. However, believing this truth will transform our character because what we believe is how we will live.

Receiving a Gift

Once I met a friend for lunch and when the server asked if the bill would all be on one check, my friend pointed to me and jokingly said, "Only if she's paying!" Now that's someone who knows how to receive a gift!

Sometimes we have a hard time just receiving a gift. We say things like, "Awe! I really don't deserve it. You shouldn't have. Here is some money; let me pay for it...." If we deserve it, then it's a reward. If we pay for it, then it's no longer a gift.

These responses insult the Giver of abundant grace and the gift of righteousness. The gift of being acceptable to God was free to us, but it cost God His Son! The most gratifying response to the Giver is to reach out our hands, take the gift as our own possession, and just say thank you.

Some people are afraid of "too much grace." How can there be too much? God wants us to receive superabounding grace. A friend shared with me that she heard a pastor warn his congregation not to slip into a "dangerous trance of grace." He likened grace to a hot tub that you get in because you need comfort for your aching muscles, but if you stay in there too long, you'll get lightheaded and drown!

We need to unwrap the gift of righteousness and superabounding grace and enjoy! Especially when we fail. Say, "Father, I thank You that I am still the righteousness of God in Christ." I say it daily! It shuts the mouth of the roaring lion, satan, and it keeps me focused on Jesus. It keeps me in a state of gratefulness, just like the woman with the alabaster box. The more I declare my righteousness before God, the more in love with Jesus I am! Even still to this day — years after my encounter with Jesus on the beach and the opening of my eyes to grace — I still weep daily over His amazing grace. I will never get over it!

When we continue to believe we are righteous before God when we fail, it's repentance: changing our minds from focusing on our failure to acknowledgment of Jesus' perfect work on our behalf. The result? We will be so grateful, and peace will spring forth in our hearts. When we live in thanksgiving for the free gift of righteousness, we will be in forward motion, reigning in life.

If God is for you, who can be against you? (Romans 8:31)

No one. Not even yourself.

Believer, it's never too late! No matter how much we have failed, no matter how many people we have hurt because of our sin, no matter what condition our lives are in because of bad decisions, we can still receive the free gift of the abundance of grace and the free gift of righteousness!

Warfare

By virtue of being a king, we will engage in warfare. Reigning in this life involves a fight, but there is only one type of battle for the believer:

Fight the good fight of faith, lay hold on eternal life, to which you were also called and have confessed the good confession in the presence of many witnesses. (1 Timothy 6:12)

We are to "lay hold of eternal life." Eternal life doesn't start when we get to heaven. Eternal life is inside of us right now! Zoe[114] — the life that God Himself lives — flows to us from heaven and through us in rivers of living water when we lay hold of that life and fight the good fight of faith, believing we are righteous from faith to faith! Our battlefield is the mind where we take hold of the truth and take captive anything that comes against it.

For the weapons of our warfare are not carnal but mighty in God for pulling down strongholds casting down arguments and every high thing that exalts itself against the knowledge of God, bringing every thought into captivity to the obedience of Christ. (2 Corinthians 10:4-5)

Anything that comes against the knowledge and obedience of Christ can form a stronghold in our minds — a fortress that can keep us from receiving. We bring down the strongholds to the OBE-DIENCE OF CHRIST — His obedience, not the obedience of our flesh! "By one Man's obedience many will be made righteous."[115] If you are born again in Christ, you have a failure-proof, devil-proof righteousness. Don't be afraid to remind the devil of that!

Spiritual Blindness

Did you know the biggest problem we have is spiritual blindness to what Christ has done for us? Blindness is the greatest bondage there is. Think about a blind person. Physically speaking, he's in a prison of darkness. Imagine being in a brightly lit room with black duck tape on your eyes so that no light comes in. If you try to walk around, you'll stumble. You may even fall. You're in the light, but you can't see it!

We are in the kingdom of light if we are in Christ, but if our eyes are blinded to the pure Gospel of grace, then we'll stumble around groping to feel our way through life. Our natural senses will be our guide. Spiritual blindness will cause us to be controlled by our emotions and will cause the voice of the Holy Spirit to be muddled by our doubts and fears and the gamut of all the other emotions. We won't walk in wisdom and peace. Instead, we'll make bad decisions based on how we feel rather than the truth of the wisdom of God.

In Isaiah 61 we find a quote of the coming Messiah. This prophecy was fulfilled when Jesus stood up in the temple and declared "the Spirit of the Lord is upon Me." In Isaiah 61 and Luke 4 we find almost identical passages, with one editorial change made by the Lord Himself. Here is the passage in Isaiah 61:

The Spirit of the Lord God is upon Me, because the Lord has anointed Me to preach good tidings to the poor; He has sent Me to heal the bro-

kenhearted, *To proclaim liberty to the captives, and the OPENING OF THE PRISON to those who are bound;... (Isaiah 61:1)*

Now let's look at this verse in the passage in Luke 4:

So He came to Nazareth, where He had been brought up. And as His custom was, He went into the synagogue on the Sabbath day, and stood up to read. And He was handed the book of the prophet Isaiah. And when He had opened the book, He found the place where it was written: "The Spirit of the Lord is upon Me, Because He has anointed Me To preach the gospel to the poor; He has sent Me to heal the brokenhearted, To proclaim liberty to the captives And RECOVERY OF SIGHT TO THE BLIND, To set at liberty those who are oppressed..." (Luke 4:16-18)

Interesting... In Isaiah 61, all the phrases are the same, except for one:

- Good tidings to the poor — same
- Heal the brokenhearted — same
- Proclaim liberty to the captives — same
- Opening of the prison doors — oops! Different! In Luke 4, Jesus says, "recovery of sight to the blind."

Did Jesus mis-quote Himself?

I used to read that passage in Luke 4 and wonder why Jesus chose to mention only one kind of healing: recovery of sight to the blind. Why didn't He mention leprosy or all the other kinds of sicknesses? Did it mean that we could only be assured of physical healing of blind eyes, and every other kind of sickness was perhaps on a case by case basis? I seriously pondered this years ago.

However, Jesus wasn't talking about physical eyes in Luke 4. He was talking about spiritual eyes to see the unseen. In the Hebrew of Isaiah 61, the phrase "opening of the prison" is the word "peqach-qowach."[116] It's a double word that literally means "the opening of the eyes" to those who are bound! This is one of my favorite nuggets of truth in the Bible. It's just awesome to me.

Jesus came to bring the opening of the eyes to those who are bound! Jesus came to open the prison doors of spiritual blindness so that the captives could be set free. What was the captivity that Jesus came to set people free from? What was He referring to? Jesus came to release the captives from the law that declared them unrighteous and unacceptable to God. When our eyes are opened to Jesus and His grace, we will no longer be in held captive to performance based religion.

Chariots of Fire

In 2 Kings 6 we find an incredible story that illustrates recovery of sight to the blind beautifully. In this story, the King of Syria decided to make war against Israel. Elisha the prophet got wind of it by the Holy Spirit and warned the king of Israel not to fall into the traps the king of Syria had laid. The king of Syria thought one of his own men had betrayed him, so he called his servants together to ask which one of them was the spy. Their response was that the God of Israel had told Elisha, the prophet, every move he was making — even sharing with Elisha the words the king spoke in his bedroom! So the king sent his army to go get Elisha. We'll pick up the story in 2 Kings 6:14.

Therefore he sent horses and chariots and a great army there, and they came by night and surrounded the city. And when the servant of the man of God arose early and went out, there was an army, surrounding the city with horses and chariots. And his servant said to him, "Alas, my master! What shall we do?" So he answered, "Do not fear, for those who are with us are more than those who are with them." And Elisha prayed, and said, "Lord, I pray, open his eyes that he may see." Then the Lord opened the eyes of the young man, and he saw. And behold, the mountain was full of horses and chariots of fire all around Elisha. (2 Kings 6:14-17)

This is an example of reality which appears to be real vs. reality which is truly real! The servant's eyes were opened to the realm of grace. The realm of the eternal. The realm of power and might and protection. Before his eyes were opened, he came to a conclusion based on his circumstances. He thought they were in big trouble. Both of these men were in the same situation, but one of them responded through the lens of temporary reality, the other one responded through the lens of eternal reality.

In the book of Ephesians Paul prayed this prayer for the church:

[I] do not cease to give thanks for you, making mention of you in my prayers: that the God of our Lord Jesus Christ, the Father of glory, may give to you the spirit of wisdom and revelation in the knowledge of Him, the eyes of your understanding being enlightened; that you may know what is the hope of His calling, what are the riches of the glory of His inheritance in the saints, and what is the exceeding greatness of His power toward us who believe, according to the working of His mighty power which He worked in Christ when He raised Him from the dead and seated Him at His right hand in the heavenly places, far above all principality and power and might and dominion, and every name that is named, not only in this age but also in that which is to come. (Ephesians 1:16-21, brackets added for emphasis)

In my opinion this is the best prayer we can pray for each other. There is exceedingly great power available to us, but we just don't see it! If our spiritual eyes were open to the fact that the power which raised Jesus from the dead is within us by the Holy Spirit, we could change the spiritual landscape of this world. Spiritual blindness has caused such passivity in the body of Christ that many Christians think that God is the one who has caused all the sickness and the tragedies and the earthquakes — all because they only see with their natural eyes, and that's the best explanation they can come up with. But what if we saw the chariots of fire? What if we realized that there are more on our side in the spirit realm than those against us? Only then would we begin to walk by faith and not by sight.

Why the Law Was Added

Reader Study Reference, Romans 5:18-20

Let's get back to Romans 5.

After Romans 5:17, we come to the end of the parenthetical expression that expounded on federal headship of first and last Adam, and then we come back to Paul's synopsis:

Therefore, as through one man's offense [Adam] judgment came to all men, resulting in condemnation, even so through one Man's righteous act [Jesus] the free gift came to all men, resulting in justification of life. For as by one man's disobedience many were made sinners, so also by one Man's obedience many will be made righteous. (Romans 5:18-19, brackets added for emphasis)

Next, Paul tells us why the law was given. Hold onto your seats because this might shock you!

Moreover the law entered that the offense might abound,... (Romans 5:20)

Another way of putting it is the law was added that sin might increase! Can that be true? Why would a holy God who hates sin put His people under something that would cause sin to abound? It's because He wanted to expose through the law that self-righteousness could do nothing to make us acceptable to God so that we would see our need for Jesus.

The word translated "entered" or "added" is the word Greek "pareiserchomai."[117] It means "to come in secretly or by stealth, creep or steal in, to enter in addition to, come in besides." To come in besides what? The law came in besides the sin that was already in the world because of Adam's sin to bring personal liability for sin. That's why after the law was given, we see God's people stoned for their sin, being put outside the camp for being unclean, dying of plagues, and being slaughtered by their enemies. Before the law, sin was in the world, but the law came in alongside sin to make sin exceedingly sinful.[118]

We can also say that the law came in besides the unconditional covenant of grace that God made on behalf of Abraham and his descendants. We will study the Abrahamic covenant in later chapters. The law came four hundred thirty years after Abraham, and from the giving of the law of Moses until the time of the coming of Jesus Christ in grace and truth, the law was alongside grace, and it never annulled the covenant of grace that God had given Abraham.[119]

The law was not added to make us better people, and it was not added as a moral guide. The law of God, the Ten Commandments, "the ministry of death" as 2 Corinthians 3:7 describes it, was given to increase trespasses. The law did not make man a sinner, and the law did not cause death to enter mankind. The law functioned much like a dye that is put in a person's body to reveal a disease. It couldn't cure the disease; it could only show that disease of sin was there.

On the other hand, the Gospel of grace reveals a righteous condition that you already have in Jesus as a believer! Or it's a righteousness that you can receive today if you will believe that you are a sinner in need of a Savior. Believe that God is not counting your sins against you! He can't because His beloved Son, Jesus Christ, took your sin into His body on the cross so that you could be just like Him. God loves you!

Back to the law... The law had its purpose while we were still in the flesh:

The law was given to stimulate sin.
The law was given to make us guilty.
The law was given to make us conscious of God's anger.
The law was given to bring attention to our unworthiness and sin.
And as Colossians 2:14 says, the law was against us, contrary to us, opposed to us, hostile to us.

The law was NOT given to make us righteous.
The law was NOT given to bring us life or salvation.
The law was NOT given to build us up.
The law was NOT given to help us overcome sin.

However, the religious are determined that the law was God's gift to man to keep him in check. They think the law is the answer to sin.

Grace was given to condemn sin.
Grace with given to make us innocent.
Grace was given to make us conscious of God's love.
Grace was given to bring attention to Christ's worthiness.
Grace was given to set us free.

In the early days of my glorious, continuous encounter with the Spirit of Grace, I had the opportunity to share the pure Gospel of grace with literally thousands of people, sometimes in large meetings or often one-on-one at coffee houses or around the world on a daily devotional blog that I was writing at the time. Mostly, the responses were beautiful, and I heard the same testimony over and over: "I have never felt so loved by God! And I have never loved Jesus more!"

However, there were some who were offended by the message of grace, and it saddened me greatly. Someone I knew who had great influence in ministry became so irate when I shared with her how God's grace had changed my life that she emphatically declared, "What you're saying is fine for the mature believer, but it would confuse the fire out of a new believer! And it would never work for those with addictions." My response: "It's the answer for the new believer! Grace is the answer for those with addictions!" She had the last word: "I'm not getting on the grace bandwagon." Wow.

In those days, I felt a little bit like Joseph sharing his dreams with his brothers. Not everyone gets excited when you share about your spiritual encounters! Wisdom is key... But sometimes being thrown in the pit is unavoidable. Although it doesn't make sense to the natural mind, God sent Joseph for the purpose of saving his brothers and many others. He told his brothers,

"But now, do not therefore be grieved or angry with yourselves because you sold me here; for God sent me before you to preserve life... You meant evil against me; but God meant it for good, in order to bring it about as it is this day, to save many people alive." (Genesis 45:5; 50:20)

In the book of Acts we see that Peter and John got into major trouble for preaching in the name of Jesus and sharing the Gospel of grace. They were arrested and thrown in jail, but they couldn't and wouldn't stop speaking about Jesus:

"Whether it is right in the sight of God to listen to you more than to God, you judge. For we CANNOT BUT SPEAK the things which we have seen and heard." (Acts 4:19-20, emphasis added)

Under great persecution Paul declared:

But none of these things move me; nor do I count my life dear to myself, so that I may finish my race with joy, and the ministry which I received from the Lord Jesus, to testify to the gospel of the grace of God. (Acts 20:24)

So I encourage you, SHARE the Good News. If there are those who reject it (and you!), ask yourself the question that I asked myself many times: "Can I ever go back?"

Grace Abounded Much More

Reader Study Reference, Romans 5:20-21

Let's look at the next verse in Romans 5...

There comes a place where you are so transformed by the good-ness of God that nothing else matters. It's just about too good to be true because —

> *But where sin abounded, GRACE ABOUNDED MUCH MORE, so that as sin reigned in death, even so grace might reign through righteous-ness to eternal life through Jesus Christ our Lord. (Romans 5:20-21, emphasis added)*

The word "abounded" is "pleonazo"[120] and means increased or abounded. "Where sin 'pleonazo' (increased), grace abounded much more." But here is something very interesting: the second time we see the word "abounded" in that verse, it is a completely different Greek word! "Abounded much more" is "hyperperisseuo,"[121] and it means "to abound beyond measure, abound exceedingly, to overflow, to enjoy abundantly." Grace abounded "with much more added to that."[122]

Can you see the difference? God's grace completely outruns sin. Sin can never keep up with His grace! His grace is outrageous!

A License To Sin?

Reader Study Reference, Romans 6:1-2

Nevertheless, every time you preach the Gospel of grace, one of the biggest accusations is going to be the question in Romans 6:1. This question was leveled against Paul and is leveled against everyone who preaches grace:

> *What shall we say then? Shall we continue in sin that grace may abound? (Romans 6:1)*

If you share the Gospel that Paul preached, you will be misunder-stood. Where will this misunderstanding come from? Not the world. They won't be the ones concerned about a license to sin. It will be the religious who will cry, "They are saying it's ok to sin!!" ...forgetting that we **ALREADY** have the choice to sin or not! We can choose to shoot someone or rob a bank or have a lustful, fearful, angry, hateful thought! But Paul at no time said, "Let us sin that grace may abound." What he said was, "Where sin abounded, grace abounded much more."

Paul put all his assurance in God's grace. Jesus said the flesh profits us nothing,[123] but most people put more confidence in the flesh to overcome sin than they do in God's grace. However, His grace is greater than all our sins.

Following is a rather lengthy quote from Dr. Martin Lloyd Jones, deceased pastor of Westminster Abbey in Westminster, England, and respected theologian. I decided to include it here because he so eloquently explained the tension between grace and the accusation to condone sin.

The true preaching of the gospel of salvation by grace alone always leads to the possibility of this charge being brought against it. There is no better test as to whether a man is really preaching the New Testament gospel than this, that some people might misunderstand it and mis-interpret it that it really amounts to this: that because you are saved by grace alone, it does not really matter at all what you do, you can go on sinning all you like because it will redound all the more to the glory of grace. That is a very good test of gospel preaching. If my preaching of the gospel does not expose it to that misunderstanding, then it is not the gospel. Let me show you what I mean. If a man preaches justification by works, no one would ever raise the question. If he says, "If you want to go to heaven, you must stop committing sins, live a life filled with good works, and keep this up regularly and constantly until the end, then you will be a Christian and go to heaven when you die." Obviously, no one will accuse a man who preached like this of saying, "Let us continue in sin that grace may abound." But every preacher who preached the gospel has been accused of this! They have all been accused of 'antinomianism.' I would say to all preachers: If your preaching of salvation has not been misunderstood in that way, then you had better examine your sermons again, and you had better make sure that you really are preaching the salvation that is proclaimed in the New Testament to the ungodly, the sinner, to those who are dead in trespasses and sins, to those who are the enemies of God. There is a kind of dangerous element about the true presentation of the doctrine of salvation. [124]

Here's Paul's answer to the question, "Shall we continue in sin that grace may abound?":

Certainly not! How shall we who died to sin live any longer in it? (Romans 6:2)

Paul didn't say, "You shouldn't live in sin"; his answer was that it isn't possible for one who has died to sin to live any longer in it. We are a new creation in Christ, and we no longer live "in sin" (the noun) because we have died to it. We'll talk about what that means when we get further into Romans 6.

Co-Crucified and Co-Raised

Reader Study Reference, Romans 6:3-6

Or do you not know that as many of us as were baptized into Christ Jesus were baptized into His death? Therefore we were buried with Him through baptism into death, that just as Christ was raised from the dead by the glory of the Father, even so we also should walk in newness of life. For if we have been united together in the likeness of His death, certainly we also shall be in the likeness of His resurrection. (Romans 6:3-5)

When Paul said we were baptized into His death, the meaning of the word baptized is to immerse or submerge, [125] and this verb tense is the Greek aorist tense which tells us that this baptism into His death was a one time event that will never happen again. In Christ's death, we died also.

At the cross, Jesus Christ identified with us. He became our identity so that we could be His. He stepped into our very lowest state so that we can receive His very highest. The highest realms of glory are ours. There is nothing that we are deprived of because there is nothing that He isn't worthy of. Why? Because there is no depth of darkness and depravity that He refused to absorb on our behalf.

We have been co-crucified with Him and co-raised with Him.

Co-crucified:

I have been crucified with Christ; it is no longer I who live, but Christ lives in me; and the life which I now live in the flesh I live by faith in the Son of God, who loved me and gave Himself for me. (Galatians 2:20)

Where Paul says, "I live by faith IN the Son of God,"[126] the better translation is "I live by faith OF the Son of God." He not only provided our death and resurrection, He provides the faith to live His life now!

Co-raised:

God, who is rich in mercy, because of His great love with which He loved us, even when we were dead in trespasses, made us alive together with Christ (by grace you have been saved), and raised us up together, and made us sit together in the heavenly places in Christ Jesus... (Ephesians 2:4-6)

Through the resurrection of Jesus Christ, we have been given His authority. Now we can say, "Jesus, as You are — seated high above all rule, power, dominion, and authority — so am I in this world."[127] God has crowned us with glory so that we speak life everywhere we go and see the forces of death and darkness give way to the force of good coming forth from within us.

Notice that these verses in Romans 6 are in past tense. We were co-crucified, co-buried, co-raised, and co-seated with Him in heaven. We are not aiming to get there one day. We are there now!

...knowing this, that our old man was crucified with Him, that the body of sin might be done away with, that we should no longer be slaves of sin. (Romans 6:6)

Think about what that verse just said. "Knowing this..." What do we need to KNOW so that we will no longer be slaves to sin? We need to know it because if we don't, then the reverse will be true — sin will swing us around by the tail. And don't think of being slaves to sin as just being in bondage to lust or addictions. Anything that isn't of faith is sin![128] If we are anxious, it's sin! If we are envious, it's sin! If we are hoping to be right with God by doing good things, it's sin! Here's what we need to know to be free: OUR OLD MAN WAS CRUCI- FIED WITTH CHRIST. The old man died and ceased to exist, and he has no resurrection power! We have to know that we don't have the "old man" with a sin nature and the "new man" with Christ's nature battling for our heart, or we're going to live a lie. Believing truth is the key to walking in freedom!

CHAPTER EIGHT

Dead to Sin

Key scriptures:
Romans 6:7-18, Hebrews 4:15

Die

Many years ago I gave a wedding shower for a dear young friend of mine who had been my babysitter. Since most of the guests were quite a bit older than she, we decided to take the opportunity to write marriage advice on cards as a keepsake for her. I contemplated what I would write on my card for weeks! I was the kind of wife that believed when my husband said, "Jump," my answer was supposed to be "How high?" (Even if through gritted teeth.) I figured that the other ladies were going to put sweet encouraging guidance on their cards, but I felt the responsibility to tell my friend something about marriage that would give her a true perspective. I needed to give her the balance. At the time I had been married about fifteen years, and the best advice I could come up with I summed up with one word: "die." Perhaps this sounds like strange advice to offer to someone that is just beginning to live her life, but that one word was all I wrote on my card. When it was my turn to read my advice, I looked at her and said, "Die." I proudly told her that if she could learn how to die on a daily basis, she'd have a good and godly marriage.

As sure as I seemed to be about this key to a perfect marriage, I remember the biggest question of my life at the time was how do I live and die at the same time? Dying was what I thought would please God, but all that dying was draining the life out of me.

Fast forward several years to another wedding shower for my oldest daughter. I found myself in a deja vu experience at this wedding shower where most of the guests were much older than the bride, and the hostess had us go through the same exercise by writing marriage advice on cards. I listened as some of the women told my daughter in a variety of ways that she would need to learn how to die, and the sooner the better. I had the honor of sharing my advice last: and as I waited for my turn, I knew what I would share. My mother had gone home to be with the Lord just two months prior, and all her grandchildren had been able to witness my parents who, after fifty-five years of marriage, were more in love than ever. So my advice was a question, "Of all the people you know, who has had the best marriage?" My daughter instantly answered, "Grandmama and Grandaddy." I asked her why. She said, "Because they had fun together." I said, "Bingo."

So what about dying? Should we be dying every day?

Dead To Sin

Reader Study Reference, Romans 6:7

For much of my Christian life, I tried to "die to sin." Have you ever tried to do that? If so, then perhaps you know that it's impossible! But we've said it many times: "I'm dying to that sin!" But the more we declare that we're finished with that sin and will never do it again, the more we seem to struggle with it. If you have tried unsuccessfully to die to sin like I did, there is good news!

For he who has died has been freed from sin. (Romans 6:7)

Trying to die does not work because you are trying to do something that has already been done. For example, imagine how frustrating it would be to try to sit in this chair while you are already sitting in this chair! All we need to do is to have our eyes opened to the fact that we are dead to sin already.

Two grammar points on being "dead":

1. The word "died"[129] is in the Greek aorist verb tense which means that it's a one-point-in-time action, never to be repeated. When we died, we died for good. It will never be repeated again.

2. In the book of Romans the word "sin" is used forty-eight times. Forty of those times the word is used as a noun, "hamartia"[130], and only eight of those times is it the verb, "harmartano."[131] In Romans 6, "sin" is a verb ONLY ONCE, and that's in Romans 6:15. For instance in Romans 6:7 which says, "For he who has died has been freed from sin," the word sin is a noun. Many of us have thought this verse meant that we were freed from "sinnING" (the verb). Consequently, we've been discouraged because we have been trying to be dead to sinnING, and we have failed miserably. At some point most individuals will do what I did and cry out, "What is wrong with me?!"

I have discovered that all those years I spent trying to die to sin, there was nothing wrong with me. There was something wrong with what I was believing about it. Victory over sinnING doesn't come from working on one's behavior. It comes from knowing we have been freed from sin (the noun).

Before we move on to the next verse, there is one more point about "dying to sin," which merits consideration. Some people have taken a verse in 1 Corinthians 15 out of context to say that Paul taught that we need to "die daily." Paul did say, "I die daily," but it was in the context of risking his life every day to preach the resurrection because people were out to kill him and bring harm to him physically. Here is that passage in The Message paraphrase:

And why do you think I keep risking my neck in this dangerous work? I look death in the face practically every day I live. ["I die daily"] Do you think I'd do this if I wasn't convinced of your resurrection and mine as guaranteed by the resurrected Messiah Jesus? (1 Corinthians 15:30-31, The Message, brackets added for emphasis)

It is clear that Paul was referring to persecution here and not "dying to sin."

A Reckoning

Reader Study Reference, Romans 6:8-11

Let's go back to Romans 6 and continue:

Now if we died with Christ, we believe that we shall also live with Him, knowing that Christ, having been raised from the dead, dies no more. Death no longer has dominion over Him. For the death that He died, HE DIED TO SIN ONCE FOR ALL; but the life that He lives, He lives to God. (Romans 6:8-10, emphasis added)

The next verse tells us why it's so important for us to know that Jesus died to sin "once and for all":

LIKEWISE YOU ALSO, reckon yourselves to be dead indeed to sin, but alive to God in Christ Jesus our Lord. (Romans 6:11, emphasis added)

We are to reckon ourselves dead to sin in the SAME WAY that Jesus died to sin. If we misinterpret verse 10 and the manner in which Jesus died to sin, we are going to misinterpret verse 11. Whatever is true of Jesus is true of us. Consider this: in whatever way Jesus died to sin, WE died also to sin. Is Jesus dying to sin progressively in the way we have imagined ourselves to be dying to sin? Of course not. He died to sin "once for all" on the cross. So how are we to die to sin? Once and for all.

What does it mean that we have died? Think about the day you were water baptized. What did it mean? It was symbolic of the death of the "old man" that you once were in Adam's sin. When you rose up out of the water, it symbolized your new life in Christ. As Paul says in Galatians 2:20, we were "crucified with Christ." Because Jesus died as our representative, we can say that when He died, we died. We are counted righteous and included in His death when we trust in Jesus as our representative and receive His righteousness as a gift. In other words, we are born again a new creation when we receive Jesus Christ as our Savior.

When the "old man" died and was buried, his past went with him. When we were born again, God gave us a whole new past - a past with a clean record. So now we need to "reckon ourselves indeed dead to sin."

The word "reckon" reveals the unequivocal nature of our death. Reckon in this verse doesn't have the meaning Southerners use when we say, "I reckon so...maybe so...I sure hope so..." Reckon is the Greek word "logizomai,"[132] which means "to count, compute, calculate, count over, to make an account of." Reckoning is to count something as a fact! Reckoning has to do with fact, not supposition or opinion. If I reckon that I have $100 in the bank, it's because I HAVE $100 in the bank. In other words, because of what has happened to us in Christ, we are to calculate/ to count ourselves, as a fact, "dead indeed to sin."

That brings us to the next question: HOW did Jesus die to sin "once for all"? That's important to know so we can walk in victory! Did He finally get over all His bad habits and addictions with one big New Year's resolution? Obviously not. He never sinned and had no sin in Him.[133] Jesus' death to sin was the death to the charges against us, the condemnation of sin, the penalty of sin for mankind, and the power of sin. All of the assignment for blame, all of our condemnation for missing the mark, and all of our punishment (the wages of sin is death) was received by Jesus at the cross, and He died forever to all of it! It is finished!

The Spotless Lamb of God

Of all mankind that ever lived, Jesus was the only One who could have been our Sacrifice because He is the only One who was not born in Adam's sin. He came as our Lamb without spot or blemish.

For we do not have a High Priest who cannot sympathize with our weaknesses, but was in all points tempted as we are, yet WITHOUT SIN. (Hebrews 4:15, emphasis added)

"Yet without sin" isn't "yet without sinnING." Sin in this verse is a noun, not a verb. Jesus was never tempted TO sin, the verb. He was tempted, but WITHOUT sin, the noun! The word "tempted" is the Greek word "peirazo"[134] which means "to try whether a thing can be done, to test, to make trial of one, put him to proof." Jesus was tested, tried, and proven to be pure and holy. It's like testing gold to make sure it has no impurities. Jesus was not an alloy. He wasn't white-washed on the outside and full of sin and death on the inside.[135] His testing by the devil was to show that He was our perfect, sinless representative. He was WITHOUT SIN.

Jesus was tested and proved to be without a NATURE to sin. Because Jesus was born of the Spirit from above, He was not born in Adam's sin like we were. He was born of a virgin with His Father's divine nature. The reason for the virgin birth was so that Jesus could be our Substitute.

"For the ruler of this world [the devil] is coming, and he has nothing in Me." (John 14:30, brackets added for emphasis)

Jesus was from the bloodline of the almighty God. He was the only begotten Son of the Father, and He became the firstborn among many brethren. The only way that Jesus became sin at the cross was by receiving the sin of others - and He did it willingly!

"No one takes it from Me, but I lay it down of Myself. I have power to lay it down, and I have power to take it again. This command I have received from My Father." (John 10:18)

He went through the testing so that He could take our place, die our death, and raise us up in Him as partakers of God's divine nature. This is how we became a new creation in Christ! His nature replaced our old nature so that we no longer have a sin nature. The old Adam (the old man) was cut away by the cross.

Don't Let Sin Reign

Reader Study Reference, Romans 6:12-13

It's only when we believe that God is not counting our sins against us that we will have the power to overcome sinning. There are people who consider suicide, and even follow through with it, because they thought they were supposed to be dead to sinning, and they couldn't seem to stop it. If they can't stop sinning, then they begin to think they are better off dead than alive. What they need to know is that through Jesus, they are already dead to sin.

The power of sin will have its way if we don't RECKON ourselves dead to it. If we take on guilt with our sins, we are destined to repeat the sin. Condemnation is what keeps a person in a cycle of sin. When we forget who we are in Christ, an identity is imposed on us in our mind: the identity of a sinner. We will live out what we believe.

Grace doesn't give a license to sin. Grace is the answer to sin.

After verse 11 where Paul says, "Likewise you also reckon yourselves dead indeed to sin...." He uses the word therefore. What is it there for?

Therefore do not let sin reign in your mortal body, that you should obey it in its lusts. (Romans 6:12)

When we understand verse 11 and that there is no condemnation, and we have died to it, THEREFORE, we now have the power not to let sin reign in our flesh. Think of flesh as the members of our bodies which includes our brains. That's why the battle begins in our thoughts. Our natural brains process what our natural eyes see and is stored in our minds as memories. Memories lodged in our natural minds are a big part of this processing. We often react to the outside stimuli based on our experiences from the past. Renewing our minds to truth is so important because if we simply go by what our natural eyes see, what our natural senses perceive, and what our brains deduce, we will live from the outside in. Pressures from the outside, including the temptation to sin, will overcome the strength of the flesh because we come to the wrong conclusions about who and what we really are.

However, if we believe right, we will live from the inside out. When we set our minds on things above and the eternal truths of the Spirit, and we renew our minds to God's word, the power of sin in the flesh will be no match for us. As partakers of Christ's divine nature in our spirit, through our union with Him, and by the power of the Holy Spirit within, we have complete dominion over sin, over satan, and over the flesh.

And do not present your members as instruments of unrighteousness to sin, but present yourselves to God as being alive from the dead, and your members as instruments of righteousness to God. (Romans 6:13)

True holiness, the kind that is an overflow of love and gratefulness to God because of His extravagant love lavished on us through the cross, always follows correct believing that there is no condemnation for us in Christ.

Under Grace

Reader Study Reference, Romans 6:14-15

A few years ago someone coming to one of my Bible studies had been seeing the results of grace in her life and seemed so hungry for more, but out of fear she backed off from pure grace. She wrote to me and said, "I have too many things that I still believe are found in both grace and truth (principles from the law)." Those parentheses were hers, not mine. It's still so perplexing even to this day that so many think that truth and law are the same thing, when the scriptures make it so clear that truth and grace are one! They are afraid to let go of the law because they have been working to be good for so long that they are terrified that sin will overtake them if they let go. But what does the next verse in Romans 6 say?

For sin shall not have dominion over you, for [because] you are not under law but UNDER GRACE. (Romans 6:14, brackets and emphasis added)

Those who are in Christ, born again of the Spirit of God, joined to the Lord are "under grace." As a new creation in Christ, it is impossible for us to be under the dominion of sin.

Even though the scriptures make it so plain, the fearful and religious will still ask the question that we find in the next verse:

What then? Shall we sin [the verb] because we are not under law but under grace? Certainly not! (Romans 6:15, brackets added for emphasis)

This is the only place that sin is used as a verb in the entire chapter of Romans 6, and it's used by those who would question whether

Paul was condoning sin. For those who don't understand grace, sin is always a verb that we can somehow control by working hard enough.

We don't need to fear the freedom we have in Christ. Paul is in no way giving us the freedom to sin. The Gospel doesn't give us freedom TO sin. It gives us freedom FROM sin - from the imputation of sin! Not only are our sins not counted against us, we have been given a new nature that does not desire sin any more than Jesus desires to sin!

Obey the "doctrine"

Reader Study Reference, Romans 6:16-17

Paul's explanation of why we won't choose to sin (the verb) if we are under grace might scare you away from grace if you don't understand that Paul is telling us that believing correctly will lead to righteous behavior. I remember in the old days I would be reading through Romans 5 and 6 reveling in amazing grace and then come to this next verse in Romans 6 and come screeching to a halt. I would hear something like, "Tricia, here's the balance. You knew it was coming. Just swallow the pill because it will be good for you." Here's the verse that caused me anxiety:

> *Do you not know that to whom you present yourselves slaves to obey, you are that one's slaves whom you obey,... (Romans 6:16)*

Here's the great news: Paul is not talking about performance and obeying the law here! Where he says we are slaves to whom we "obey," it's the Greek word "hypakouo"[136] which means "to listen, to harken." Harken means to pay attention to or to heed what is being said. Here's what Romans 6:16 literally says: "You are slaves to whomever you pay attention to. You are slaves to whomever you listen to and heed what they are saying." It's about the message that we are listening to:

> *...whether of sin leading to death, or of obedience leading to righteousness? (Romans 6:16, cont.)*

The better translation for this verse is the King James Version. The word translated "leading" is actually a word that means "into" or "unto." It should read like this:

...whether of sin unto death, or of obedience unto righteousness? (Romans 6:16, KJV)

Whose sin and whose obedience is this verse talking about? Yours and mine? Could it be saying that we better not sin because when we do it will bring death? We better be good because it will lead to righteousness? If that were the case, it would completely unravel the first five chapters of Romans that came before this chapter!

Paul is talking about doctrine here. He's talking about what we BELIEVE. Are we listening to the one whose sin was unto death or to the One whose obedience is unto righteousness? He's talking about a person. Who?

• Whose sin unto death? Adam's!

• Whose obedience unto righteousness? Jesus'!

Do you believe that you are still in Adam's sin as a sinner? Or do you believe you are in Christ's righteousness as a saint? Remember Romans 5, just one chapter before (remember CONTEXT is very important in understanding the scriptures!):

Therefore, just as through one man sin entered the world [Adam], and death through sin, and thus death spread to all men... (Romans 5:12, brackets added for emphasis)

For as by one man's disobedience [Adam] many were made sinners, so also by one Man's obedience [Jesus] many will be made righteous. (Romans 5:19, brackets added for emphasis)

To confirm that it's doctrinal (what you believe), let's look at the very next verse in Romans 6 –

But God be thanked that though you were slaves of sin, yet you obeyed [listened to, harkened to] from the heart that form of doctrine to which you were [past tense] delivered. (Romans 6:17, brackets added for emphasis)

Doctrine is the Greek word "didache"[137] which means teaching. We were (past tense!) slaves to sin (the noun), but we "obeyed from the heart" (we believed, listened to, gave attention to) from the HEART that form of doctrine (teaching) to which we were delivered (past tense!). It's about believing the Gospel of Jesus Christ!!

We hear the word "obedience" a lot, but what kind of obedience? Under the New Covenant of grace, our obedience is an obedience to the faith. Later in the book of Romans, Paul speaks of the obedience of faith:

Now to Him who is able to establish you according to my gospel and the preaching of Jesus Christ, according to the revelation of the mystery kept secret since the world began but now made manifest, and by the prophetic Scriptures made known to all nations, according to the commandment of the everlasting God, for obedience to the faith. (Romans 16:25-26)

"Obeying from the heart this doctrine to which you were delivered" is the process of the renewal of our minds to the truth of our new identity in Christ as His righteousness.

...and be renewed in the spirit of your mind, and that you put on the new man which was created according to God, in true righteousness and holiness. (Ephesians 4:23-24)

The "new man" is the new creation, formed in true righteousness and holiness! Now we have the mind of Christ.[138] We have a new heart and a new spirit within us.[139]

Set your mind on things above, not on things on the earth. For you died, and your life is hidden with Christ in God (Colossians 3:2-3)

Amen!

Does all of this sound repetitive? It's because every verse supports the same basic truth of the Gospel. I have endeavored in this study to give a wide spectrum of passages to show that grace permeates the scriptures. The Bible truly is the revelation of Jesus Christ and His amazing grace from Genesis to Revelation.

Slaves To Righteousness

Reader Study Reference, Romans 6:18

Continuing with Romans 6 we read the following:

Having been set free from sin, you became slaves of righteousness. (Romans 6:18)

Before we were saved, there was no list of good things we could do to be righteous. We were confined in sin and sinners by nature. No righteous act could change our status, and all our efforts at making sure our naughty list was shorter than our nice list amounted to nothing more than dead works. However, today even when we sin, God sees us as righteous. We are freed from the confinement of sin and forever in Christ's righteousness.

This says to me that Jesus' obedience was far more powerful than what Adam's sin was. You, believer, are as righteous as Jesus is.

But of Him you are in Christ Jesus, who became for us wisdom from God—and righteousness and sanctification and redemption— that, as it is written, "He who glories, let him glory in the Lord." (1 Corinthians 1:30-31)

Jesus has become our everything!

CHAPTER NINE

Joined to Jesus

Key scriptures:
Romans 7:1-20

Can you remember this one?

Oh, be careful little eyes, what you see.
Oh, be careful little eyes what you see,
For the Father up above, is looking down in love,
Oh, be careful little eyes what you see.

Oh, be careful little mouth, what you say.
Oh, be careful little mouth what you say,
For the Father up above, is looking down in love,
Oh, be careful little mouth what you say.

Oh, be careful little hands, what you do.
Oh, be careful little hands what you do,
For the Father up above, is looking down in love,
Oh, be careful little hands what you do.

Oh, be careful little mind what you think.

Oh, be careful little mind what you think,
For the Father up above, is looking down in love,
Oh, be careful little mind, what you think.[140]

As a child, the more they told me not to, the more I wanted to. Can you relate? The scary thing about that song, though, was not the instruction to be careful what I saw, said, did, and thought. It was the notion of God sitting on His throne in heaven holding His binoculars in one hand keeping an eye on me and His switch in the other hand waiting to whip me!

In Romans 7 Paul vividly describes the results of living life burdened with a consciousness of sins.

To Whom Are You Married?

Reader Study Reference, Romans 7:1-4

Paul begins Romans 7 by using the analogy of marriage: are we married to the law or to Jesus? At one time we were "married to" the law. We were "in the flesh" and our identity was in the flesh. Mr. Law gave us our name: "Sinner."

Or do you not know, brethren (for I speak to those who know the law), that the law has dominion over a man as long as he lives? For the woman who has a husband is bound by the law to her husband as long as he lives. But if the husband dies, she is released from the law of her husband. So then if, while her husband lives, she marries another man, she will be called an adulteress; but if her husband dies, she is free from that law, so that she is no adulteress, though she has married another man. (Romans 7:1-3)

If Mr. Law lives, his wife cannot marry another man because she can't be married to two men at the same time. If she marries another man while her husband is alive, she commits adultery. However, if her husband dies, she's free to marry another man. Paul was using the analogy of marriage because the Jewish law concerning marriage gave the husband 100% control. Listen to how that law read:

Suppose a man marries a woman but she does not please him. Having discovered something wrong with her, he writes her a letter of divorce, hands it to her, and sends her away from his house. (Deuteronomy 24:1, NLT)

Under Jewish law, even today, a man can divorce a woman for any reason or no reason. The Talmud (oral law of the Jews) specifically states that a man can divorce his wife for no other reason than because she spoiled his supper or because another woman is more attractive, and his wife's consent to the divorce isn't needed.[141] And yet, the only way she can get out of the marriage is if her husband dies. She is bound to her husband no matter what.

Back to Paul's analogy: the problem with Mr. Law is that he can't die! He's eternal because he came from God. Since Mr. Law cannot die, who has to die? The wife. And that's YOU and ME! But how can we die and still live? The next verse tells us:

You [the wife] also have become dead to the law through the body of Christ... (Romans 7:4, brackets added for emphasis)

And that's exactly what happened: we died, but actually, He died our death for us at the cross!

The dilemma was that someone had to die to release us from the dominion and condemnation of the law so that we could be joined to Jesus. There was no way for us to ever be compatible as sinners with our new Husband. A whole new bride of His species had to be born!

...that you may be married to another — to Him [JESUS] who was raised from the dead, that we should bear fruit to God. (Romans 7:4, cont., brackets added for emphasis)

When we are joined to Jesus, we bear the offspring of that union: love, joy, peace, patience, kindness, goodness, faithfulness, gentleness, self-control. Against these things there is no law![142] Now we are married to Jesus who by His Spirit gives us everything we need for life and godliness. He never stops supplying us with every good fruit. Every day has its demands, but the supply of our new Husband is there before we even need it or were conscious of it. As awesome as it is to be free from Mr. Law, that's not the good part. The good part is being joined to our new Husband, Jesus, who is our endless well of supply. We can do all things through our new Husband who strengthens us![143]

We aren't married to Jesus to be His servant any more than we married our spouses to be their slaves. At my wedding the pastor said, "Tricia, do you take Mark to love and to cherish all the days of your life?" When I said, "I do," it never occurred to me that this meant I would be his slave.

Here's the picture of our union with Jesus:

Husbands, love your wives, just as Christ also loved the church and gave Himself for her, that He might sanctify and cleanse her with the washing of water by THE WORD, that He might present her to Himself a glorious church, not having spot or wrinkle or any such thing, but that she should be holy and without blemish. (Ephesians 5:25-27, brackets added for emphasis)

What was THE WORD that sanctified us? What was THE WORD that cleansed us? What was THE WORD that presented us before Him as having no spot or wrinkle or any such thing? "JUST AS CHRIST LOVED THE CHURCH AND GAVE HIMSELF UP FOR HER!" That's THE WORD that has cleansed us. It's the Gospel!

In the Flesh

Reader Study Reference, Romans 7:5

Back to Romans 7:

We have established that we have died to the law. However, that doesn't mean that the enemy and his minions won't still try to use the law by shouting its demands at us, but we don't have to listen to it!

Here are the old days of being married to Mr. Law:

When we were [past tense] in the flesh, the sinful passions which were aroused by the law were at work in our members to bear fruit to death. (Romans 7:5, brackets added for emphasis)

To be "in the flesh" is to be under law, seeking to do good through self-effort. Being "in the flesh" isn't referring to the "works of the flesh"; however, being "in the flesh" does arouse sinful passions and will lead to the "works of the flesh" such as sexual immorality, hatred, jealousy, arguing, fits of anger, selfish ambition, and drunkenness.[144] Those sinful passions are aroused by the law! If you want to get rid of sinning, get rid of the law! Law puts demands on the flesh to overcome sin. The problem is that the power of sin in the flesh is more powerful than the flesh to overcome it. The flesh, as strong as it may seem, will never match the power of sin which originates from the devil. But here is good news:

> *He who is IN YOU is greater than he who is in the world. (1 John 4:4, emphasis added)*

So we can't say, "The devil made me do it," because we have an infinitely greater power within us than the power of sin and satan. The new creation joined to the Spirit of God, married to Jesus, has the power of God within. This power has already overcome the power of satan. Our "job" is to be AWARE of the truth and set our minds on it! The worst thing we can do is set our mind on the flesh. All it does is bear fruit to death.

A Deadly Combination

Reader Study Reference, Romans 7:6

The problem in Romans 7 is not sin, in and of itself. The problem in Romans 7 is SIN combined with the LAW which says, "Don't do it, or else!" When temptation meets the flesh (self-effort), sinful passions are aroused. The more we try to be good by our own self-effort, the more sinful passions are triggered in the flesh.

Whatever the sin is, the more we try not to do it, the more we want to do it. And then we end up doing it! It's like a being in quicksand; the more we try, the deeper we fall.

It's all about whom we are "obeying."[145] Are we listening to Jesus whose obedience has given us righteousness? If we are conscious of Him, we can rest in His love and supply, and bear fruit to life. At our core is the desire to walk after the Spirit and not after the flesh. We are not "IN the flesh" anymore in the sense that we are joined in identity to it, but we can certainly walk "according to the flesh" by living in the demands of the self-effort and cravings of the flesh.

In a sense, we can still put ourselves "under the law" by listening to, "obeying," the demands of our old husband.

> *But now we have been delivered from the law having died to what we were held by, so that we should serve in the newness of the Spirit and not in the oldness of the letter. (Romans 7:6)*

Following is Romans 7:6 in the Amplified Bible (think about the analogy of marriage that Paul used just a few verses before):

> *But now we are discharged from the Law and have terminated all intercourse with it, having died to what once restrained and held us captive. So now we serve not under [obedience to] the old code of written regulations, but [under obedience to the promptings] of the Spirit in newness [of life]. (Romans 7:6, Amplified Bible)*

We have died to what once restrained us and held us captive, and we need to believe it! The law is what brings fear. The law is what makes us look at our circumstances, our flesh, and the flesh of others as if they are the determining factors of our lives. The law makes us turn our attention away from Jesus and look to ourselves. The law will not allow us to rest in His provision. The law will keep us up at night worrying about tomorrow. Why? Because the expression of the law today is simply, "I can handle this myself." The weapon is fear — fear that we can't do it, but that we are supposed to be able to do it. Fear that we won't measure up, but we are supposed to try. Fear that we are unworthy, but we are supposed to earn our worthiness. And we will literally DIE trying!

The Law Arouses Sin

Reader Study Reference, Romans 7:7-8

> *What shall we say then? Is the law sin? Certainly not! On the contrary, I would not have known covetousness unless the law had said, "You shall not covet." (Romans 7:7)*

The law Paul was talking about here is not the part that told the Israelites what animals to sacrifice and how to kill them or the instructions for the seven feasts or the dietary rules. The context clearly tells us that the "law" he was referring to was the Ten Commandments:

"I would not have known covetousness unless the law had said, 'You shall not covet.'"

But sin, taking opportunity by the commandment, produced in me all manner of evil desire. (Romans 7:8)

Sin by itself didn't produce in Paul all manner of evil desire. He said sin "taking opportunity by the commandment" produced in him all manner of evil desire. The more Paul tried not to covet, the more he coveted!

With sin, first there is temptation, but then before a sin becomes a sin, something happens: temptation hooks up with CONFIDENCE IN THE FLESH. This is the conception that gives birth to sin. Paul said he put no confidence in the flesh. When there is confidence in the flesh, we will fall into sin because we fall back into self-effort: "I can handle this thing." And the problem after sin comes guilt and promises to do better. "I'm NEVER going to do that again!" The devil just loves all these promises we make because all of our declarations lean on our strength which always ends in failure and produces guilt. Once we're in guilt, the cycle continues, and then we are susceptible to being tempted even more. Like Paul said,

...the strength of sin is the law... (1 Corinthians 15:56)

When we get into guilt and shame, we need to repent! Remember, "repent" is not changing your behavior. It's changing our mind. Repent, the Greek word "metanoeo," means "to change one's mind." Change our mind about what? About who we are in Christ! Are we sinners or are we a new creation? We still sin, but we believe by faith that we are the righteousness of God in Christ, and we will be transformed outwardly by the renewing of our mind. We have the mind of Christ!

After we repent —change our mind and get out of that stinkin thinkin — we don't want to go back to performance and put confidence in the flesh again. A lot of times we'll enjoy our forgiveness and peace in our conscience for a while, but the guilt returns, and we go back to leaning on our fleshly commitments. That's called spiritual adultery. We go from Grace to law and back to Grace!

Our union with Jesus is a life of strength and supply from the inside out. Paul prayed,

...that He would grant you, according to the riches of His glory, to be strengthened with might through His Spirit in the inner man. (Ephesians 3:16)

Satan's Deception

Reader Study Reference, Romans 7:8

Without the law, sin will have no opportunity.

...For apart from the law sin was dead. (Romans 7:8, cont.)

Who benefits the most from the church never knowing who they are in Christ and never knowing that they are free from the law? The accuser of the brethren! Satan's main plot is NOT to try to get us to sin. His strategy is to try to get us to keep the law in our flesh! Why? Because:

...the law is not of faith... (Galatians 3:12)

...whatever is not from faith is sin. (Romans 14:23)

The devil tries to get us to be law keepers because our very efforts not to sin are sin in the eyes of God. Performance based religion is sin because the only true righteousness is Christ's righteousness, and the only way to get it is to receive it and surrender all our self-effort!

What was the #1 deception that the cunning serpent used with Eve: "I can be like God (be righteous) WITHOUT God. If I just have the knowledge of right and wrong, I don't need God." That is the power that still operates in the flesh today.

In 2 Corinthians 11, Paul's speaks of his authority as an apostle being challenged by certain Jewish teachers seeking to put the people under the bondage of legalism. There were those who really couldn't handle grace the way Paul preached it, and they fell prey to these guys who were coming in espousing righteousness by works. Paul was very upset with the church for allowing themselves to be led astray from the simplicity of the Gospel of grace:

For I am jealous for you with the jealousy of God himself. I promised you as a pure bride to one husband—Christ. But I fear that somehow your pure and undivided devotion to Christ will be corrupted, just as Eve was deceived by the cunning ways of the serpent. You happily put up with whatever anyone tells you, even if they preach a different Jesus than the one we preach, or a different kind of Spirit than the one you received, or a different kind of gospel than the one you believed... These people are false apostles. They are deceitful workers who disguise themselves as apostles of Christ. But I am not surprised! Even Satan disguises himself as an angel of light. So it is no wonder that his servants also disguise themselves as servants of righteousness. (2 Corinthians 11:2-4, 13-15, NLT)

Do you see the deception? These deceitful workers looked like they were all for righteousness. Their deception was not to get people to sin, but to be good! Our adversary knows that if we attempt to relate to Jesus based on our own righteousness, our undivided devotion to Him will be corrupted. Why? Because our devotion will be to men instead of Jesus! That's why with a mixture of grace and law, people take their eyes off of Jesus and put them on a man who will control them.

Recently my daughter came home from a youth retreat and shared with me how another youth had argued strongly with the salvation message of grace that was preached at the retreat. She told my daughter, "That preacher is wrong. We definitely have to work for our salvation!" She told my daughter that this is what she had learned in the youth group at her church — one of the largest churches in the nation! It's frightening to imagine how many youth are hearing a mixed message of law and grace.

We must guard our hearts from receiving any gospel that teaches that we are saved by anything but grace through faith in Christ's work alone. It's only when we live life under pure grace that our devotion to Jesus remains undefiled and undivided.

The Law Is Holy, Just, and Good

Reader Study Reference, Romans 7:9-13

I was alive once without the law, but when the commandment came, sin revived and I died. And the commandment, which was to bring life,

I found to bring death. For sin, taking occasion by the commandment, deceived me, and by it killed me. Therefore the law is holy, and the commandment holy and just and good. Has then what is good become death to me? Certainly not! But sin, that it might appear sin, was producing death in me through what is good, so that sin through the commandment might become exceedingly sinful. (Romans 7:9-13)

The power of sin is deceitful and uses the law to try to kill us. How does it "kill" us? Guilt, shame, burn-out, depression, sickness, and death! Yes, the commandment is holy, but it cannot make us holy. It is just, but it cannot justify us. The commandment is good, but it cannot make us good. Only Jesus can make us holy and justify us and give us goodness. The law can only condemn and curse us and give us heavy burdens.

The law itself isn't sinful. Law-haters, known as antinomians, have been misinterpreting the Scriptures since the days of the early church by saying that the law is evil and people can just go about living any way they want. Paul corrects this heresy by declaring the law to be holy, righteous, and good. The law in its intended severity shows how terrible sin is. So there's nothing wrong with the law by itself, but when combined with human effort, the results are always failure.

The Battle

Reader Study Reference, Romans 7:14-20

In verse 14, Paul begins to describe the battle that rages in our minds.

For we know that the law is spiritual, but I am carnal, sold under sin. For what I am doing, I do not understand. For what I will to do, that I do not practice; but what I hate, that I do. If, then, I do what I will not to do, I agree with the law that it is good. But now, it is no longer I who do it, but sin that dwells in me. (Romans 7:14-17)

Paul places the blame on something that was NOT him. Sinful thoughts come from the source called sin. We sin, but sin is not who we are. Sin acts in our flesh and may even feel like us, but it is not us.

For I know that in me (that is, in my flesh) nothing good dwells;... (Romans 7:18)

Notice that Paul is making a distinction between himself and his flesh by putting "that is, in my flesh" in parentheses. This is why he said He didn't put any confidence in it!

...for to will is present with me, but how to perform what is good I do not find. For the good that I will to do, I do not do; but the evil I will not to do, that I practice. Now if I do what I will not to do, it is no longer I who do it, but sin that dwells in me. (Romans 7:18-20)

Paul is talking about the complete inability of the flesh to overcome the power of sin even though the flesh will give it its best shot. However, good intentions simply don't cut it.

Some modern Bible translations such as the New International Version interpret the Greek word "sarx"[146] in verse 18 and later in verse 25 as "sinful nature" rather than "flesh" as if a believer still has a nature that is sinful. "Sarx" simply means the flesh or body of man. "Sarx" does not mean sinful. The connection is made because the flesh is where sin operates, but the confusion comes in when theologians make the leap that we as believers are sinful by nature. Our flesh was not born again in the new creation, and we will get new glorified perfect bodies when we go to heaven. However, in our spirits at the center of who we are, there is no nature to sin. How can we have a nature that is sinful when we are a new creation and partakers of Christ's divine nature?[147] We have a new nature. The old has passed away!

Unfortunately, because of mistranslations of the word "sarx," many Christians believe that their ongoing battle is with their own sinful nature. So here's the thought process: I have a sinful nature... I am a sinner... I'm just doing what comes naturally to me.

Tragically, many believe that in their innermost being they are sinful. If you are a Christian, nothing could be further from the truth! We inherited the sinful nature from Adam, but through the cross, the old creation with its sin nature died! Through the resurrection, the new creation with the nature of God's Son rose! We are righteous, and we want what is holy!

The enemy would have us think the work is unfinished, and we are still sinners in the hands of an angry God so we'll kill ourselves focusing on good works to make it to the finish line with His acceptance. People who believe this lie don't live their lives with the wisdom, peace, and guidance of God because they believe their lives are dependent on themselves. In truth, we can't do anything without God! Jesus said,

"I can of Myself do NOTHING." (John 5:30, emphasis added)

These are the words of Jesus, and they are the words of the new man created in the image of Jesus. The lie that Adam and Eve believed in the garden is the same lie that the power of sin in the flesh shouts. It's "I don't need God," or perhaps it's the mixed up message, "Jesus and I are partners. I do my part, He does His. He's not obligated to do His part if I don't do mine." Sounds fair enough, doesn't it? But our spirits cry, "Apart from Jesus, I can do nothing!"

The equation of religion: Jesus + me = everything.

The equation of grace: Jesus + zero = everything.

CHAPTER TEN

God Is For Us

Key scriptures:
Romans 7:21-8:3, Colossians 2:9-15

Is there any sweeter truth than "there is therefore now no condemnation"? At the end of the day when we've messed up, and we've done all we could do in our strength to make things right, to give our side of the story, to lick our wounds, earn our way back, and to start afresh, don't we just want to hear, "Child, it's okay. I've got it." When everyone else assesses us based on what we've done, God assesses us based on what He's done for us. Before we can ever make it with others, we've got to know that God is for us.

The End of the Battle

Reader Study Reference, Romans 7:21-25

From Romans 7:21 through the end of the chapter, Paul continues to describe the battle in our minds and the victorious end to the struggle.

I find then a law, that evil is present with me, the one who wills to do good. For I delight in the law of God according to the inward man. (Romans 7:21-22)

The "law of God according to the inward man" is not the Mosaic law. The Mosaic law was according to the performance of the outward man. The law of God is "the law of the Spirit of life in Christ Jesus" according to the new man that we have become in Christ.[148]

But I see another law in my members, warring against the law of my mind, and bringing me into captivity to the law of sin which is in my members. (Romans 7:23)

Notice that Paul says that the battle is between the law in his members (the law of sin and death[149]) and the law of his mind. He has the mind of Christ. The law of his mind in the new creation is the law of the Spirit of life in Christ Jesus. The law in his members (in his flesh) brings his flesh into captivity to the law of sin in his members. Again, some believers have been taught that this is a war between two natures — the sin nature and the divine nature, but Paul is not talking about a sin nature. He is talking about the flesh which has been severed from our new identity in Christ. The battle is simply between the new man joined to the Spirit and the flesh where sin operates.

O wretched man that I am! Who will deliver me from this body of death? Thanks be to God through Jesus Christ our Lord! (Romans 7:24-25)

Notice he said "WHO will deliver me?" Not "what." Jesus is our Deliverer from this body of death!!! Jesus is our Redeemer! Jesus is our Rescuer! Jesus is our Savior!!

Freedom

Reader Study Reference, Romans 7:25-8:3

So how did Paul get free of this tangled web of sin and the condemnation of the law? He tells us as we move into Romans 8:

So then, on the one hand I myself with my mind am serving the law of God, but on the other, with my flesh the law of sin. There is therefore now no condemnation to those who are in Christ Jesus. (Romans 7:25-8:1, NASB[150])

The word "condemnation" is the Greek word "katakrima"[151] which means the "sentence has been pronounced with the punishment following." No condemnation literally means there is not one bit of sentencing with punishment following for us. Even when we fail, there is therefore now no condemnation. We are now empowered to live a victorious life!

For the law of the Spirit of life in Christ Jesus has set you free from the law of sin and of death. (Romans 8:2, NASB)

Again, there are two laws. One is the law of the Spirit of life in Christ Jesus that is always on our side. The other is another law, another force, that wars against the members of our bodies. In order to win the battle, we need to know who is fighting whom. We are not our own enemy!

For what the Law could not do, weak as it was through the flesh, God did: sending His own Son in the likeness of sinful flesh and as an offering for sin, He condemned sin in the flesh. (Romans 8:3, NASB)

Sin in the flesh has been condemned. It has been subdued, overcome, and deprived it of its power to condemn us or control us! The law of the Spirit of life in Christ Jesus is the new "want to's" on the inside! It's the royal law of love.[152] We love because He first loved us![153] We forgive because He first forgave us![154] The motive is different under grace!

Spiritual Circumcision

Reader Study Reference, Colossians 2:9-13

For the remainder of this chapter, we will focus on a passage in Colossians 2 where Paul explains what happened to us when we were delivered from the law and joined to Jesus.

For in Him dwells all the fullness of the Godhead bodily; and you are complete in Him, who is the head of all principality and power. (Colossians 2:9-10)

The law will tell us that becoming complete is our goal in life, and we must live our whole life working our fingers to the bone to get there. However, grace says the work is finished, and we are at the goal line the minute we are born again! The word "complete" is in the perfect passive participle tense[155]:

Passive — We did nothing to be made complete. It was done to us.
Perfect — It was done once, and will never be done again.
Participle — It describes our on-going state of being.

Kenneth S. Wuest, a Greek expert, translated Colossians 2:10 like this[156]:

And you are in Him, having been COMPLETELY filled full, with the PRESENT result that you are in a state of fullness, in Him who is the Head of every principality and authority. (Colossians 2:10, Kenneth S. Wuest, emphasis added)

For us to be made complete, we experienced a death to the law when our "old man" died. The "old man" was our inward man that was JOINED to the flesh. This was our condition before we were raised with Christ, and our "new man" was joined to Him. We were "in the flesh" in the old race of Adam, dead in sin and in the uncircumcision of the flesh.

In Him you were also circumcised with the circumcision made without hands, by putting off the body of the sins of the flesh, by the circumcision of Christ buried with Him in baptism, in which you also were raised with Him through faith in the working of God, who raised Him from the dead. And you, being dead in your trespasses and the uncircumcision of your flesh, He has made alive together with Him... (Colossians 2:11-13)

The cross of Jesus Christ CUT AWAY the "old man" from the flesh. In this spiritual circumcision, the old man with its sin nature died, went into the grave, and ceased to exist. The "new man," a completely new creation with no sin nature, was born.

The Old Testament sign of circumcision given to Abraham and all of his physical descendants was a picture of this spiritual circumcision given to all of Abraham's spiritual descendants, which includes you and me today. Abraham is the father of our faith because "Abraham believed God, and it was accounted to him for righteousness."[157] It's the same way with us. God commanded that every Jewish child be circumcised on the eighth day as a sign of the covenant He had made with Abraham.[158] The eighth day was the first day of a new week following the passing of a completed week. "Eight" is the number of new beginnings and signifies our new life in Christ. The circumcision on the eighth day symbolized our deliverance from the old creation. The old has gone, the new has come!

> *If anyone is in Christ, he is a new creation; old things have passed away; behold, all things have become new. (2 Corinthians 5:17)*

"New" is the Greek word "kainos,"[159] and it means "fresh, unused, unworn, of a new kind, unprecedented, novel, uncommon, unheard of." The new creation is nothing like the old. This new creation is joined to the Lord, NOT joined to the flesh as the old man was. When we are joined to the Lord, we are made one spirit with Him.[160]

All those who believe in Him are translated from the kingdom of this darkness — this earthly realm — into the kingdom of God's beloved Son.

> *He has delivered us from the power of darkness and conveyed us into the kingdom of the Son of His love, in whom we have redemption through His blood, the forgiveness of sins. (Colossians 1:13-14)*

He literally translated us from this earthly realm of darkness into another kingdom of light. We actually went through a "door," and that door is Jesus.[161] Jesus said,

> *The Spirit of truth, whom the world cannot receive, because it neither sees Him nor knows Him; but you know Him, for He dwells WITH you and will be IN you. (John 14:17, emphasis added)*

Jesus spoke these words the night He was betrayed. He was talking about what would happen after the resurrection. When His flesh was torn, heaven would open up and come down through the gift of the Holy Spirit for all who believe. In the resurrection, God created a dwelling place for His Spirit: our hearts became His home. This new dwelling place is holy as He is holy because the Holy Spirit cannot live in an unholy place. Believer, you ARE HOLY!

He is in us and we are in Him!

The old man who was joined to the flesh ceased to exist. However, in a way that we cannot explain, God allowed the power of sin to remain in the body. Our identity was cut away from the flesh, but the flesh remains. Our flesh was not saved. Flesh and blood will not inherit the kingdom, so we will all get new incorruptible bodies when these corruptible ones die.[162] Until then, the power of sin is confined in the flesh and does not have dominion over us or determine our identity. The new creation never meets the sin in the flesh. That's why we can never be condemned by it again. Through the cross, Jesus removed our sins as far as the East is from the West from us.[163] He made us alive together with Himself and raised us up together to be seated in Him in heavenly places![164]

The Devil Is Disarmed

Reader Study Reference, Colossians 2:14-15

Back to Colossians 2:

...having forgiven you all trespasses, having wiped out the handwriting of requirements that was against us, which was contrary to us. And He has taken it out of the way, having nailed it to the cross. Having disarmed principalities and powers, He made a public spectacle of them, triumphing over them in it. (Colossians 2:13-15)

How many trespasses were we forgiven? ALL! Why? Because every sin was obliterated in the body of our Lord Jesus at the cross. If we weren't forgiven of ALL, we weren't forgiven at all!

The devil has been disarmed! Did you ever stop and think that this means he was armed at one time? What was the weapon? The law! The hand-writing against us! The adversary entices us with words like, "If you'll only be good, God will love you. He'll be pleased with you. You'll be right with Him." That's when we say, "I'm already right with God by the blood of Jesus!" Reminding the forces of darkness of the blood of Jesus is a reminder of the spectacle that Jesus made of the enemy on that day and the triumph that we have in Him.

Can you see how the devil tries to confuse us about who we are? He tries to make us think the work is not finished, and we are not yet complete in Christ. His main strategy is to get us working and focusing on the fruit, instead of the Source. We hear the question from well-meaning Christians, "Are you bearing fruit? You need to get to work! Bear some fruit!" There's a teaching in the church that we must examine ourselves to see if we are bearing fruit, or we cannot be sure that we are saved. This makes bearing fruit a work that people strive to produce to cleanse their conscience.

So we start looking at patience or kindness or goodness or self-control, and then we try our hardest to get it. Or we start looking at healing and we try to earn it. So we go back to self-effort (self-righteousness), and we pray harder, fast more, make resolutions to change, and declare the Word with zeal pushing to MAKE fruit happen. Where in the world did we get this idea of bearing fruit? Fruit comes from abiding in God's love. We can't produce fruit! Fruit is a byproduct of receiving the sap of His enduring love.

Progressive Expression, Not Progressive Sanctification

An apple tree bears apples. In the same way we bear the fruit of who we are. The change in our identity and person has already taken place, but the expression of the change is the outward transformation that people see. We move from faith to faith as we behold Him, and the new man breaks forth and manifests to the world to bring glory and honor to Jesus' name.

What does it mean to behold Jesus? We know that Jesus isn't here in flesh and blood for us to look at, so what was Paul saying when he said that we would be transformed into His image from glory to glory by beholding Him? He was talking about something very spiritual — about how inside of us we can rest, and we can behold Him in our inner man. We'll see when we look at 2 Corinthians 3 in a later chapter of this book that the truth of the word of God is THE basis for what we behold about Jesus in the Spirit. Any departure from the word of God or any addition to the word of God will not give us the pure face of Jesus. The word of God is spiritual, and we have been born again of the incorruptible seed of the word of God which lives forever.[165] It is eternal.

...while we do not look at the things which are seen, but at the things which are not seen. For the things which are seen are temporary, but the things which are not seen are eternal. (2 Corinthians 4:18)

The visible realm is the natural realm. The invisible realm is the eternal realm. If we just look at the natural realm with our natural eyes, we will live in constant limitation based on the knowledge of good and evil. Do this and good will come. Do that and evil will come. We must "see" with the spiritual eyes and the spiritual mind that we were given in the new birth. The most important thing in walking in the Spirit is awareness of the unseen realm. For example, we could have $1,000,000 in the bank, but not be aware of it, and it does us no good.

We are not trying to BE someone. We are beholding to KNOW Someone. And when we know Him, we will find out who we are in Him. We're not doing to be. We see that we already ARE, and we find ourselves doing.

This might seem weak to us. We might think, "What in the world is THAT going to do?" The flesh is always geared towards right and wrong. "Just give me the ten steps to reach the goal, and I'll do it." We need to realize we are at the goal! Religion will never understand the mystery of Christ's life inside because religion focuses on that what is seen and not that which is unseen.

When Jesus created us in Himself, He put inside of us our spiritual DNA, our destiny, and every good work that He prepared for us. Today we just flow in our identity in Him. The progressive aspect of our lives on earth is just a progressive expression of what already IS: we have already been made holy. We are not being slowly sanctified. Outwardly it appears that we're getting more holy, more pure, more righteous because our lives are changing. The seed of God is already in us, and now we are just bearing fruit from who we are.

...for it is God who works in you both to will and to do for His good pleasure. (Philippians 2:13)

It is the life of Jesus in us performing the good that is His nature to perform. We set our mind on Him, we attend to His word, and we will start acting like Him. There are no more "have to's"! We're now under the "want to's" of our new nature in Christ! Yet it's only when we let go of the "have to's" that the "want to's" have a chance to be released.

> *You are not in the flesh but in the Spirit, if indeed the Spirit of God dwells in you. If Christ is in you, though the body is dead because of sin, yet the spirit is alive because of righteousness [the gift of Christ's righteousness!]. But if the Spirit of Him who raised Jesus from the dead dwells in you, He who raised Christ Jesus from the dead will also give life to your mortal bodies through His Spirit who dwells in you. (Romans 8:9-11, brackets added for emphasis)*

Our flesh is effected by the resurrection power of the Spirit within us. His glory transforms our bodies and our minds and gives us life. We are joined as one spirit with the Lord, but residing in these earthen vessels. God left us in these earthen vessels of flesh so that His life flowing through us is seen to be of Him and not of us.

> *We have this treasure in earthen vessels, that the excellence of the power may be of God and not of us. (2 Corinthians 4:7)*

If the power was seen as being from us, it would only be fig leaves that would attract others to our own goodness (self-righteousness) and ultimately bring condemnation and a sense of unworthiness on them as they compare themselves to us. God's goodness never brings condemnation. It only brings joy and peace and gratefulness. We are utterly dependent on His life in us because He allowed the new to remain in the frame of the old.

When we live from the inside out, people will look at us and glorify HIM. Why? Because they will see that it's His power and not our own. They would be drawn to HIM, not to us. That way they too will be saved! These bodies can be a means to glorify God as His power in us comes out. This body with its members will become a "sieve" for the glory to go forth from within!

Nothing Can Separate Us From God

Like our elder Brother Jesus, the Firstborn among many brethren, we are born from above. He is the Son of God who lives in heaven and walked on earth. We too live with Him in heavenly places as we walk the earth by the Spirit who was given to us. Today sin cannot separate us from God because sin has been confined to the flesh which has been forever cut away from who we are. Today NOTHING can separate us from God's love:

What then shall we say to these things? If God is for us, who can be against us? He who did not spare His own Son, but delivered Him up for us all, how shall He not with Him also freely give us all things? Who shall bring a charge against God's elect? It is God who justifies. Who is he who condemns? It is Christ who died, and furthermore is also risen, who is even at the right hand of God, who also makes intercession for us. Who shall separate us from the love of Christ? Shall tribulation, or distress, or persecution, or famine, or nakedness, or peril, or sword? ...For I am persuaded that neither death nor life, nor angels nor principalities nor powers, nor things present nor things to come, nor height nor depth, nor any other created thing, shall be able to separate us from the love of God which is in Christ Jesus our Lord. (Romans 8:31-35; 38-39)

Half Time Quiz

Now that we're half way through the book, it's time for a little exercise to see if we can recognize the difference between the mixed gospel of religion and the true Gospel of grace. Below are several paragraphs that are a good sampling of the mixed message that is being taught and believed by many in the church.

For several years I led a "deliverance" ministry. The goal of the ministry was for the participant to be set free to serve God, be blessed by Him, and be in fellowship with Him. The way to get there was by getting rid of the sin in our lives and casting off the powers of darkness, i.e., demons. Participants were encouraged to go on to become leaders so that they could maintain their freedom and stay sin-free, blessed, and enjoying the presence of God.

Recently I skimmed through the curriculum that I wrote for that ministry to see what I used to teach and affirm as the steps to "freedom." Below I have included a few excerpts from that Bible study workbook.[166] To be fair, this curriculum had many true statements and teachings. In fact, if you were only exposed to those statements, you would think you were reading pure grace. Here's a sampling of those true statements:

After He had created the earth, the plants, and the animals, He made for Himself a family in His own image.

You will find that our God is the kindest and most faithful person you will ever know. Imagine a life free of guilt, condemnation, pain, fear, and shame. Grab hold of God's vision for you—a life of fruitfulness, direction, purpose, righteousness, joy, and peace.

God is in love with sinful man and sent His Son Jesus to rescue people.

God says we can only come to Him through grace, by faith—not by works. You can't connect with God by simply doing more good things than bad things.

The blood of Jesus has overcome satan. We as believers are fighting from victory and not to victory! The veil has already been torn; the victory has already been won; satan is a defeated foe!

All those statements are true, but that's where the deception comes in. We'll read books or listen to sermons that include awesome New Covenant truths from the Bible, but thrown in will be a little "leaven" as Paul called it in Galatians. A little law mixed with grace isn't grace. When we hear the mixed message of grace and works, works will be our lasting impression. We'll take all of the Good News mix it with self-effort, and it will morph into the ability to obey commands. In fact, the last of those pure grace excerpts above was actually the first part of a mixed message paragraph. Here's the last sentence of that paragraph:

Now, the only veil hindering God's presence is the veil of our own flesh.

The main idea of the teaching was that you would not be close to God if you sinned. The fallacy is that we could do something bad that would cause God's presence to be hindered, or we could do something pleasing to God that would invite His presence.

Righteousness by faith has absolutely NOTHING to do with behavior. Nothing. Behavior, while important in relating to people and expressing the love of God to them, has no bearing on our union with God or our standing with Him. That's the scandalous, outrageous nature of the finished work of Jesus Christ.

Read the passages below, and as you read them, ask yourself what the problem is with each statement, and see if you can find scripture to back up your assertion.

1. *Living a life of fellowship with God, innocence, anointing, and freedom is not natural for us. As we will see, ever since the sin of the first man, we battle a sinful nature.*

2. *You wouldn't want to eat on a plate that is dirty no matter how clean it looks on the surface! But the Lord knows when there is something in our lives that keeps us from being fit for His use and every good work. Will you let the Lord put the spotlight on your life? John 16:8 says that He will convict the world of sin, and He will judge us according to His righteousness. The Lord wants to bring us to another level of personal integrity and move us from the paper plate realm to the fine china realm.*

3. *Sanctification is when we let God make us more like Him. This is not an event; it's the process of becoming fit for the Master. It's a journey to allow God to mold and transform our character.*

4. *There are levels of Christianity that go beyond the salvation experience. God plays many roles in our lives: He is friend; He is Savior; but He is also Lord. This means that He calls the shots! We need to be continually giving Him every area of our lives and giving Him rulership. We must become servants of the Lord before He can fulfill His purpose in us.*

5. *Cry out to God from a pure heart—He never intended for us to cleanse ourselves without His help.*

6. *Release from spiritual oppression involves two actions, repentance of sin and casting off the powers of darkness. Often people believe that simply admission of sin clears their conscience and frees them from any consequence or responsibility. Admitting a sin is a part of repentance, but it is not repentance. Repentance is actually turning from the sin and making a decision not to continue in it.*

7. *When we repent, 1 John 1:7 says that the blood of Jesus cleanses us from all sin. But often people feel that they aren't forgiven even after confessing and repenting of a sin many times. Have you ever had that experience? It may be because you need to cast off any demon spirit associated with the sin. Even though the blood of Jesus has covered that sin through*

your repentance, the enemy must be cast off and the hook removed. This will destroy the demonic hold in that area and release you to experience the peace of God's forgiveness. Sin separates us from God so we REPENT and turn from sin. Sin allows the enemy to gain footholds so we CAST OFF the powers of darkness and remove the footholds.

8. The best way to find God's call on your life is to say, "My life's not my own. I've been bought with a price and I am Your slave by choice. What would you like me to do, King Jesus?" With that kind of attitude, He will lead you and bless you abundantly.

9. Worship is a life of obedience. How do we worship in spirit and in truth? We need to ask Him to purify us. God is saying He can't tolerate worship from a heart whose affections are divided and mixed. He says to us, "If you're going to worship Me, please bring me an offering that is pure."

10. Worship is a lifestyle that keeps us clean because as we devote ourselves to God, we live in innocence and purity.

11. It's good to examine ourselves and ask God if there are any offensive ways in us. Ask the Holy Spirit to put a finger on any area of your life that has grieved or quenched Him and be willing to come to a place of truth. Remember – God is faithful and just and will cleanse us from all unrighteousness. If you know the Holy Spirit is speaking to you right now about His desire to purify you, pray this prayer: Father, Forgive me for offending you, for grieving and quenching Your Spirit. I make no excuses for it; I confess my sin right now. (Say out loud anything that you need to rid your life of.) God, I want this sin out of my life right now – I don't want to be any where near it! I receive Your cleansing right now. I know you delight to show me mercy. Thank You, Lord, for letting me off the hook. Father, I make my decision to be the kind of child you've always wanted me to be – the kind who will worship You and know You in spirit and in truth. I worship You with all my heart and love You! In Jesus name, Amen.

CHAPTER ELEVEN

The Letter Kills, The Spirit Gives Life

Key scriptures:

2 Corinthians 3:2-6, Exodus 12:12-13, Exodus 14:10-14, Exodus 15:22-25, Exodus 16:2-4, Exodus 17:2-6, Exodus 19:3-6, Hebrews 12:18-24

Of all the passages in the Bible that contrast grace and law, 2 Corinthians 3 may be my favorite because of the famous verse near the end of the chapter that is well known to many Christians. It is the strongest desire of my heart that the world experience this truth:

For where the Spirit of the Lord is, there is liberty. (2 Corinthians 3:17)

2 Corinthians 3 is also the passage that inspired the name **Unveiling Jesus**. You will understand why as we go through the scriptures.

Living Letters

Reader Study Reference, 2 Corinthians 3:2-3

You are our epistle written in our hearts, known and read by all men; clearly you are an epistle of Christ, ministered by us, written not with ink but by the Spirit of the living God, not on tablets of stone but on tablets of flesh, that is, of the heart. (2 Corinthians 3:2-3)

This entire chapter of 2 Corinthians is a contrast between the Old Covenant and the New Covenant. Paul starts out by saying we aren't letters written with ink on scrolls or letters etched on stone. In other words, our message isn't the message of the law. We are living letters of grace written by the Spirit of God on our hearts. His message through us is love and faith and grace, not condemnation and fear.

Ministers of the New Covenant

Reader Study Reference, 2 Corinthians 3:4-6

And we have such trust through Christ toward God. Not that we are sufficient of ourselves to think of anything as being from ourselves, but our sufficiency is from God, who also made us sufficient as ministers of the new covenant, NOT of the letter but of the Spirit; for the letter kills, but the Spirit GIVES LIFE. (2 Corinthians 3:4-6, emphasis added)

We are called as ministers of the New Covenant of the Spirit, not ministers of "the letter." What was Paul referring to when he said "the letter that kills?" He was talking about the Old Covenant law of Moses.

How does this apply to us today? The "letter that kills" for us today is the system of performance based Christianity where we try to serve God and work to please Him in order to earn His blessing and His love. We'll find out very quickly that the ministry of the old — or a mixture of the old and the new — will cause us to burn out quick. The sufficiency of God only comes as we minister the new.

The letter is unbending and unsympathetic to our weaknesses. We can see the nature of the law when we look at how Jesus brought the letter to it's intended standard when He said things like,

"You have heard that it was said to those of old, 'You shall not commit adultery.' But I say to you that whoever looks at a woman to lust for her has already committed adultery with her in his heart." (Matthew 5:27-28)

In Galatians 4 Paul said,

Tell me, you who desire to be under the law, do you not hear the law? (Galatians 4:21)

As I have said many times in this book, God didn't give the law to define and illustrate how well-behaved His children are. He gave the law to show how far short we fall without His righteousness. It's the "letter that kills."

"I came that they may have life, and have it abundantly. I am the good shepherd; the good shepherd lays down His life for the sheep." (John 10:10-11, NASB)

Some people believe that we are supposed to follow Jesus and mimic the way that He lived in the Gospels, but by His sheer existence, His example condemns all of us. No one can be like Him. Thank God He didn't save us by Jesus' life on earth. He saved us by His DEATH and resurrection life — "zoe," the supernatural, resurrection life of God.

In John 10 Jesus called Himself the Good Shepherd who gives up His life for the sheep so that we could have life abundantly. The abundant "life" He gave TO us is the Greek word "zoe"[167] and it means the supernatural life of God. The "life" He gave FOR us is the Greek word "psyche" which means the emotions, affections, desires, His heart.[168] Jesus literally gave up His soul for you! He left His position, His title, His royalty to give you supernatural life.

The point of Jesus living a perfect, sinless life on earth was not for us to imitate Him, it was for Him to qualify to take our place. Now He lives His resurrection life through us!

To see the background of the "letter that kills," we'll need to go back to the book of Exodus to the first Passover.

The Passover

The night before God delivered the Israelites from the hand of the Egyptians, He instructed them through Moses to paint the blood of a spotless lamb over the doorposts of their homes.

...every man shall take for himself a lamb, according to the house of his father, a lamb for a household... And they shall take some of the blood and put it on the two doorposts and on the lintel of the houses where they eat it... I am the LORD. Now the blood shall be a sign for you on the houses where you are. And when I see the blood, I will pass over you. (Exodus 12:3, 7, 12-13)

The last plague that came upon the Egyptians was the death of the firstborn. That night the angel of death passed through the streets entering every home that did not have the blood over the doorposts, and the firstborn of those families died. However, if the doorpost was covered in the blood, the angel passed over. Hence, the name "Passover." God said, "When I see the blood, I will pass over you."[169] The angel passing over had nothing to do with the people on the other side of the door. It was the presence of the blood on the doorpost that kept them alive. In the same way, God's deliverance, His favor, His blessing, and His salvation come upon us when He sees that the blood of His Son has washed away all of our sins.

Beginning with that first Passover, the Israelites were set free after being in captivity for four hundred years.

Before we get back to 2 Corinthians, we're going to take a detour into the time period following the Exodus of God's people from the bondage of Egypt. During the two months from the Exodus through the Red Sea to their arrival at Mount Sinai, we see a season of grace in the life of ancient Israel that relates to us this side of the cross. This was BEFORE the law was given. We'll see several times where Jesus is unveiled to us in the Old Testament scriptures from this time period. As we learned in the first chapter of this book, every time we have a revelation of Jesus — an unveiling ("apokalypsis"[170]) — the grace of God is being brought to us.[171]

Exactly two months after the Israelites left Egypt, they arrived in the wilderness of Sinai. After breaking camp at Rephidim, they came to the wilderness of Sinai and set up camp there at the base of Mount Sinai. (Exodus 19:1-2, NLT)

In this two month period, from the Red Sea to Mount Sinai, there is no record of anyone dying, no record of the word "anger" being used regarding the Lord towards Israel (even when they sinned), and no record of God punishing or rebuking His people. This season represents where we live perpetually this side of the cross: under grace.

Complaining, the Big One

The #1 sin of the Israelites was complaining. They complained before the law was given, and they complained after the law was given. After the law was given, Moses defined complaining as despising God:

> *"...because you have despised the LORD who is among you, and have wept before Him, saying, 'Why did we ever come up out of Egypt?'"* *(Numbers 11:20)*

Complaining was despising the hand that fed them, the arms that comforted them, and the God that healed them and delivered them. Loving God and complaining are opposite responses to God's grace. Complaining was (and still is) no small matter!

When the law came, the "greatest commandment" would be:

> *You shall love the Lord your God with all your heart, with all your soul, and with all your strength. (Deuteronomy 6:5)*

To complain is to break the greatest commandment. Complaining demonstrates unbelief. Unbelief is saying to God, "You have made promises to me, but I don't trust You."

But don't feel condemned if you have complained. Today we are not under law; we are under grace. The more we know Him, the more we will trust Him, and the more we will love Him. We can try with great resolve to stop complaining and speaking negatively, but until we are filled with the joy of the Lord from understanding His great grace towards us, we'll never be able to consistently zip the lip or force ourselves to think good thoughts and speak positively. The power of positive thinking only works to the degree that a person is strong-willed. Everyone has a breaking point in the flesh. Don't try to stop being negative. Let's just get to know Jesus, and we won't be able to stop ourselves from praising Him and thanking Him and speaking words of life, even in the worst circumstances.

Throughout this two month time period they continually broke what would become the greatest commandment; but notice that even though they sinned repeatedly, there was no law; therefore, there was no punishment.

Unveiling Jesus #1, Red Sea Crossing

God led the Israelites around by way of the wilderness to the Red Sea. If you remember the story, after God sent ten plagues on the Egyptians, Pharaoh relented and set the Israelites free. However, as he was in the habit of doing, he changed his mind, and sent his army after them towards the Red Sea.

And when Pharaoh drew near, the children of Israel lifted their eyes, and behold, the Egyptians marched after them. So they were very afraid, and the children of Israel cried out to the LORD. Then they said to Moses, "Because there were no graves in Egypt, have you taken us away to die in the wilderness?... For it would have been better for us to serve the Egyptians than that we should die in the wilderness." And Moses said to the people, "Do not be afraid. Stand still, and SEE the salvation [Yeshua] of the LORD [Yahweh], which He will accomplish for you today. For the Egyptians whom you see today, you shall see again no more forever. The LORD will fight for you, and you shall hold your peace."... (Exodus 14:10-14, brackets added for emphasis)

Moses told them to "stand still" while their enemies were rushing towards them. "Stand still and SEE the salvation of the LORD." Can you imagine just standing there with a massive body of water before you and the strongest army in the world in fast pursuit approaching from behind? Imagine for a moment that you are Moses leading two million people, and you tell them not to be afraid and just do nothing but watch! Our motto is often "Don't just stand there, do something!" When trouble or hardship or pressures come, the flesh demands that we do something. Fixing problems by DOING appeals to the flesh. But we need to hear the Spirit of the Lord from within saying, "Don't fear. Stand still and LOOK AT ME! I will deliver you safely."

Salvation is the Hebrew word "yeshuwah"[172] (also spelled yeshua) which is the Hebrew word for "Jesus." Yeshua (Jesus) means "Yahweh [the LORD] is Salvation."[173] What does this mean? It means Jesus is

Yahweh! Jesus is the Great I Am. Jesus is the beginning and the end. Jesus is the first and the last. Jesus is our all in all. When we see LORD (Yahweh) in the Old Testament, we are seeing Jesus!

The message God wants us to hear is the declaration that Moses gave to the people: "Stand still, look at Jesus, and see Him save you!" He will take care of us as He took care of the Israelites. Every last one of the enemies of God's people were drowned in the sea, but every last one of the Israelites made it to the other side!!

As we will see over and over during the season of grace: they broke the greatest commandment[174], but no law; therefore, no punishment.

Unveiling Jesus #2, The Bitter Waters of Marah

In the next chapter of Exodus, we see the Israelites traveling through the desert, and going three days without water.

So Moses brought Israel from the Red Sea; then they went out into the Wilderness of Shur. And they went three days in the wilderness and found no water. Now when they came to Marah, they could not drink the waters of Marah, for they were bitter. Therefore the name of it was called Marah. And the people complained against Moses, saying, "What shall we drink?" So he cried out to the LORD, and the LORD [Yahweh] showed him a tree. When he cast it into the waters, the waters were made sweet. (Exodus 15:22-25, brackets added for emphasis)

This is an unveiling of Jesus, the Tree of Life! Jesus is the tree that turns our bitterness into sweet rivers of joy. When Moses threw the tree in the water, it was a declaration that our reliance is to be completely in the LORD, Yawheh, the Tree of Life who would come down out of heaven and be our answer to every need. Even in the midst of their complaining, God showered them with grace. When we see the sweetness of Jesus, how can we stay in bitterness?

They broke the greatest commandment, but no law; therefore, no punishment.

Unveiling Jesus #3, The Bread from Heaven

In Exodus 16, we find the story of the manna. Every day starting on the 16th day of the 2nd month for the entire forty years that the Israelites were in the wilderness, God provided bread from heaven which they called manna, which means "What is it?"[175]

Fast forward to the New Testament, about fifteen hundred years after the wilderness experience, Jesus revealed Himself as the Bread from heaven:

> *Then Jesus said to them, "Most assuredly, I say to you, Moses did not give you the bread from heaven, but My Father gives you the true bread from heaven. For the bread of God is He who comes down from heaven and gives life to the world. Then they said to Him, "Lord, give us this bread always." And Jesus said to them, "I am the bread of life. He who comes to Me shall never hunger, and he who believes in Me shall never thirst." (John 6:32-35)*

The manna in the wilderness was a manifestation and shadow of Jesus Christ, the true manna from heaven! Jesus said if we come to Him, we'll never hunger; and if we believe, we'll never thirst.

I can't count how many times I cried in years past with tears streaming down my face and hands lifted to heaven, "I'm hungry for you, Lord!" Christians have bought into the idea that being starved for Jesus is admirable and spiritual. But what does the scripture say? Jesus said, "He who comes to Me shall never hunger." If we are "hungry" it's because we're believing what our emotions are telling us based on what's happening outside, instead of the reality of Christ's fullness in our spirit. Have we come to Jesus? Have we received the Bread of Life? If so, we are complete in Him. All of the fullness of the Deity is in Him, and He is in us! We are full! If we are feeling empty, dry, and hungry, the answer is to behold our wonderful Jesus in His love, His wisdom, His promises, His provision, and His glory. See Him seated on the throne above all principalities and powers. See Him strong and powerful. And then, see yourself in Him!

Notice, once again the manna came when the people were complaining.

Then the whole congregation of the children of Israel complained against Moses and Aaron in the wilderness. And the children of Israel said to them, "Oh, that we had died by the hand of the Lord in the land of Egypt, when we sat by the pots of meat and when we ate bread to the full! For you have brought us out into this wilderness to kill this whole assembly with hunger." Then the LORD said to Moses, "Behold, I will rain bread from heaven for you." (Exodus 16:2-4)

Even though the Israelites accused Moses of leading them out to die, God did not reign judgment on them! God had parted the Red Sea for them. God had brought them out ladened with the riches of Egypt. God had kept every one of them safe and healthy. God had turned the bitter waters sweet.[176] Jesus, the Bread of heaven, was sent down into the wilderness while man was rebellious, disobedient, and complaining; and His response to all their complaining was GRACE!

They broke the greatest commandment, but no law; therefore, no punishment.

Unveiling Jesus #4, The Rock from which the Water Flows

In the next chapter of Exodus, the Israelites experienced another water shortage.

[They] camped in Rephidim; but there was no water for the people to drink. Therefore the people contended with Moses, and said, "Give us water, that we may drink." So Moses said to them, "Why do you contend with me? Why do you tempt the LORD?" And the people thirsted there for water, and the people complained against Moses, and said, "Why is it you have brought us up out of Egypt, to kill us and our children and our livestock with thirst?" So Moses cried out to the Lord, saying, "What shall I do with this people? They are almost ready to stone me!" And the Lord said to Moses, "Go on before the people, and take with you some of the elders of Israel. Also take in your hand your rod with which you struck the river, and go. Behold, I will stand before you there on the rock in Horeb; and you shall strike the rock, and water will come out of it, that the people may drink." And Moses did so in the sight of the elders of Israel. (Exodus 17:2-6)

Once again, the waters flowed for God's people!

The rod that God told Moses to strike the rock with was the rod he used to strike the Nile River and turn it into blood, which was the first plague against the Egyptians.[177] Blood signifies judgment, and that rod was a rod of judgment.

What does this mean for us? Jesus (the fulfiller of the law) is saying to Moses (who represents the law), "Strike Me with the rod of judgment." The judgment that should have fallen on us because of sin, fell upon Jesus, the Rock of our salvation.[178] He took the blows for us, and He took away all of the handwriting against us when the nails were hammered into His flesh. The rod was the cross. The cross struck the Rock and mercy flowed towards us in living rivers of the Spirit of God! He was smitten at the cross to give us the refreshing waters of the Spirit.

If anyone thirsts, let him come to Me and drink. He who believes in Me, as the Scripture has said, out of his heart will flow rivers of living water." But this He spoke concerning the Spirit, whom those believing in Him would receive... (John 7:37-39)

Back to the Israelites: they were thirsty, they whined, and God provided.

They broke the greatest commandment, but no law; therefore, no punishment.

Why All This Grace?

About five hundred years after these events in the wilderness took place, David wrote about it in Psalm 105. David declared the everlasting faithfulness of our Lord and then gave the reason that God showered the Israelites with grace during that two month period:

He also brought them out with silver and gold, And there was none feeble among His tribes. Egypt was glad when they departed, For the fear of them had fallen upon them. He spread a cloud for a covering, And fire to give light in the night. The people asked, and He brought quail, And satisfied them with the bread of heaven. He opened the rock, and water gushed out; It ran in the dry places like a river. [Why all of this grace?] For [because] He remembered His holy promise, And Abraham His servant. (Psalm 105:37-42, brackets added for emphasis)

Abraham lived hundreds of years before the law was given, and he lived under an unconditional covenant based on grace. I believe the two month period in the desert before Mount Sinai and the giving of the law was God saying, "This is grace. Can you handle it? It's going to require that you trust Me. It's going to require that you stop looking at the natural and look to the heavenly. All you have known is the bondage of this world, but that was not My doing, nor My plan for you. Don't look back. Here is My plan":

> *"You have seen what I did to the Egyptians, and how I bore you on eagles' wings and brought you to Myself. Now therefore, if you will indeed obey My voice and keep My covenant, then you shall be a special treasure to Me above all people; for all the earth is Mine. And you shall be to Me a kingdom of priests and a holy nation." (Exodus 19:4-6)*

What covenant was God referring to? The only covenant that was in place at the time: the Abrahamic covenant of grace! God wanted to carry them on eagles' wings. He wanted to be near them, and He wanted them to be a KINGDOM of priests — not just one priest who could alone approach God and represent the people. He wanted all of them to be in His presence.

They rejected God's desire for them, but today His desire is our reality. We are washed in the blood of Jesus, and He has brought us to Himself and made us kings and priests and a royal priesthood.

> *To Him who loved us and washed us from our sins in His own blood, and has made us kings and priests to His God and Father, to Him be glory and dominion forever and ever. (Revelation 1:5-6)*

> *But you are a chosen generation, a royal priesthood, a holy nation, His own special people, that you may proclaim the praises of Him who called you out of darkness into His marvelous light; who once were not a people but are now the people of God, who had not obtained mercy but now have obtained mercy. (1 Peter 2:9-10)*

Another Covenant

God declared His desire for His people, yet they agreed to another covenant that came alongside the Abrahamic covenant: the covenant of law which would be based on their own faithfulness and goodness, not the goodness of God. They were birds in a cage that wouldn't fly out when the door was opened for them. They wanted to have it their way, and with that came a system that was against them/ hostile to them/ contrary to them and led to wrath, condemnation, and death.[179]

They boasted:

All that the Lord has commanded us, we will do. (Exodus 19:8)

When the Mosaic law was given to the children of Israel, God expressed Himself to His people in an unprecedented manner. In Hebrews 12, the writer describes what happened on that day when God gave the law at Mount Sinai:

For you have not come to the mountain that may be touched and that burned with fire, and to blackness and darkness and tempest, and the sound of a trumpet and the voice of words, so that those who heard it begged that the word should not be spoken to them anymore. for they could not endure what was commanded: "And if so much as a beast touches the mountain, it shall be stoned or shot with an arrow." And so terrifying was the sight that Moses said, "I am exceedingly afraid and trembling." (Hebrews 12:18-21)

Mount Sinai is the mountain that represents the Old Covenant. We have not come to that mountain! If we touch that mountain of law, we'll be pummeled with satan's fiery darts of condemnation. The people who heard the commandments were so terrified that they begged that they not be spoken. Moses himself was "exceedingly afraid!"

No more could the people come near God. No more would they be carried on eagles' wings.

"And Moses alone shall come near the Lord, but they shall not come near; nor shall the people go up with him." (Exodus 24:2)

Never before had God appeared to His people in this way. With the law came a terror that kept the people far from God. When they boasted in their own ability to do all that the Lord commanded, counting on their own righteousness, God backed away. All of a sudden God had changed the way He related to His people. From

Egypt to Mount Sinai God had been close to them. At that time when they sinned, He showered them with grace, showing them His heart: "Where sin abounds, grace superabounds."[180] However, after the law was given, no human being except the high priest could approach God because no one in their own righteousness measured up to His glory.

However, the command "they shall not come near" has been totally reversed this side of the cross.

...let us DRAW NEAR with a true heart in full assurance of faith... (Hebrews 10:22, emphasis added)

...the law made nothing perfect; on the other hand, there is the bringing in of a BETTER hope, through which we DRAW NEAR to God. (Hebrews 7:19, emphasis added)

We haven't come to Mount Sinai. We've come to the mountain of the Lord into the heavenly realms with Him!

But you have come [past tense] to Mount Zion and to the city of the living God, the heavenly Jerusalem, to an innumerable company of angels, to the general assembly and church of the firstborn who are registered in heaven, to God the Judge of all, to the spirits of just men made perfect, to Jesus the Mediator of the new covenant... (Hebrews 12:22-24, brackets added for emphasis)

Today you and I are in the presence of the Judge Himself! How much more security could we possibly need?! We are eternally safe and accepted. We have come to the spirits of just men made perfect. Why? Because we are just men made perfect! And we have come to Jesus Himself, our High Priest and Mediator of a new covenant in His very own blood.

After the law was given, if they murmured, they died. When they said things like, "Did God bring us out here to die?!"...that's exactly what happened to them.

Which covenant would you prefer?

They Broke the First Commandment

We see in Exodus chapters 20-31 that God spoke the 10 Commandments from the mountain, and then Moses went up the mountain for forty days to receive the entire law and the instructions for building the tabernacle, the portable temple that would be a dwelling place the presence of the Lord. The tabernacle showed that God always had a plan to redeem His people. In the tabernacle, blood sacrifices would be offered for the sins of the people, and each year on the Day of Atonement the high priest would go in to the presence of God in the Holy of Holies as a representative of the people. He would offer the sacrifices and sprinkle the blood on the Mercy Seat of the Ark of the Covenant so that the nation of Israel could be blessed and protected for another year. All of these things were shadows of the better things to come in Jesus.[181]

After receiving all of these instruction, Moses came down the mountain to deliver the law to the people.

And when He had made an end of speaking with him on Mount Sinai, He gave Moses two tablets of the Testimony, tablets of stone, written with the finger of God. (Exodus 31:35)

When Moses came down the mountain with the two tablets of stone containing the Ten Commandments, he stopped short of reaching the bottom. Why? Because he saw the people breaking the first commandment which was written on those stones: "You shall have no other Gods before Me. You shall not make any graven image."[182]

The Israelites had formed a golden calf from the gold they had brought out of Egypt. In righteous anger, Moses broke the two tablets of stone.[183] Because of the judgment of the law, three thousand people had to die at the hands of the Levites (the priests). Because of God's mercy, Moses didn't come all the way down the mountain lest they all would be slaughtered. God told him to go back up and receive another set of stones.

The Spirit Gives Life

Reader Study Reference, 2 Corinthians 3:6

Fast forward to the New Covenant when on the day of Pentecost, fifty days after the Passover when our Lamb of God was slain, one hundred twenty disciples were in the upper room waiting for the promise of the Spirit. All of a sudden a mighty rushing wind blew through, tongues of fire landed on each of them, and the Holy Spirit not only filled the house, but also filled the people! The next thing we see is Peter preaching the Gospel, and three thousand people were saved!

When the law was given, 3000 died. (Exodus 32:28)

When the Spirit was given, 3000 were saved. (Acts 2:41)

Which goes to show:

...the letter kills, but the SPIRIT GIVES LIFE... (2 Corinthians 3:6, again, emphasis added)

The Veil Is Removed

Key scriptures:
2 Corinthians 3:7-18; 2 Corinthians 4:3-4; Genesis 22:2, 6, 8, 12

Not long ago, my husband, Mark, was on an elevator with a stranger who was complaining about the blazing summer here in Alabama. As Mark waited patiently for the elevator to arrive at the right floor, the man idly chattered, "It may be hot here in Alabama, but it's a lot hotter in hell. That's what I tell the guys in my men's Bible study group."

Mark responded, "Well, you don't have to worry about that."

The man argued in a jolly tone, "As long as I stay on the straight and narrow, I don't!"

Mark tried to encourage him, "Hey man, Jesus did all the work on the cross."

"Well, He did most of it!" The man answered with a smile. Then the elevator opened, and the man walked away wiping the sweat from his brow.

Sadly, many cling to tradition and rhetoric. How did things get so mixed up when the scriptures are so clear? Too often we give an audience to utter absurdity and don't even question it. I think we need to take the spiritual blinders off.

The Parentheses

After 2 Corinthians 3:6, Paul goes into an explanation of the contrast between the two covenants. He explains the difference between the "letter that kills" and the "Spirit that gives life." To better understand what Paul is teaching in this chapter, think of Verses 7 to 16 as being set off by parentheses.[184] Then on the other side of the parentheses we come to verse 17 and the very famous statement, "For where the Spirit of the Lord is, there is liberty." We have heard this verse recited in songs and in "deliverance" meetings and in "inner healing" books. We'll see what it means IN CONTEXT. You might be surprised... And you might experience freedom you have never known!

The Ministry of Death

Reader Study Reference, 2 Corinthians 3:7-8

Now we come to the first verse within the parentheses:

But if the ministry of death, written and engraved on stones,... (2 Corinthians 3:7)

Paul was talking about the Ten Commandments here. It was the only part of the law hand-written by God Himself and engraved on stones.[185] The instructions for animal sacrifice, ceremonial feasts, dietary restrictions, and all the detailed moral and civil laws were given by God to Moses who wrote them down on scrolls.[186] God told Moses to put the stones which contained the Ten Commandments in the Ark of the Covenant, but the rest of the law, God commanded Moses to place it beside the Ark of the Covenant.[187]

But if the ministry of death, written and engraved on stones, was glorious, so that the children of Israel could not look steadily at the face of Moses because of the glory of his countenance, which glory was passing away, how will the ministry of the Spirit not be more glorious? (2 Cor-inthians 3:7-8)

Paul said that the Ten Commandments had glory. It was perfect, but its perfection was a glory that caused the people to run away from God instead of coming near Him.

When Paul refers to the "ministry of death" and the glory of Moses' countenance being so brilliant that the people couldn't look at him, he was referring to the second time when Moses came down the mountain with the second set of stones.[188] Why was his face shining? Why was this time different than the first time?

After the first giving of the Ten Commandments and the worship of the golden calf, God threatened to send the people to the Prom-ised Land without Him lest His anger consume them along the way. Although the people were commanded not to come near the Lord, He spoke to Moses face to face as a man speaks to a friend. Moses pleaded with God not to leave them. Moses begged God on the basis of His grace. The proof that Moses found grace in the sight of God would be that God would personally stick with them and not leave them.[189] Isn't that still the proof of God's grace today? Yet today His presence doesn't just abide WITH us, but is also INSIDE of us.

Out of His heart of grace, God agreed to go with Moses. Then God told Moses to prepare another set of stones on which He would etch the Ten Commandments again. Next, God stood before Moses in the cloud and declared His name:

And the LORD passed before him and proclaimed, "The LORD, the LORD God, merciful and gracious, longsuffering, and abounding in goodness and truth..." (Exodus 34:6)

In this second giving of the Ten Commandments, God revealed Himself as the God of mercy and grace. As Moses spoke with the Lord, his face shone with the glory of the Lord as he found grace in the sight of the Lord.[190] With a shining face reflecting God's mercy and grace, Moses came down the mountain holding in his hands the stones declaring the standards of God's holiness. So here we have the mixture of grace and law. Moses, a mere man, could only deliver God's holy commandments as a servant. He could not provide the righteousness to fulfill them. Only Jesus would be able to fulfill the law and give us the righteousness that God requires. However, righteousness and peace would not kiss until many centuries later when mercy and truth met at the cross.[191]

Because he had been in the presence of the God of grace, Moses' face was shining, but because of the law, that glory was passing away. This was the mixture that Paul called the "ministry of death" that demanded righteousness from people who didn't have any to offer.

Moses had to put a veil over his face so he could speak to them because God will not allow the glory of His grace to be seen in a mixture. It would only be after the cross that we could look at God's glory in the face of Jesus. It's only through His grace that we can see the shining light of His glory and run towards it instead of away from it. Why? Because the "ministry of the Spirit" inside of us declares that we are righteous. The light of His glory only reveals that His blood has cleansed us. There is no condemnation for those who are in Christ!

Mercy Triumphs

The first time Moses went up the mountain, God showed him the instructions for the Tabernacle.[192] The second time that Moses came down the mountain with the two tablets of stone, God told him to put them in the tabernacle in the ark under the Mercy Seat where blood would be sprinkled every year on the Day of Atonement.[193] When God would see the blood on the Mercy Seat, He would see the innocence of the lamb, not the disobedience of His people. The Ten Commandments were put in the ark, UNDER the Mercy Seat. Which goes to show:

Mercy triumphs over judgment. (James 2:13)

God's grace and mercy triumph over the law because of our spotless Lamb who took away our sins. We see Jesus all through the tabernacle. The Mercy Seat is Jesus. The Ark is Jesus. The Lamb is Jesus.

The Ministry of Condemnation

Reader Study Reference, 2 Corinthians 3:9

For if the ministry of condemnation had glory... (2 Corinthians 3:9)

It's when we mix law and grace that we get the ministry of con- demnation. Today in the church it's not the pure law that is preached; it's the mixture of grace and law. I know I have said my whole life as a Christian that I am not under the law because we don't obey all the Jewish laws of the Old Testament, such as circumcising our babies on the 8th day or celebrating the Jewish feasts and holy days or stoning people to death or sacrificing animals to atone for sins. Most of us don't obey the Old Covenant dietary laws or observe the Sabbath. However, many Christians think that we're saved by grace, but we live by the Ten Commandments after we are saved in order to main- tain our right standing with God.

I can remember strongly advocating posting the Ten Command- ments in the schools in my state, and I supported leaders who were working hard to get the Supreme Court to pass a law mandating the rights of states to post them. My children went to a Christian school where each child was required to memorize the Ten Commandments in the King James Version! I recall being so proud of them. They had practiced for months to perfect their presentation for the parents. My heart swelled as these elementary age students displayed their keen memorization skills as they recited every word in Old English. Have you tried memorize the Ten Commandments? If not, you may be surprised to discover that it's quite difficult!

However, there aren't just ten commandments. If the law was preached in its purity, we would have to obey the six hundred thirteen laws of the Old Covenant perfectly to be acceptable to God![194] But honestly, we'd all be better off if the pure law were given to us than this confusing mixture because instead of slaving to make ourselves right, we'd cry for mercy and turn to Jesus. And guess what, my friend — that's the purpose of the law!

Recently I heard a sermon on addictions that in my opinion de- picts very well the mixture that we often hear today. The preacher was cruising right along through Romans 7, systematically laying out the reality of the fleshly struggle of sin: "I do the thing I don't want to do..." And he made it almost to the end of Romans 7 to the next to the last verse:

O wretched man that I am! Who will deliver me from this body of death? (Romans 7:24, NASB)

I was sitting there listening and getting excited because I know the next three verses. I expected to hear the preacher say:

Thanks be to God through Jesus Christ our Lord! So then, on the one hand I myself with my mind am serving the law of God, but on the other, with my flesh the law of sin. Therefore there is now no condemnation for those who are in Christ Jesus. For the law of the Spirit of life in Christ Jesus has set you free from the law of sin and of death. (Romans 7:25-8:2, NASB)

I was on the edge of my seat waiting for those words, and I just about fell off the chair when I heard this INSTEAD:

How foolish are those who manufacture idols. These prized objects are really worthless. The people who worship idols don't know this, so they are ALL PUT TO SHAME! Who but a fool would make his own god— an idol that cannot help him one bit? All who worship idols will be disgraced. (Isaiah 44:9-11, NLT, emphasis added)

I sat there... shocked and stunned. He made it all the way to "what a wretched man I am! Who will deliver me from this body of death?!" and instead of continuing and giving us the New Covenant reality of freedom from condemnation through Jesus, he leaped back to the Old Covenant reality of shame and disgrace. He went on to say that we must love the Lord our God with all our heart, soul, mind, and strength and then we'll overcome those addictions. I was literally shaking from this blatant example of the mixture of law and grace. He just put a figurative noose around the neck of his congregation! Yes, they will do better for a while, but when they fall, it will be worse than before. They may be good for six months or even longer, but then they'll binge. I have seen this tragic story in ministry over and over and over!

What is the result of taking our frustration with the cycle of sin and making a determination to do better by trying harder? A cycle of defeat. It's the law in action! There is no place for the law in the life of a New Covenant believer. We have the Holy Spirit inside today, and He is enough to lead us in holy living. We don't need the external demands of the law because we have the supply straight from God.

For those who advocate the law: the law demands 100% perfection. There's no grading curve with the law. If the law is compromised, it is dishonored. For the law to be the law, it cannot be altered in any way.

For those who advocate principles of the law mixed with grace: they are lowering God's holy standards to a place that man can keep them, and they are cheating God's grace of it's glory. They dishonor the cross and the perfection of Christ's sacrifice and work of redemption.

For those of us who advocate pure grace: we honor the law for the purpose that God gave it. It was to bring people to the God of grace and mercy.

The Ministry of Righteousness

Reader Study Reference, 2 Corinthians 3:9

In much of Christianity today we see the "ministry of condemnation" having glory. People get saved out of utter fear. The wrath of God is preached and people come running to the altar. People are threatened with the terror of hell instead of pursued with the love of God as demonstrated in that "while we were yet sinners, Jesus died for us." On the other hand, Paul said,

> ...*the ministry of righteousness exceeds much more in glory. (2 Corinthians 3:9, cont.)*

Today the "ministry of righteousness" far exceeds the "ministry of condemnation" in glory. Now across the whole world eyes are being enlightened to this glorious Gospel of grace. The coming revival of God's "abundance of grace and the gift of righteousness" will be like nothing we have ever witnessed. The "ministry of righteousness" is the "ministry of the Spirit" who guides us into the truth that we are sons of God like our Elder Brother, Jesus Christ! When we have a revelation of that truth, nothing will be impossible for us and the church will rise up to be who she is called to be!

The Veil

Reader Study Reference, 2 Corinthians 3:10-14

> *For even what was made glorious had no glory in this respect, because of the glory that excels. For if what is passing away was glorious, what remains is much more glorious. Therefore, since we have such hope, we use great boldness of speech unlike Moses, who put a veil over his face so that the children of Israel could not look steadily at the end of what was passing away. But their minds were blinded. For until this day the same veil remains unlifted in the reading of the Old Testament, because the veil is taken away in Christ. (2 Corinthians 3:10-14)*

Paul said, "We have great boldness of speech." "Boldness of speech" literally means "freedom of speech, unreservedness of utterance, to speak without ambiguity, plainly, without figures of speech."[195] What Paul is saying here is that when the veil is lifted, we can see Jesus not only today, but also throughout the Old Testament scriptures. The types and shadows of Jesus are unveiled to us!

"Until this day" the veil is covering the eyes of those who see the Old Testament with Old Covenant lenses. In that context, what is the veil? It's the condemnation that comes from the law that says they don't measure up to the standard, and they are deserving of punishment and a cursed life. Even to this day, people's minds are blinded because of the veil. They don't see Jesus in His glory and love and grace! Yet, the veil was torn from top to bottom when our Lord was crucified! The veil is taken away in Christ!!

So who is putting the veil over people's eyes today? If we skip down a few verses to the next chapter of 2 Corinthians, we can read in context who is blinding the minds of people.

> *But even if our gospel is veiled, it is veiled to those who are perishing whose minds the god of this age has blinded, who do not believe, lest the*

light of the gospel of the glory of Christ, who is the image of God, should shine on them. (2 Corinthians 4:3-4)

Satan, the god of this age, is the one who blinds the minds of the unbelieving. People are perishing from unbelief, depression, bondages, disease, loss of spiritual vision, and broken relationships because the Gospel is being veiled to them. Why is the devil blinding their minds? Because he's so afraid that the "light of the Gospel of the glory of Christ" will shine on people and set them free!

The mystery which has been hidden for ages from generations has been revealed. God has made HIMSELF known in Christ. The greatest truth that the devil wants to blind the world to is that Jesus came to manifest the goodness and heart of the Father to us. The glory of Jesus reveals the nature of the Father. The adversary does not want people to know that Jesus is the very image of the Father. The enemy wants us to see God as an angry and mean judge. But what is the truth?

And He [Jesus] is the radiance of His glory and the exact representation of His nature. (Hebrews 1:3, NASB, brackets added for emphasis)

[Jesus] went about doing good and healing all who were oppressed by the devil, for God was with Him. (Acts 10:38)

As many as touched Him were made whole. (Mark 6:56, KJV)

• Not just those who repented.
• Not just those who confessed their sins.
• Not just those who were at peace with all men.
• Not just those whose marriages were perfect.
• Not just those who ate right food and exercised.
• Not just those who obeyed their parents.
• Not just those who gave the temple tax.
• Not just those who behaved themselves.

The compassion and love that Jesus demonstrated when He took children in His arms, protected the woman caught in adultery, defended the woman with the alabaster box, healed the man with the withered hand, and calmed the storm is the same compassion and love that the Father has for us today!!

The Veil Is Taken Away

Reader Study Reference, 2 Corinthians 3:15-16

> *But even to this day, when Moses is read, a veil lies on their heart. Nevertheless when one turns to the Lord, the veil is taken away. (2 Corinthians 3:15-16, emphasis added)*

When we turn to Jesus, the veil of condemnation is removed. Think of it this way: it would be difficult for the groom to kiss the bride if the veil were not lifted. We are His bride, and when He lifts the veil, He says to us:

> *"You are all fair, my love, and there is no spot in you." (Song of Solomon 4:7)*

In the Song of Solomon from which this verse is taken, the Shulamite woman whom the bridegroom pursues is a picture of Jesus and His love for and pursuit of His bride, the church. "Shulamite" is the feminine form of the name Solomon. Shulamite means "the perfect, the peaceful."[196] In other words, we are the reflection of the perfection and peacefulness of our Lover and Redeemer. He created a bride comparable to Himself to join Himself to. He has taken the sin away, removed the condemnation, and lifted the veil. And He likes what He sees!

Where the Spirit of the Lord Is

Reader Study Reference, 2 Corinthians 3:17

Now the parentheses that began after verse 6 come to an end. If you recall, verse 6:

> *...for the letter kills, but the Spirit gives life. (2 Corinthians 3:6)*

Now we come to the end of the parentheses and verse 17:

> *Now the Lord is the Spirit; and where the Spirit of the Lord is, there is liberty. (2 Corinthians 3:17)*

What is the context of this awesome truth? We are no longer under the law! The veil of condemnation has been removed, and now we can look into the face of Jesus without shame! We are free from the limiting thoughts, from the accusations, and from all the fears of the enemy! We are under grace!

The work is finished. We are free.

We should always look at scriptures IN CONTEXT! How many Christians are frustrated because they are engaging in "spiritual warfare" taking up arms to defeat the devil and reciting verses out of context? I can remember leading many conferences and singing songs that declared that "where the Spirit of the Lord is, there is freedom," but we never mentioned the veil being torn and being set free from the bondage of the law. I remember being so frustrated that people were having to cycle multiple times back through this deliverance ministry that I oversaw. They seemed so free at one time. What happened? Many, many times I would vent my frustration by crying out, "What is the missing link?! What are we missing?" At the time I didn't realize that the root of every evil in the world is condemnation. It started in the Garden of Eden with the fig leaves and the shame, and was later magnified by the law. The missing link was GRACE, and what we didn't realize was that the work is finished. There's nothing left to do.

Deliverance and inner healing ministries could be greatly simplified if they focused on grace and put the ax to the deepest root of every problem: condemnation.

Jesus Is the Center of It All

Reader Study Reference, 2 Corinthians 3:17

In verse 17 of 2 Corinthians 3, we see the phrase, "Now the Lord is the Spirit." The word Lord here refers to the Lord Jesus Christ.[197] We know that the Lord is One God and wherever the Lord is mentioned, we see the Trinity; however, in the context, we see in the previous verses, verses 14-16, that the veil of condemnation of the law is removed when we see JESUS. Paul contrasted the liberty that we now have in Christ with the bondage that came from the being under the law. He contrasted the boldness of speech that we now have through the unveiling of the hidden mystery of Christ in the Old Testament with the lack of understanding that people had of the Old Testament scriptures when they could only see the law. In other words, when the veil is taken away, the Old Testament in unlocked, and we can begin to see God's plan of redemption throughout the Bible. We can see Jesus in every story, type, shadow, and prophecy. We'll see that Jesus is the center of it all!

In the context of 2 Corinthians 3, Paul is speaking of two different ways of seeing the scriptures: one is when Moses is read; the other is when one turns to Jesus. When you read your Bible, who do you see? Do you see Moses who is giving you a list of instructions on how to be a better Christian? Or do you see Jesus who wants to reveal Himself to you by showing you His heart of grace and love?

If we read the Old Testament with man-centered Old Covenant lenses, we will miss the primary teachings about Jesus and mistakenly think it's all about us. If we read the Old Testament with New Covenant lenses, the Holy Spirit will reveal Jesus on every page!

Abraham and Isaac

A great example of the typology of Jesus in the Old Testament is the story of Abraham laying Isaac on the altar.

Perhaps you've heard this spin on the story: "Abraham laid Isaac, the son that he loved, on the altar. Are there any idols in your life that are between you and God? Is God calling you to lay down certain relationships or things that are hindering your relationship with Him? You need to consecrate yourself to God. What are you holding back from God?"

There was a time when I used to teach this passage from that perspective. In one of our Bible study groups where I taught this perspective on Genesis 22, a women in the group confessed that her "Isaac" was her collection of designer shoes. She had carried guilt for years because of her love for expensive shoes, and she "laid it down" that night. She thought that God would bless her because of her obedience.

But where is Jesus in all of that?

The problem with taking those stories from the Old Testament and making them man-centered is that we miss the whole point of the story! This account of Abraham offering Isaac is not about us! It's about our heavenly Father offering His only Son for us. Isaac was a picture of Jesus!

Isaac	*Jesus*
Take now your son, your only son Isaac, whom you love, and go to the land of Moriah, and offer him there as a burnt offering ... (Genesis 22:2)	*For God so loved the world that He gave His only begotten Son, that whoever believes in Him should not perish but have everlasting life. (John 3:16)*
So Abraham took the wood of the burnt offering and LAID IT ON ISAAC his son. (Genesis 22:6, emphasis added)	*He, BEARING HIS CROSS, went out to a place called the Place of a Skull, which is called in Hebrew, Golgotha. (John 19:17, emphasis added)*
Abraham said, "My son, God will provide for Himself the lamb for a burnt offering." (Genesis 22:8)	*"Behold! The Lamb of God who takes away the sin of the world!" (John 1:29)*
"For now I know that you fear God, since you have not withheld your son, your only son, from Me." (Genesis 22:12)	*God demonstrates His own love toward us, in that while we were still sinners, Christ died for us. (Romans 5:8)*

When God told Abraham to take his son, "the son that he loved" and put him on the altar, this is the first time the verb "to love" is used in the Bible.[198] This was God saying, "I'm going to give My Son, My only Son, the Son that I LOVE and offer Him on a cross." Abraham was willing to go all the way in trusting God. In Hebrews 11 in the "hall of fame of faith," we see what was on Abraham's mind when he was willing to offer Isaac:

> *By faith Abraham, when he was tested, offered up Isaac, and he who had received the promises offered up his only begotten son, of whom it was said, "In Isaac your seed shall be called," concluding that God was able to raise him up, even from the dead, from which he also received him in a figurative sense. (Hebrews 11:17-19)*

Not even the death of his only son could negate God's promise! This is a picture of our heavenly Father who went all the way for us. Here we see Jesus on the cross, and Jesus being resurrected for us. God's only Son, the Son that He loves! Now we can look at God in the same way the angel spoke to Abraham and declare, "For now I know that You love me, Father, since You have not withheld your Son, Your only Son, from me!"

When we see Jesus in the Old Testament, it brings us life, and faith bursts forth with joy explosions in our hearts! This story isn't about us laying down our "Isaacs." It's about our heavenly Father who gave up His only Son for us and our heavenly spotless Lamb who laid down His life for us!!

He who did not spare His own Son, but delivered Him up for us all, how shall He not with Him also freely give us ALL things? (Romans 8:32, emphasis added)

When we know that God gave us the absolute BEST that He had, how could He withhold any good thing from us? In fact, through the cross every good and perfect gift, every spiritual blessing in heavenly places, is already ours to receive![199] The Lamb was slain from the foundation of the world. Can you imagine God before the foundation of the world making a list of good things that He would withhold from us? It would be saying that there are good things that are of more value than Jesus Himself! What things would be of greater value than Jesus?

Back to our famous verse in 2 Corinthians 3:

Now the Lord is the Spirit; and where the Spirit of the Lord is, there is liberty. (2 Corinthians 3:17)

The veil has been removed! See Jesus in the word and be set free!!! "The new is in the old concealed; the old is in the new revealed."[200]

Beholding

Reader Study Reference, 2 Corinthians 3:18

The last verse in 2 Corinthians 3 says:

But we all, with unveiled face, beholding as in a mirror the glory of the Lord, are being transformed into the same image from glory to glory, just as by the Spirit of the Lord. (2 Corinthians 3:18)

"We all" have unveiled faces today. We have no veil and Jesus has no veil. We can now look full in His wonderful face. When that happens, we move from one glory to another. And the divine instrument of that change is the Holy Spirit who has enlightened the eyes of our understanding to His love and power and goodness. Everything He is and everything He has is now ours.

"Transformed" is the Greek word "metamorphoo"[201] which means a change from one state to another state, like the caterpillar to the butterfly. This is what happens to us when we turn to the Lord and behold Him in His glory. We are transformed from the passing glory of our own righteousness as servants into the unveiled glory of Christ's righteousness as sons.

Paul was speaking of two very distinct glories:

1. The veiled, passing glory of the Old Covenant where God saw man through the unbending judgment of the law. In this glory, no one could see the Lord and live. In this glory was the wrath of God, shame, and punishment. In this glory, Moses could only look upon the back parts of God. In this glory, God was always leaving.[202]

2. The unveiled, eternal glory of the New Covenant where God sees us as perfectly righteous through grace. We have become a whole new creation in Him that is perfect and holy, and believing this truth will transform our actions and works into the Christ-likeness of our spirit. In this glory, we not only see God and live, the more we see Him, the more alive we will be! In this glory is acceptance, approval, and love. In this glory, God is always with us; He will never leave us or forsake us. In this glory is liberty!

The unveiled glory of the New Covenant is the life of the Spirit within. It's no longer, "Do this, and God will bless you. Do that and God will curse you." We live by the power and love of the endless life of the Spirit within, not by the demands of performance from the outside. Religion tells us that if we perform better, then we will become more like Jesus and have fellowship with Him through our righteous actions and good attitudes. What an affront to the cross! We have been transformed into the perfect counterpart of Jesus by the power of the cross and the resurrection.

His Image

In this study of 2 Corinthians 3, we find that the whole context of "beholding" is about how we understand God's word and distinguish between the old and the new. "When Moses is read, a veil lies over their hearts. Nevertheless when one turns to the Lord, the veil is taken away."[203] It's so clear that Paul is talking about two ways of seeing the word: through the identity of a condemned law-breaker or through the identity of a Christ-like, redeemed new creation.

When we behold Jesus, we are transformed into His glorious image. We are "beholding as in a mirror" because when we look at Jesus, it's like looking into a mirror. When we see the image and beauty of Christ with unveiled face and eyes of grace through faith without a task-based paradigm, we see what we have become in Christ as a new creation.

James talks about seeing our identity in the mirror.

For if anyone is a hearer of the word and not a doer, he is like a man observing his natural face in a mirror; for he observes himself, goes away, and immediately forgets what kind of man he was. (James 1:23-24)

A doer of the word is one who lives by faith in the perfect law of liberty which has set us free from the law of performance. If we walk away from the mirror of Christ and look to other things for our identity, we forget who we are! Our identity is not found in our own integrity or lack of it. It is not found in the bad things that have happened to us or the bad things that we have done. Our identity is found in the image of God.

I had the opportunity recently to teach children about their identity in Christ, and I focused my teaching on 2 Corinthians 3:18. I had each child hold a mirror in front of their face and say out loud a characteristic of Jesus, and then declare that same characteristic over themselves as they looked in the mirror. For example, one young boy said, "Jesus is strong, I am strong." A kindergartener said, "Jesus is sweet, I am sweet." One young teenage girl was about to say something, but she stopped short in embarrassment. "I asked her what she had planned on saying. She mumbled, "Jesus is beautiful." I said, "SAY IT!" It took some encouragement, but she looked in the mirror and said, "Jesus is beautiful. I am beautiful." Another teenage boy looked in his mirror and said, "Jesus is perfect. I am perfect." Awesome.

Arise, shine; for your light has come! And the glory of the Lord is risen upon you. (Isaiah 60:1)

I wonder what the future would look like if young Christians believed the truth about themselves? I wonder how the world would be impacted if the church would look in the mirror of God's word and see who they have become in Christ?

13

Do You Trust Me?

Key scriptures:
Romans 4:3; Philippians 3:4-9; Genesis 12:1-3; Genesis 15:5-6; Exodus 1:7-11; Exodus 16:3-5, 9-12; Exodus 19:3-6; Exodus 32:7-14

Throughout my whole life as a Christian I have heard that Abraham is the father of our faith [204] However, for decades all I knew about Abraham was the Sunday School song "Father Abraham" (including the hand motions, of course) and the story of God telling Abraham to kill his son Isaac and sacrifice him on the altar. For all practical purposes, for years I had a mental file for Abraham, but it was empty. However, there is so much more to know.

Many Christians don't understand the significance of being in the spiritual lineage of Abraham. Most are living like spiritual orphans because they don't have a clue about who they are nor do they comprehend all their inheritance includes because of this spiritual lineage. Shouldn't we know something about our roots?

God told Abraham, "In you all the families of the earth shall be blessed."
(Genesis 12:3)

Paul taught extensively on our spiritual lineage in Abraham, and the cornerstone of his teaching was this phrase:

Abraham believed God, and it was accounted to him for righteousness. (Romans 4:3)

So let's look at the verse in context. Abraham was blessed by God, and the way he received the blessing was by BELIEVING that he was righteous before God; therefore, we are blessed, and the way we receive the blessing of God is by believing that we are righteous before God. Simple.

Two Ways To Qualify

Theoretically, there are two ways to qualify for God's favor: 1) receive it by grace through faith or 2) earn it yourself.

One way is to see the powerlessness of the flesh, recognizing the flesh for what it is and being completely dependent on the Spirit for every blessing of God, including life itself. The other way is to put confidence in the flesh. That's a futile and deadly exercise. Paul said, "In my flesh nothing good dwells."[205] However, at one time Paul put ALL his confidence in his flesh to gain right standing with God and with people:

If anyone else thinks he may have confidence in the flesh, I more so: circumcised the eighth day, of the stock of Israel, of the tribe of Benjamin, a Hebrew of the Hebrews; concerning the law, a Pharisee; concerning zeal, persecuting the church; concerning the righteousness which is in the law, blameless. But what things were gain to me, these I have counted loss for Christ. Yet indeed I also count all things loss for the excellence of the knowledge of Christ Jesus my Lord, for whom I have suffered the loss of all things, and count them as rubbish, that I may gain Christ and be found in Him, not having my own righteousness, which is from the law, but that which is through faith in Christ, the righteousness which is from God by faith. (Philippians 3:4-9)

There are two credentials that Paul mentions that he considered at one time to have given him an advantage over other people: his background and his achievements. Another way to say it is that under the law a person could only qualify for God's favor by being a Jew (his bloodline) and by obeying the law (his performance). In fact, Paul put so much worth in these two things that he condoned the murder of Christians to guard the sacredness of adherence to the Jewish religion. He terrorized the church, entering every house, dragging off people, and throwing them into prison for embracing Jesus and not obeying the law.[206] This was not considered criminal; it was applauded! He was perfectly justified in his actions and passion according to the Jewish leadership of that day. Why? Because of the covenant that they had been under for fifteen hundred years: the Mosaic Covenant of law.

When Paul was ambushed by God's grace on the Road to Damascus, Jesus appeared to him and asked him why Paul was persecuting Him.[207] Why was Jesus telling Paul that he was persecuting Him, instead of telling him he was persecuting the church? It's because the church is the body of Christ! When a believer is persecuted, Jesus is persecuted. Can you see the identity that we have in Jesus?

That same identity in which we share in His suffering is the identity that qualifies us for every blessing of heaven. When we gain Christ, we gain all that He is and all that He is worthy of!

The Covenants

If we misunderstand the covenant that we are under with God, we are going to feel like He is pleased with some days and mad at us on other days. Some days we will feel qualified for His favor and some days we will feel like we need to earn it because we have not lived up to His standards. That type of reasoning reveals a mindset that does not understand what has changed when Jesus stood in our place before God and took all of the curse that we deserved so that we could receive all of the blessing that He deserves. Understanding the change in covenants unveils the relationship God wants us to enjoy and the means by which we are qualified to receive His favor.

If we read scriptures like, "Jesus is the same yesterday, today, and forever,"[208] and take it to mean that there is no difference in God's dealings with His people whether they were under the Old Covenant or the New Covenant and that there is no distinction between the old and the new, this dilutes and defuses the work of God and devalues the awesome work of Christ. It makes the cross a "rubber stamp" kind of formality. It's as if nothing really changed, even though Christ suffered everything for us!

Isaiah prophesied regarding the huge change that would take place at the cross:

Do not call to mind the former things, or ponder things of the past. "Behold, I will do something new, now it will spring forth; will you not be aware of it?" (Isaiah 43:18-19, NASB)

He asked the question, "Will you not be aware of it?" Are you still calling to mind the former things (the Old Covenant) and not realizing that God did something new (the New Covenant)?

Therefore, if anyone is in Christ, he is a new creation; old things have passed away; behold, all things have become new. (2 Corinthians 5:17)

The two major covenants that God has made with mankind over history are the Old Covenant of law and the New Covenant of grace. All of the other covenants can be categorized under these two covenants. There are many covenants that are described throughout the Bible, and the types and shadows of the other covenants all find their fulfillment and substance in the final covenant: the everlasting covenant that is in Christ Jesus. For a brief description of these other covenants, see Appendix A.

When we understand covenants, we understand how God deals with people. A covenant is stronger than an agreement or a contract, and the only way a covenant is enacted is by death. The reason that Jesus had to die was to bring all people out of the covenant of law (the Mosaic covenant) into the covenant of grace (the New Covenant).

In the context of the new order of things under the New Covenant of grace, Jesus told the people of His time who were under the law that if they did not believe in Him, they would die in their sins. Then He said, "You will know the truth, and the truth will set you free!"[209]

What we believe is everything.

Unconditional vs. Conditional

Now let's come back to Abraham and why he's important to us. The Abrahamic Covenant is the mirror covenant of the New Covenant because of its unconditional nature. For the purpose of understanding more about the New Covenant with its promises and blessings for believers, we'll look closely at the Abrahamic Covenant and contrast the unconditional nature of the Abrahamic with the conditional nature of the Old Covenant, and then we'll look at the realization of the Abrahamic Covenant in the New Covenant.

Every covenant involves three things: benefits, beneficiaries, and a benefactor. With these three covenants the **benefits** are the blessings of God. The **beneficiaries** are the people of God. The **Benefactor** is God.

So what's the difference? The nature of the covenants: conditional or unconditional. Please note that when I say "unconditional," the obvious stipulation would be that we believe it's true. Like I have said before, we could have a million dollars in the bank, but if we didn't believe it, it would do us no good. We have to believe it to receive it. Grace is received by faith.

Here are these three covenants and what is required to qualify for the blessings of God under the terms of each covenant:

- **The Covenant of Abraham** was an unconditional covenant that was based on bloodline. If one was born in the family line of Abraham, he qualified to receive God's blessing. An unconditional covenant is an agreement between two parties, but only one of the two parties has to do something to fulfill the covenant. Nothing is required of the other party. Nothing was required of Abraham's descendants but to be born in the family and because "Abraham believed God, and it was accounted to him for righteousness."[210]

- **The Covenant of Moses**, also called the Old Covenant, was a conditional covenant based on performance. Under the Mosaic Covenant, one qualified for God's blessing based on his ability to perfectly keep the law. A conditional covenant is an agreement that is binding on both parties for its fulfillment. If either party fails to meet their responsibilities, the covenant is broken, and neither party has to fulfill the requirements of the covenant.

God could keep His end of the bargain in the Mosaic Covenant of law, but the bankrupt flesh of man could not, even though they agreed to it. Thus God in His mercy established the priestly blood sacrifices to atone for (cover) sin while the Mosaic Law was in effect. However, the people still suffered greatly under the Old Covenant. Multitudes died or were sent out of the camp, flogged, stoned, and otherwise punished for breaking the law.

- **The New Covenant** in Jesus' blood is the unconditional covenant based on the love of God. God's blessing is not based on an earthly bloodline or fleshly performance. It's based simply in the fact that you were born a new creation in Him. Belief in Christ is not a condition within the New Covenant, but it is the one condition of entering into it. You must believe and receive His free gift of righteousness to be born again. When we receive the Lord Jesus, we enter into his death and are raised a new creation in His resurrection.

The Abrahamic Covenant is recorded in Genesis 15, and it shows the unconditional nature of the covenant. In those days both parties of a covenant would pass between the pieces of animals. In Genesis 15 we see God alone passing between the halves of animals to enact the covenant. God appeared as "a smoking oven and a burning torch" as He passed between the pieces. This symbolized the promise that in the midst of darkness, God would bring the light of His salvation.[211] God alone bound Himself to the covenant with all its promises of blessing. God caused a deep sleep to fall on Abraham so that he would have nothing to do with the enactment of this covenant. Fulfillment of the covenant fell on God alone. In the Abrahamic Covenant there were no "if" clauses, and as we will see, we are included in this covenant!

A couple of years ago, I was teaching on the unconditional nature of the New Covenant, and although I said nothing about Abraham in that teaching, a former pastor in the group who had been wounded terribly during his years serving in ministry and plagued with the feelings that he was forever branded by his mistakes, the rejection of people, and disapproval of God, interrupted the teaching session and yelled, "STOP! Stop talking! I GET IT! God put Abraham to sleep!!! God did it all!!! It's not dependent on man!!" We watched this man over the next few weeks be immersed in God's unconditional love as he studied the covenants and begin to be healed of years of hurt.

For some people learning about the covenants is just theology. For others it's the key that sets them free to receive the extravagant love of God.

In contrasting the Mosaic Covenant and the New Covenant, the writer of Hebrews explains that a covenant is like a will that someone leaves for his family. It only takes effect after the death of the one who made it. The Mosaic Covenant was put in effect through the death of spotless animals to cover sins. The New Covenant was enacted with the death of Jesus whose blood took away sins.

> *For where a covenant is, there must of necessity be the death of the one who made it. For a covenant is valid only when men are dead, for it is never in force while the one who made it lives. Therefore even the first covenant [the Mosaic Covenant] was not inaugurated without blood. ...without shedding of blood there is no forgiveness. (Hebrews 9:16-18, 22, NASB, brackets added for emphasis)*

In the Mosaic Covenant God gave the provision of the animal sacrifices. The priest would sprinkle the blood in the tabernacle, on all the furniture in the tabernacle, and on the people.[212] The tabernacle in the desert and all of the sacrifices of the Mosaic Covenant were just shadows of better things to come in the New Covenant.

> *For Christ did not enter a holy place made with hands, a mere copy of the true one, but into heaven itself, now to appear in the presence of God for us; nor was it that He would offer Himself often, as the high priest enters the holy place year by year with blood that is not his own. Otherwise, He would have needed to suffer often since the foundation of the world; but now once at the consummation of the ages He has been manifested to put away sin by the sacrifice of Himself. (Hebrews 9:24-26, NASB)*

Christ's death enacted the New Covenant, and now that we are in Him, we receive the abundance of His grace:

For all the promises of God IN HIM [in Christ] are Yes, and in Him Amen, to the glory of God through us. (2 Corinthians 1:20, brackets added for emphasis)

Abrahamic Covenant

In Genesis 12 God first spoke to Abram (later God changed his name to Abraham[213]) and declared a great blessing on him. Abram was seventy-five years old at the time.

"Get out of your country, from your family and from your father's house, to a land that I will show you. I will make you a great nation; I will bless you And make your name great; and you shall be a blessing. I will bless those who bless you, and I will curse him who curses you; and in you all the families of the earth shall be blessed." (Genesis 12:1-3)

About ten years later when Abraham was eighty-five years old and still childless, God spoke to him again:

"Look now toward heaven, and count the stars if you are able to number them." And He said to him, "So shall your descendants be." And he believed in the Lord, and He accounted it to him for righteousness. (Genesis 15:5-6)

He had prospered with health and silver, gold, and cattle since God first appeared to him,[214] and now the Bible says that God is counting him righteous because of one thing: he believed in the Lord. Fourteen years later, the Lord came to Abraham again and told him that Isaac would be born within that year. Abraham would have an heir to carry on the family name and inherit all of the blessings.

In Genesis 15, God also told Abraham that his descendants would be in captivity for four hundred years in Egypt:

"Know certainly that your descendants will be strangers in a land that is not theirs, and will serve them, and they will afflict them four hundred years. And also the nation whom they serve I will judge; afterward they shall come out with great possessions." (Genesis 15:13-14)

The Israelites In Egypt

So how did the Israelites end up in Egypt?

Here is the line of Abraham spoken of many times in scripture: Abraham, Isaac, and Jacob. Jacob had twelve sons, one of whom was Joseph. You know the story of Joseph who shared his dreams with his brothers, and the obvious meaning of those dreams was that they would bow down to him. His brothers were jealous of him so they threw him in a pit and ended up selling him as a slave in Egypt[215] at the age of seventeen.

Joseph spent many years in prison, and eventually, by God's favor, when Joseph was thirty years old, Pharaoh made him the second in command of all of Egypt. A great famine hit the land, and when he was thirty-nine years old, his family came to Egypt to get grain because of the famine. Just as was predicted in Joseph's dreams many years before, his brothers bowed before him. Joseph had mercy on his brothers who had sold him into slavery many years before, and gave them grain. Because of the favor on Joseph, Pharaoh then gave Joseph's family, the Israelites, the land of Goshen in which to settle.

When Joseph was one hundred ten years old, he died in Egypt.[215] The Pharaoh who had been so kind to him and his family died also, and many years later a cruel Pharaoh emerged. The children of Israel were becoming more mighty in number than the Egyptians, so this Pharaoh made them slaves.

But the children of Israel were fruitful and increased abundantly, multiplied and grew exceedingly mighty; and the land was filled with them. Now there arose a new king over Egypt, who did not know Joseph. And he said to his people, "Look, the people of the children of Israel are more and mightier than we; come, let us deal shrewdly with them, lest they multiply, and it happen, in the event of war, that they also join our enemies and fight against us, and so go up out of the land." Therefore they set taskmasters over them to afflict them with their burdens. (Exodus 1:7-11)

The Taskmaster

I'll take a detour from the story to share a bit of symbolic insight. In most teachings I have heard regarding the symbolism of Egypt and God's people being delivered from bondage, the analogy is made to their coming out of worldliness, the passions of the flesh, addictions, and demonic oppression. While that analogy may apply,

I believe the primary symbolic meaning of "coming out of Egypt" is being set free from the bondage of the law. We see this in Paul's allegorical explanation of the Old Covenant and New Covenant by using the story of the Egyptian slave girl, Hagar, and Abraham's wife Sarah in Galatians 4. Egypt and Hagar represent law. Abraham's descendants and Sarah represent faith and grace.[216] We will touch on this in a later chapter.

Today satan works in the same way as the cruel Pharaoh: he strives to bring God's people under the "taskmaster" of the law. Religion has held many in bondage. And why? Like the Israelites who were multiplying and becoming more mighty than the Egyptians, satan attacks God's people because of the grace and favor of God on us. Lest we multiply and grow exceedingly mighty, satan's strategy is to put us in bondage to the law.

The evil Egyptian Pharaoh set up taskmasters over the Israelites for the purpose of afflicting them and thinning out their population to weaken them. The job of the Israelites was to make bricks. At one point Pharaoh commanded that no more straw be given them to make the bricks, forcing them to find their own straw. More back-breaking labor. Pharaoh's mantra was "Get back to your labor!... Why have you not fulfilled your task in making brick both yesterday and to-day?"[217] The whole goal of the Israelite enslavement was to control them and to kill them with mindless labor. But the God of Abraham kept His covenant of grace and set His people free from those taskmasters.

This is where the analogy of the law comes in: today when the law is used on people in the form of performance-based religion, it's the ministry of death. It's goal is to control through rules and regulations to create a passive culture. The ultimate goal is to weaken the church, stop its growth, and keep the Gospel from going forth.

But hallelujah! More and more eyes are being opened to the freedom that comes with the revelation of grace! When the taskmaster is disarmed of his weapon of the law, people are set free to soar on the wings of the Spirit of grace. We're no longer making bricks to build structures and systems for the kingdom of this world, but instead we've become living stones of the kingdom of heaven. Now we labor more abundantly than them all, but not us — the GRACE of God in us![218]

God Remembered His Covenant

Hundreds of years into the Israelites' captivity, Moses was born to lead them in their deliverance from Egypt. The Bible says that God sent Moses to set the people free because He remembered the covenant He had made with Abraham.

> *And God spoke to Moses and said to him: "I am the Lord. I appeared to Abraham, to Isaac, and to Jacob, as God Almighty, but by My name Lord I was not known to them. I have also established My covenant with them, to give them the land of Canaan, the land of their pilgrimage, in which they were strangers. And I have also heard the groaning of the children of Israel whom the Egyptians keep in bondage, and I have remembered My covenant. (Exodus 6:2-5)*

Think about this little nugget: the Israelites had been given the land of Goshen to settle in by the Pharaoh who had been so kind to Joseph many years before. "Goshen" means "drawing near."[219] When Moses boldly approached the evil Pharaoh about setting the people free, God sent ten plagues on the entire land of Egypt, although one area was protected: Goshen.[220] God's people were near to Him, and therefore they were protected. How much more we today who have the presence of God inside of us. How much more near can we be?

All throughout the years, the covenant of grace that God made within Himself on behalf of Abraham and all of his descendants was still in place. It was never annulled, even when the Mosaic covenant was agreed upon by God's people. God's unconditional covenant of grace could not be broken because it was not dependent on man to keep it.[221]

The New Covenant is the same: it's a covenant that was made within the Trinity. The only way that it could be broken is if Jesus sinned or if His blood didn't take away ours. Neither is possible. We're in. There's nothing left to be done.

The Test of the Manna

As God led the children of Israel out of Egypt, He continued to relate to them under that covenant of grace. He blessed them with His presence and His provision. They came out of Egypt laden with silver and gold and the scripture says there was "not one feeble among them."[222] During the two month period between the Red Sea and Mount Sinai, God's response to every complaint was a fresh demonstration of grace: waters of Marah; manna from heaven; water from the rock. He didn't once curse them, punish them, or judge them during that first two month period. He didn't even get angry with them.

We covered this extensively in the chapter entitled "The Letter Kills, but the Spirit Gives Life." However, I want to focus a little more on one of the demonstrations of God's grace in this two month period.

In Exodus 16 when the people complained about not having any meat to eat, God rained down bread from heaven. Pure grace. In that event, the Bible says that God tested them. This test would prove something that would come into play later on when they made a promise that they couldn't possibly keep.

And the children of Israel said to them, "Oh, that we had died by the hand of the Lord in the land of Egypt, when we sat by the pots of meat and when we ate bread to the full! For you have brought us out into this wilderness to kill this whole assembly with hunger." Then the Lord said to Moses, "Behold, I will rain bread from heaven for you. And the people shall go out and gather a certain quota every day, that I may test them, whether they will walk in My law or not." (Exodus 16:3-4)

Note that when God said, "whether they will walk in My law or not" is not referring to the law of Moses. It had not been given yet because they had not reached Sinai yet. This is talking about obeying the voice of God. This is the obedience of FAITH.

"And it shall be on the sixth day that they shall prepare what they bring in, and it shall be twice as much as they gather daily."… 'Come near before the Lord, for He has heard your complaints.'" Now it came to pass, as Aaron spoke to the whole congregation of the children of Israel, that they

looked toward the wilderness, and behold, the glory of the Lord appeared in the cloud. And the Lord spoke to Moses, saying, "I have heard the complaints of the children of Israel. Speak to them, saying, 'At twilight you shall eat meat, and in the morning you shall be filled with bread. And you shall know that I am the Lord your God.'" (Exodus 16:5, 9-12)

Wow!!! When they complained and accused Moses of bringing them out to the desert to die, God's response was to give them heavenly bread. Instead of telling them to flee from His presence lest He consume them as He would AFTER the law of Moses was given, God told them to come near Him! What was God doing? He was testing them. This test would prove whether or not they would trust the Lord and know that it was the Lord who would take care of them. It was an obedience of faith based purely on grace. In essence God was asking the question: "Do you believe in the righteousness of faith like your father Abraham? Do you believe that I am good? Do you believe that I even exist?"

What did the Israelites do? Did they trust Him and believe that He would provide? For five days they were to eat all of the manna and not save any for the next morning. This would show that they trusted Him to provide the next day. Some didn't obey and saved the left-overs to find the next morning that the leftovers "bred worms and stank."[223] On the sixth day they were to gather twice as much and not gather any on the seventh day in honor of a day of rest. Yet, some did not gather twice as much on the sixth day, and they went out on the Sabbath looking for manna, once again disobeying the voice of God and not trusting Him.

Relief Or Freedom?

They disobeyed His "law." But what was the "law"? It was simply to believe Him. The "law" was simply the obedience of faith — the "law" of faith. It was God saying to them, "Do you trust ME to provide for you? Or do you want to take matters in your own hands? You keep saying that you want to go back to Egypt. That might give you momentary relief, but it won't give you freedom!" It's like God saying to us today, "Grace requires utter dependence on Me. I know that the flesh has no patience and no faith. The flesh would rather have the 'pots of meat' and be in slavery than be free and trust Me.

The flesh finds its security in the bondage of the law. But the spirit is free because of law of faith. Every day there will be tests that ask the question: do you believe Me or not?"

"Do you want RELIEF or do you want FREEDOM?"

Living under a system of performance is like doing drugs. It gives us a temporary feeling of relief from guilt if we do something for God. However, when the feelings of guilt and shame return, we have to give ourselves another "hit" of dead works to numb the guilt and get the "high" that gives us the illusion that we have earned God's pleasure.

The definition of drug addiction is "a brain disease that causes compulsive drug seeking and use, despite harmful consequences."[224] In other words, there comes a point in the addicted person's life where he's not getting high because he wants to, he's getting high because he HAS to, even though he knows it's hurting him and the people closest to him.

For forty-five years of my life I was on a similar kind of treadmill with performance-based religion; and for the five years just prior to being ambushed by Grace several years ago, the consequences of being on that treadmill had taken its toll. I was fried, and it was having a serious negative affect on those around me. Yet, I was so "wired" for performance that instead of getting off the treadmill, I just ran faster — or actually, it was more like someone kept increasing the speed — higher and higher — and it was forcing me to keep up. (I wonder who would do such a cruel thing?) I remember regularly thinking of the famous phrase of George Jetson: "Jane, get me off this crazy thing!" I used to envision myself trying to jump off this machine that was going too fast, but I was afraid to jump off because I thought it might kill me! That's the way it is with religion. We can't get out of it until we jump off in faith and trust God. It's scary, but it's the only way to freedom.

"Through Him everyone who believes is freed from all things, from which you could not be freed through the Law of Moses." (Acts 13:39, NASB)

Grace doesn't appeal to the flesh because when righteousness is a gift, there is nothing we can do to relieve ourselves from dead works that do nothing to cleanse the conscience. However, grace is true freedom because God is offering us permanent relief through the blood of Christ which offers eternal acceptance, unconditional approval, uninterrupted fellowship, incorruptible holiness, and relentless love. Whom the Son sets free is free indeed.[225]

God was asking the Israelites the same question He is asking us: "Do you want RELIEF or do you want FREEDOM?" This was the test, and they failed it.

Yet, even though they failed the test and disobeyed, the fresh bread from heaven kept coming every single day.

"We Will Do"

Later they came to the foot of Mount Sinai and this is the message that God gave to Moses to deliver to them:

"You have seen what I did to the Egyptians, and how I bore you on eagles' wings and brought you to Myself. Now therefore, if you will indeed obey My voice and keep My covenant, then you shall be a special treasure to Me above all people; for all the earth is Mine. And you shall be to Me a kingdom of priests and a holy nation.'" (Exodus 19:3-6)

Notice that God wanted them near: "I brought you to Myself." What covenant did He want them to "keep"? The covenant of GRACE that God made with Himself on behalf of Abraham and his descendants. The covenant of faith for righteousness. Notice the word "IF you will.., then you will be a special treasure..." What is the IF about? It's about believing. If they had only believed in the faithfulness of God, they could have continued in the Abrahamic Covenant. Instead they made this statement:

"All that the Lord has spoken we will do." (Exodus 19:8)

That actually sounds commendable, doesn't it? In fact, I would agree wholeheartedly with the truth that we should do everything the Lord says to do. So what is the problem with the Israelites' response? If we look into the meaning of their promise, "we will do," we see that it was actually a promise of faithfulness according to their OWN ability, not the faithfulness of God to keep His covenant with them.

The phrase "we will do" means "to make, to produce by LABOR."[226] In other words, they were saying, "Whatever You tell us to do, God, we can do it. Whatever is required of us, we are certainly fully capable of performing." They may have come out of Egypt, but Egypt wasn't out of them.

Just two chapters before in the test of the manna, they proved that they did not trust the faithfulness of God. They had failed the test of believing that He would take care of them like He had when He delivered them through the Red Sea and as He had blessed their father Abraham everywhere he went.

I have often wondered how SHOULD they have responded? I believe they should have said something like this: "Yes, keep on carrying us on eagle's wings! We want to be near You! We want to be under the covenant You made with our fathers Abraham, Isaac, and Jacob. All that the Lord has spoken, we BELIEVE! We put all our hope and trust in You!"

The people boasted with confidence, not in God's ability, but in their own. Like Adam and Eve in the Garden, they bought into the lie that they could be like God independent of Him. By that one statement "All that the Lord has commanded, we will DO," everything changed.

The Golden Calf

After this, Moses went up the mountain to receive the two tablets of stone on which God etched the Ten Commandments. When God gave him the tablets, He said this to Moses:

> "Go, get down! For your people whom you brought out of the land of Egypt have corrupted themselves. They have turned aside quickly out of the way which I commanded them. They have made themselves a molded calf, and worshiped it and sacrificed to it, and said, 'This is your god, O Israel, that brought you out of the land of Egypt!'" And the Lord said to Moses, "I have seen this people, and indeed it is a stiff-necked people! Now therefore, let Me alone, that My wrath may burn hot against them and I may consume them. And I will make of you a great nation." (Exodus 32:7-10)

Hmmmm... this is a little different than "come near" in Exodus 16, and "I brought you to Myself" in Exodus 19. Can you see that being under the law and breaking the first commandment completely changed everything? The first commandment was

"You shall have no other gods before Me." (Exodus 20:3)

In Egypt they had worshipped other gods, but God never punished them for it.[227] Yet, because of the change in covenants, He said He would consume them with the fire of His wrath because they disobeyed! Moses interceded on their behalf, but not based upon any promises to do better in the future and try their hardest to keep the commandments from then on. No, he pleaded with God to spare the people based on something else entirely: the very character of God to keep His covenant with Abraham.

"Turn from Your fierce wrath, and relent from this harm to Your people. Remember Abraham, Isaac, and Israel, Your servants, to whom You swore by Your own self, and said to them, 'I will multiply your descendants as the stars of heaven; and all this land that I have spoken of I give to your descendants, and they shall inherit it forever.'" So the Lord relented from the harm which He said He would do to His people. (Exodus 32:12-14)

God remembered His covenant with Abraham. That meant the nation of Israel lived to see another day. However, when Moses came down the mountain with the two tablets of stone, three thousand people still had to die. In God's mercy, He didn't wipe them out, but because of the judgment from the law, blood was shed, and there was death. The letter kills.

Then Moses went back up to get the second set of stones. After the Law was given, we see in Numbers and Deuteronomy that time and time again when God's people complained or broke laws, they died.

Only One Thing Changed

In this great shifting in God's relationship with His people, He never changed. He had always had the ability to bless and to curse. He had always had the ability to express anger. The people didn't change either. They sinned before the law was given, and they sinned after the law was given. They were Abraham's descendants before the law was given, and they were still Abraham's descendants after the law was given. The only thing that changed was the kind of covenant they were under.

With the Abrahamic covenant, there was no law, so there was no transgression.[228] They were under grace and qualified for every blessing of God. In fact, when God told Abraham he was counted righteous by his faith, God called HIMSELF Abraham's exceedingly great reward![229] If you have God, you have everything!

Under the Mosaic Covenant, the law entered and along with it entered transgression and judgment. The only way that they could qualify for God's blessing was to obey an unreachable standard. If they disobeyed, they would be cursed by God as if they were God's enemies. God had only ever used His anger against the enemies of His people for the purpose of protecting them. Now His anger was turned towards them because with the law, sin became personal transgression, and each person became personal liable.

For about fifteen hundred years this was the relationship between God and His people. When they obeyed, they were blessed; but when they disobeyed, He gave them over to calamity, hardship, captivity, and death. In the conditional covenant of law that God made with the people, God's favor relied on the character and conduct of the people.

In the unconditional covenant of grace that God made within Himself on behalf of Abraham, God's favor never relied on Abraham's character nor his conduct. That covenant was based on Abraham's faith, not his faithfulness. It was based on the faithfulness of God and was a picture of the New Covenant that was to come.

Therefore, since we have been made right in God's sight by faith, we have peace with God because of what Jesus Christ our Lord has done for us. Because of our faith, Christ has brought us into this place of undeserved privilege where we now stand, and we confidently and joyfully look forward to sharing God's glory. (Romans 5:1-2, NLT)

CHAPTER FOURTEEN

Righteousness of Faith

Key scriptures:
Colossians 1:12-14; Galatians 3:13-19, 26-29; Romans 4:1-5, 13-22; Luke 13:10-17

In the fullness of time, when the law had served it's purpose and proved that no man could be made right with God by perfect performance, God sent His Son, born under the law[230], to redeem those who were under the law. Redeem literally means "to buy out of slavery."[231] Jesus, the Son of God, loves us, came as us, died as us, and rose as us so that we could be as He is: in perfect union with the Father. We have been purchased out of the slavery of works-religion by the blood of Jesus and have been made sons and daughters of God.

The New Order

About fifteen hundred years after Sinai, a prophet named John appeared on the scene and declared the new order of things:

"Repent, for the kingdom of heaven is at hand!" (Matthew 3:2)

"Behold! The Lamb of God who takes away the sin of the world! (John 1:29)

The phrase "at hand"[232] in the verse above literally means "to bring near, to join one thing to another." In other words, the time had come when God would join believers to Himself through His Son. The kingdom of heaven was in their midst: Jesus Christ, the Savior of the world, had come to remove the sin barrier forever! Jesus' blood wouldn't just cover sins temporarily like the Old Covenant sacrifices. He would remove sin completely.

When Jesus cried, "It is finished!"[233], there was a great earthquake and the veil in the temple was split from top to bottom by God Himself. This was the end of Old Covenant system! No more would man relate to God through obedience to the law of Moses. From then on, relationship with God would be by grace through faith in Jesus. The ministry of condemnation and death had been replaced with the ministry of the of the Spirit of grace.

We Are Qualified

Today we can rest and be at peace because the Father Himself has qualified us to partake in the inheritance for those in Jesus Christ. He was the firstborn among many brethren. We have been born from above by the Spirit of God as a new creation in the very image of God.

> *... giving thanks to the FATHER WHO HAS QUALIFIED US to be partakers of the inheritance of the saints in the light. He has delivered us from the power of darkness and conveyed us into the kingdom of the Son of His love, in whom we have redemption through His blood, the forgiveness of sins. (Colossians 1:12-14, emphasis added)*

We are co-inheritors of everything that Jesus has inherited as the Son of God. He had the perfect conduct and the perfect character that we lacked. He had the sinless blood that was required for the sacrifice. In our spirits we also have His impeccable performance and His divine bloodline. We have become sons of God as He is the Son of God. His Father is our Father.

Christ has redeemed us from the curse of the law, having become a curse for us (for it is written, "Cursed is everyone who hangs on a tree"), that the blessing of Abraham might come upon the Gentiles in Christ Jesus, that we might receive the promise of the Spirit through faith... For you are all sons of God through faith in Christ Jesus. For as many of you as were baptized into Christ have put on Christ. There is neither Jew nor Greek, there is neither slave nor free, there is neither male nor female; for you are all one in Christ Jesus. And if you are Christ's, then you are Abraham's seed, and heirs according to the promise. (Galatians 3:13-14, 26-29)

Today we are free from the law and redeemed from every curse associated with disobeying the law. When we are in Jesus, the One who is the Heir of all the blessings, we are IN the Seed; therefore, WE ARE THE SEED of Abraham and heirs according to the promise of God.

What does it mean to be the seed of Abraham? Let's look at several passages in Romans 4 to learn about this awesome promise.

He Who Does Not Work

Reader Study Reference, Romans 4:1-5

What then shall we say that Abraham our father has found according to the flesh? For if Abraham was justified by works, he has something to boast about, but not before God. For what does the Scripture say? "Abraham believed God, and it was accounted to him for righteousness." (Romans 4:1-3)

That last sentence, "Abraham believed God, and it was accounted to him for righteousness," is repeated six times in the Bible. Again, Abraham was blessed by God, and the way he received the blessing was by BELIEVING that he was righteous before God. When Paul says "according to the flesh," he means trying to obtain right standing with God through self-effort. Paul is asking the question, "What did Abraham discover about his own righteousness?" Nothing! As we will see, Abraham wasn't a model citizen. He was more a model of God's grace! He obviously wasn't made righteous by his works.

Let's move on to the next verse:

Now to him who works, the wages are not counted as grace but as debt. (Romans 4:4)

Do you see how extreme this righteousness of faith is? If we're working for it, it becomes a debt, not a gift. If the blessing of God is a reward for good behavior, then we get the credit for earning it. Yet, in that system the flip-side is also true: we lose the blessing of God by bad behavior. If the blessing of God is truly a gift, then Jesus gets the credit, and we can't lose it even when we fail. Which system do you want to be under? Law or grace?

In Romans 10, Paul said the Jews were ignorant of God's righteousness, and they tried to establish their own righteousness.[234] But it's impossible to establish our own righteousness. We can't believe that we're righteous by what we DO and still believe we're righteous as a GIFT. A double-minded man is unstable in all his ways.[235]

Some of us are very strong-willed. We can last decades striving to maintain our righteousness and do it our way. However, even the hardiest human stock has its breaking point. We will either break in our morals, in our emotions, or in our bodies. The sad thing is that the more we try, the harder it is to just let go because we have invested so much in it!

The next verse in Romans 4 says:

But to him who DOES NOT WORK but believes on Him who justifies the ungodly, his faith is accounted for righteousness. (Romans 4:5, emphasis added)

The scandal of the Gospel is that a Holy God justifies wicked, ungodly people!

Only for the one who "DOES NOT WORK" for it can the blessing be given to him as a gift. Abraham is a great example of someone who was not justified by works. On two occasions he lied about his wife being his sister and was willing to let Sarah be taken by two different kings (Pharaoh, king of Egypt, and Abimelech, king of Gerar) to be among their wives.[236] We don't have polygamy today, but we can envision what Abraham did: he gave his wife away for these men to do with her what they wanted! He had an "honorable" reason for it: to save his own hide! Abraham wasn't a model of integrity. He was a model of someone living under the grace of God. God never punished or rebuked Abraham, and the Bible even calls Abraham "God's friend."[237] In fact, God defended Abraham, and scared those kings half to death when they found out Sarah was Abraham's wife! He stopped the kings from touching Sarah, and He blessed Abraham with great wealth: "livestock, sliver, and gold."[238] In the "hall of fame of faith" in Hebrews 11, there is no record of Abraham's sins.[239] Why? No sins of any of the heroes of faith are recorded in Hebrews 11 because it's straight from God's book of remembrance in heaven, and heaven does not keep a record of sins.

Heir of the World

Reader Study Reference, Romans 4:13

God made a promise to Abraham, and as the seed of Abraham, God made that promise to us as well. What was the promise?

> *For the promise that he would be the heir of the world was not to Abraham or to his seed through the law, but through the righteousness of faith. (Romans 4:13)*

The promise to Abraham was that he would be heir of the world through the righteousness of faith. There is no Old Testament scripture that states this promise in the way that Paul worded it here: "heir of the world." The Old Testament promises to Abraham included the promise that all of the families of the earth would be blessed through him and that he would be the father of many nations. But what does it mean that he was "heir of the world?" The Greek word for "world" is the word "kosmos," and it can mean the earth, the universe, or "the whole circle of earthly goods, endowments, riches, advantages, pleasures."[240] I believe it simply means that this whole world and universe belongs to Christ, the Seed of Abraham. The Father has given all things into His hands,[241] and because we are in Christ, it's the Father's pleasure to give us the kingdom.[242] We reign in this life as priests and kings. It means we have nothing to gain and nothing to lose because we have it all, and the supply never runs dry. We inherit all that God has and all that God is. Today we are blessed to be a blessing. It puts this whole natural realm into perspective.

Faith Made Void

Reader Study Reference, Romans 4:14

> *For if those who are of the law are heirs, faith is made void and the promise made of no effect. (Romans 4:14)*

In other words, if we could obtain the promise by working for it, then it wouldn't be given by promise! "Void" is the Greek word "kenoo"[243] which means "to empty, to deprive of force, useless." Our faith is made empty, it has no power, it's USELESS if the favor of God can be bought with our sweat. "Of no effect" is the Greek word "katargeo," and it means "to render idle, unemployed, inactivate, inoperative."[244] I'm giving lots of descriptions here to prove the point: if we try to work to please God, our faith is useless and His promise will not work in our lives. Most of us think that sin is the thing that makes God's promises of no effect in our lives, but that's not the truth! Believing that lie will cause you to suffer! The imputation of sin is a finished and done deal for all who are in Christ!

The more reliance we have in our behavior to qualify for God to bless us, the more we'll find that our faith is useless! We can't have it both ways. What is the purpose of faith if we can obtain the grace of God on our own? If we earn it, God can't give it to us because He promised. We just get what we paid for. If we live in that system, both our faith and God's promise are deprived of power in our lives. I know a lot of people resist this truth, but Paul is saying that God has promised us, but the issue is on our end! Because we're taking matters in our own hands to force promises to come to pass instead of living by faith, we aren't seeing promises activated.

Falling from Grace

What is true faith? Faith is simply receiving what God has already provided by His grace. Faith is the hand that takes what grace gives. Faith cannot operate outside of the unmerited favor of God. Apart from grace through faith, God's promises to us are of no effect.

> *Christ is become of no effect unto you, whosoever of you are justified by the law; ye are fallen from grace. (Galatians 5:4, KJV)*

My whole life I have heard that falling from grace is falling into sin, but that's not what the scriptures say. Falling from grace is not falling into sin. It's falling back into law!

What does "whosoever of you are justified by the law" mean for us today? It simply means that we are trying to be made right by behaving right. So many Christians think that good behavior is what God is after, when truthfully we are missing the whole reason for the cross when we think that way. It's cheap and cheesy to think that God sent His Son for a moral revolution. We are lowering God's estimation of what the blood of Jesus has done. Law is lower than grace. To go back to law is to fall from grace.

When we elevate law to a place above grace, it's as if we are saying we don't need Jesus. However, we'll find a very real result of that wrong thinking in our lives: Christ will be of no effect to us. If we are sick or depressed or confused or broke or can't sleep at night, we need Jesus to be of effect! So often we toss and turn and worry and become self-focused and self-occupied when we face hardship in life. When we take our eyes off of Jesus and His endless funnel of grace, we will come to the wrong conclusions about why we are in need. We will either think God is not good or that sin in some way has hindered the promise of God.

God's grace is greater than all our sin. Our "receiver" is malfunctioning when we take matters in our own hands and go back to performance again. The power from heaven is always flowing, we just need to turn the switch on.

Abraham's Faith

Reader Study Reference, Romans 4:15-18

> *...because the law brings about wrath; for where there is no law there is no transgression. Therefore it [righteousness] is of faith that it might be according to grace, so that the promise might be sure to all the seed, not only to those who are of the law, but also to those who are of the faith of Abraham, who is the father of us all (as it is written, "I have made you a father of many nations") in the presence of Him whom he believed— God, who gives life to the dead and calls those things which do not exist as though they did; who, contrary to hope, in hope believed, so that he became*

the father of many nations, according to what was spoken, "So shall your descendants be." (Romans 4:15-18, brackets added for emphasis)

Paul said that God called things forth in Abraham's life which didn't exist in the natural because he believed. How did Abraham believe God? How did the "father of our faith" get such faith?

Abraham and Sarah were one hundred years old and ninety years old, respectively, before they saw God's promise of having descendants come to fruition. They had no children and the Bible says that their bodies were as good as dead! Once I was teaching this passage to young people, and in preparation I Googled "centenarians." I found a picture of a couple both sitting in wheelchairs who lived to be over a hundred (which is an accomplishment in itself!), and I told the kids to imagine that couple bearing a child. It's impossible! God had to literally go into their bodies and jump start their reproductive systems! And the next step was that Abraham and Sarah had to believe it and act on it. No stork came and dropped Isaac at the front door of their tent.

When the Lord appeared as an angel to Abraham and told Him that Sarah would have a son, notice Sarah's response:

And He said, "I will certainly return to you according to the time of life, and behold, Sarah your wife shall have a son." (Sarah was listening in the tent door which was behind him.) Now Abraham and Sarah were old, well advanced in age; and Sarah had passed the age of childbearing. Therefore Sarah laughed within herself, saying, "After I have grown old, shall I have pleasure, my lord being old also?" (Genesis 18:10-12)

She didn't say, "After I have grown old, shall I have a SON?" She said, "Shall I have PLEASURE?" We tend to think that the life of faith is one where we have to give up on everything that means anything to us. "Lay it all down for God! Suffer for Him and He'll move on your behalf." But that's not the message I see from Abraham and Sarah's story. I see the Lord saying to them, "You two are going to see your dream come true, but it's going to require that you go back to your honeymoon days and enjoy yourself!"

We don't need faith when everything is going well. We don't need grace when we've done everything right. Sometimes all the facts oppose the truth. With Abraham and Sarah it was hope against hope, but the Bible says, CONTRARY to hope Abraham did not give up! What is hope? It's the Greek word "elpis,"[245] and it means a joyful, confident expectation of good. Faith is the substance of things hoped for.[246] We must have hope, or we have no foundation for our faith.

Have a Good Opinion of God

Reader Study Reference, Romans 4:19-21

> *And not being weak in faith, he did not consider his own body, already dead (since he was about a hundred years old), and the deadness of Sarah's womb. He did not waver at the promise of God through unbelief, but was strengthened in faith, giving glory to God, ... (Romans 4:19-20)*

Abraham was strengthened in his faith "giving glory to God." What does that mean? In the New Testament Greek, the word we translate "glory" is the word "doxa", and in Thayer's Greek Lexicon it gives this meaning: "in the New Testament always a GOOD OPINION concerning one, resulting in praise, honor, and glory."[247] In other words, Abraham was strengthened in faith by having a good opinion of God, resulting in praise, honor, and glory. Our faith is strengthened the same way: we fight the good fight of faith by keeping a good opinion of God.

Recently someone shared with me that a family member had hurt her deeply. I was overjoyed to see this guilty person who had done terrible things turn to the Lord and receive God's grace. However, I was saddened to see that this grace was very offensive to the person who had been hurt. She wanted the offender to suffer, and she was angry with God for extending grace to an undeserving person. She said to me, "I don't trust God. A good father doesn't make one child suffer so another one can be free." She was accusing God of making her suffer in order to heal her family member. Her opinion of God was very low, and her faith in a good outcome plummeted as she spoke negatively of God. We speak what we believe.[248]

Abraham Did Not Waver

Reader Study Reference, Romans 4:20

Another important phrase in verse 20 is that Abraham "did not waver at the promise of God through unbelief." That word "waver" is the Greek word "diakrino", and it is often translated "doubt." Abraham did not "doubt" the promise of God. We see this same word used in a famous quote of Jesus:

"Have faith in God. For assuredly, I say to you, whoever says to this mountain, 'Be removed and be cast into the sea,' and does not doubt [diakrino] in his heart, but believes that those things he says will be done, he will have whatever he says. Therefore I say to you, whatever things you ask when you pray, believe that you receive them, and you will have them." (Mark 11:22-23, brackets added for emphasis)

The word "doubt" means to separate or distinguish. In the context of Mark 11 and Romans 4, it means "to be at variance with one's self."[249] When Abraham believed God about being the father of many nations and bringing forth a son, he was not "at variance with himself." He knew he was righteous by faith, and he knew the promise of God was for him.

"Diakrino" is actually made up of two Greek words: the preposition "dia"[250] which means "through or because of" and "krino"[251] which means "make a judgment." "Krino" is often translated "condemn" in English. Putting "dia" and "krino" together we get "because of being condemned."

When we know we are righteous, we know that we will never be condemned, and we will never be limited to only what is possible in the natural realm. My mother died of cancer a few years ago. I would be getting into doubt by believing that I will die of cancer because my mother died of cancer. Other examples of doubt are "I'm too old to run a mile, or I'm too overweight to get married, or I'm too young to get that job, or I'm not educated enough to be successful." If we believe like this, we are saying that God's power is limited to the system of this natural world, and we are condemning ourselves by believing that since we are only human, our destinies are bound by the realm that we see. Instead, we need to keep our eyes fixed on

Jesus! He's the author and perfecter of all faith, and with Him nothing is impossible![252]

What God Remembers

Reader Study Reference, Romans 4:21-22

How could Abraham have a good opinion of God when year after year God did not seem to be delivering on His promise to him?

> *...and being fully convinced that what He had promised He was also able to perform. And therefore "it was accounted to him for righteousness." (Romans 4:21-22)*

Paul says Abraham was "fully convinced." Back in Genesis 15, God had told Abraham to look at the stars because that would be how many descendants he would have. But you should know that in Genesis 16, the very next chapter, Abraham decided not to wait on the promise, and he listened to the unbelief of his wife Sarah:

> *"See now, the LORD has restrained me from bearing children. Please, go in to my maid; perhaps I shall obtain children by her." (Genesis 16:2)*

So when Abraham was eighty-six years old, he bore a son with Hagar, Sarah's slave, and named him Ishmael. All of this is interesting to me because in the New Testament account of this story, there is no record of any lack of faith on Sarah's part:

> *By faith Sarah herself also received strength to conceive seed, and she bore a child when she was past the age, because SHE JUDGED HIM FAITHFUL who had promised. Therefore from one man, and him as good as dead, were born as many as the stars of the sky in multitude — innumerable as the sand which is by the seashore. (Hebrews 11:11-12, emphasis added)*

The Bible says that Sarah judged God faithful. Wow. In our minds we would think that God would be just in remembering our sins. Don't we deserve that? However, God considers it just that He DOES NOT remember our sins. Why? Because He remembered our sins once: when Jesus was punished for them. Now, in His justice He only remembers the good that we do:

For God is not unjust to forget your work and labor of love which you have shown toward His name, in that you have ministered to the saints, and do minister. (Hebrews 6:10)

So we can forget about the mistakes of yesterday and move on! Once again, it all goes back to the righteousness of faith. Thank God that we can mess up, but He still delivers on His promises! Are you convinced that what God has promised you He is fully able to perform? That's the righteousness of faith!

The Father Of Our Faith

One last point about Abraham being our "father": this refers to those of us who are of the FAITH of Abraham, and this is not necessarily referring to the Jewish people, his physical descendants.

Being descendants of Abraham doesn't make them truly Abraham's children. For the Scriptures say, "Isaac is the son through whom your descendants will be counted," though Abraham had other children, too. This means that Abraham's physical descendants are not necessarily children of God. Only the children of the promise are considered to be Abraham's children...What does all this mean? Even though the Gentiles were not trying to follow God's standards, they were made right with God. And it was by faith that this took place. But the people of Israel, who tried so hard to get right with God by keeping the law, never succeeded. Why not? Because they were trying to get right with God by keeping the law instead of by trusting in him. (Romans 9:7-8, 30-32, NLT)

Paul continues this point into chapter 10 of Romans:

Brethren, my heart's desire and prayer to God for Israel is that they may be saved. For I bear them witness that they have a zeal for God, but not according to knowledge. For they being ignorant of God's righteousness, and seeking to establish their own righteousness, have not submitted to the righteousness of God. For Christ is the end of the law for righteousness to everyone who believes. (Romans 10:1-4)

Whether Jew or Gentile, Abraham is the father of faith for all who put their trust in Christ's righteousness and not in their own.

A Daughter of Abraham

There is a powerful story in the book of Luke which recounts the story of Jesus performing a miracle of healing and deliverance on a descendant of Abraham, a woman who had been bent over for eighteen years because of a demonic spirit. I love this account of Jesus because He makes it so clear that the seed of Abraham is not under the authority of satan and should not be living a life oppressed by demonic spirits.

Now He was teaching in one of the synagogues on the Sabbath. And behold, there was a woman who had a spirit of infirmity eighteen years, and was bent over and could in no way raise herself up. But when Jesus saw her, He called her to Him... (Luke 13:10-12)

First of all, this woman would not have been in the room where He was teaching. In the ancient synagogues, men and women were separated, usually by placing women in a side room or a second floor balcony.[253] For Jesus to notice her would take keen observation, an eye for someone who needed Him.

...and said to her, "Woman, you are loosed from your infirmity." (Luke 13:12, cont.)

Imagine "deliverance ministry" with no yelling at demons! He just spoke to the woman and told her she was loosed.

And He laid His hands on her, and immediately she was made straight, and glorified God. (Luke 13:13)

Imagine this woman bent over looking at the ground, at the dust, satan's food, for eighteen years.[254] I can hear that demon saying to her, "From dust you came and to dust you will return." What hopelessness! And then all of a sudden, Jesus laid His hands on her, and immediately she stood straight up to look in the eyes of her Deliverer and Healer.

And everyone rejoiced!!! Right? ...Not quite... Believe it or not, her "pastor" wasn't too happy about it.

But the ruler of the synagogue answered with indignation, because Jesus had healed on the Sabbath; and he said to the crowd, "There are six days

238 . UNVEILING JESUS

on which men ought to work; therefore come and be healed on them, and not on the Sabbath day." (Luke 13:14)

Here he is admitting that Jesus healed the lady, but shows absolutely no joy at her freedom! Those who have a law mentality care more about the rules than the people. However, to be fair, before we throw stones at this synagogue ruler and wonder how in the world he could be so cold-hearted, think about it. How often do you see a teacher in church stop what he or she is saying, call out to someone in the balcony to come forward, and then cast a demon out of her? It could be a little disruptive to the flow! It reminds me of the seven last words of the church: "We've never done it that way before." When we look at a story in the Bible, we should put ourselves in the people's shoes and truly imagine the reality of the circumstances.

Back to Luke 13:

The Lord then answered him and said, "Hypocrite! Does not each one of you on the Sabbath loose his ox or donkey from the stall, and lead it away to water it? So ought not this woman, being a daughter of Abraham, whom Satan has bound—think of it—for eighteen years, be loosed from this bond on the Sabbath?" And when He said these things, all His adversaries were put to shame; and all the multitude rejoiced for all the glorious things that were done by Him. (Luke 13:15-17)

Here was this woman in the synagogue bent over, symbolic of the heavy burden of the law. Can you hear Jesus's outrage at this woman's bondage? It wasn't just wrong, it was illegal and unjust according to the courtroom of heaven. "Ought not, the woman BEING a daughter of Abraham be loosed?!" In this story I can hear the cry of Jesus' heart, "IT'S TIME! It's time for the righteousness of faith to be revealed to the world! They have been in bondage to the law and human effort for too long!"

What is the significance of eighteen years? 6 is the number of man. 666 is the number of the anti-Christ who will come during the final days with a great deception, leading people away from Jesus in order to rule the world.[255] The spirit of antichrist is the spirit of humanism. It's the demonic spirit that came against Adam and Eve in the Garden of Eden: I can be like God without God. 666 is the number of human effort because relying on man — ANY man — is "anti-Christ."

Why did Jesus heal her on the Sabbath? Sabbath means rest. Jesus did more healings on the Sabbath than any other day. Why? I think He was sending us the message that if we are at rest, His grace will flow in our lives. The life of rest says, "Jesus, apart from you, I can do nothing! I want to live under grace! I want to get off this treadmill! I count all my investment in earning Your blessing and righteousness as worthless. I give up on everything I have ever earned because nothing I have ever accomplished could ever measure up to what you have done for me. I quit!!"

CHAPTER FIFTEEN

Law + Grace = Another Gospel

Key scriptures:
Galatians 1:6-12, Galatians 2:11-3:14, Acts 10:13-16

The book of Galatians is an amazing letter of encouragement to all of us who have been ambushed by grace and have been so gloriously undone by grace that we simply can't go back to the mixture of grace and law.

For me, grace isn't a doctrine. Grace is Jesus. Because my paradigm has shifted, I can smell the leaven of the law a mile away, and my response when I see it coming is "Don't mess with my Jesus!" It's kind of like Mary Magdalene when she arrived at the tomb after the resurrection, and she said to the two angels, "They've taken my Lord, and I don't know where they've put Him!"[256] That's my sentiment as I witness the influx of self-help doctrines being dispensed in the church today.

Paul wrote the letter to the churches in Galatia to combat teaching by false brethren who wanted to bring works back into the church. These men were seducing the people to believe that Jesus alone wasn't enough for salvation. They were bringing back the carrot on the end of the stick: "You must do this and do that for God to accept you. You must keep the law to maintain your salvation." Paul was astounded with the Galatians who were allowing this teaching in their churches, and his language in this letter is forceful and even fierce at times.

Double Curse

Reader Study Reference, Galatians 1:6-12

> *I marvel that you are turning away so soon from Him who called you in the grace of Christ, to a different gospel, which is not another; but there are some who trouble you and want to pervert the gospel of Christ. But even if we, or an angel from heaven, preach any other gospel to you than what we have preached to you, let him be accursed. As we have said before, so now I say again, if anyone preaches any other gospel to you than what you have received, let him be accursed. For do I now persuade men, or God? Or do I seek to please men? For if I still pleased men, I would not be a bondservant of Christ. But I make known to you, brethren, that the gospel which was preached by me is not according to man. For I neither received it from man, nor was I taught it, but it came through the revelation of Jesus Christ. (Galatians 1:6-12)*

The Galatians were "turning away" from God by believing the heresy of a mixed gospel. "Turning away" is the Greek word "meta-tithemi," and it means "to transpose two things, one of which is put in place of the other."[257] These false brethren were coming in to re-place grace with another gospel.

Paul, the apostle of grace, pronounced a double curse on anyone, man or angel, who would preach any other gospel than the one he had previously preached to them. Curse is the Greek word "anathe-ma" and it means "a person doomed to destruction, devoted to the direst of woes."[258] In other words, "Let these men who are preaching another gospel be stopped in their tracks. Whatever it takes, let their preaching come to nothing!" That doesn't sound very "Christian" of Paul, does it? Aren't we all just supposed to get along? It is clear from this passage that Paul did not consider pleasing men of more value than protecting the integrity of the Gospel, the Gospel which he had received directly from Jesus Himself. Sadly, men and women over the centuries have compromised the Gospel in the name of pleasing each other, resulting in massive numbers of disillusioned souls.

Some have said, and at one time I have even said it myself, that the doctrine the Galatians were buying into was a "perversion" of the Gospel as if it was some variation on the Gospel. That is not what Paul was saying, however. Adding a little law to grace is not just altering it like when someone puts an addition onto their house. It is, according to Paul, "another gospel." Paul used a word that is translated "pervert" when he was speaking of the men coming in trying to bring in a little law. It's the Greek word "metastrepho" and it means "to reverse, to change to the opposite, to turn about."[259] In other words, a mixed gospel is not a form of the Gospel of grace. It is not a watered down Gospel. It is a message diametrically opposed to grace and completely opposite in its nature. A little leaven leavens the whole lump.[260]

If the Gospel is mixed with works to earn or maintain salvation, IT IS NOT the Gospel. I have given many illustrations of how this "other gospel" is alive and well in the church today. I in no way intend to be offensive, but if you are accepting a mixture of law and grace, you are accepting something other than the Gospel of Jesus Christ.

Paul Rebuked Peter

Reader Study Reference, Galatians 2:11-13

From verse 11 of Galatians 2 to the end of the chapter, Paul says something that might seem even more shocking to those of us who believe there should not be open confrontation in the church. Paul told the Galatians of his public rebuke of the apostle Peter for compromising the Gospel.

> *Now when Peter had come to Antioch, I withstood him to his face, because he was to be blamed; for before certain men came from James,[261] he would eat with the Gentiles; but when they came, he withdrew and separated himself, fearing those who were of the circumcision. (Galatians 2:11-12)*

Peter was wrong and it is documented in the Scripture for billions of people throughout the ages to see! When I consider Peter's "credentials" and Paul's lack of them, it's amazing to me that Paul was the one to rebuke Peter. Peter walked with Jesus during His three and a half years of ministry. Peter was saved first. Peter is the one to whom Jesus said, "On this rock I will build My church."[262] Peter is the one who preached on the day the church was born and three thousand people were saved.[263] On the other hand, Paul called himself the least of the apostles, born at the wrong time, having persecuted the church.[264]

Paul had such assurance of who he was in Christ as an apostle of grace that he confidently rebuked Peter, the most prominent apostle and the oldest apostle in the church at that time, for compromising the Gospel and walking in hypocrisy.

And the rest of the Jews also played the hypocrite with him, so that even Barnabas was carried away with their hypocrisy. (Galatians 2:13)

Wow. Paul openly condemned the hypocrisy of them all!

Peter and the Gentiles

For context on Paul's rebuke of Peter, we'll look at a tradition in the early church. They celebrated what became known as "agape" (love) feasts where they would have dinner and then share in the Lord's Supper together. It was sort of like a "pot luck" where everyone would bring food and they would fellowship together.[265] Peter would share in these feasts and eat along with the Gentiles. He would eat what had previously been considered unclean and was forbidden by the law for the Jews to eat.

Peter was freed to eat with the Gentiles because God Himself had appeared to Peter to release him from the dietary restrictions of the law. You may recall that Peter at one time went into a trance and had a vision from God where he saw a sheet with all of the "unclean" animals on it being lowered from heaven, and the voice from heaven telling Peter to eat them. These were non-kosher animals that Jewish people didn't eat, such as rabbits, pigs, cats, lizards, and vultures.

And a voice came to him, "Rise, Peter; kill and eat." But Peter said, "Not so, Lord!..." (Acts 10:13-14)

Imagine the Lord appeared to you, and you said, "Not so, Lord!" Some people are so bound by the rules that even if God put them in a trance and appeared in a vision, they wouldn't believe Him!

"For I have never eaten anything common or unclean." And a voice spoke to him again the second time, "What God has cleansed you must not call common." (Acts 10:14-15)

God moved from talking about animals to people. He was about to send Peter to the Gentiles in Cornelius' home to save them, and He wanted Peter to know that he was not to call the Gentiles unclean. Unclean means unholy. Unholy means "common." The opposite of holiness is not sin. The opposite of holiness is commonness. Holiness means to be set apart. God said to Peter, "What I have cleansed, don't call common/unclean/unholy."

This was done three times. And the object was taken up into heaven again. (Acts 10:16)

Three times God said, "What God has cleansed you must not call common." Why three times? Perhaps it's because the number three was a significant number to Peter. On the night Jesus was betrayed, Peter denied knowing Him three times. I believe the Lord was saying to Peter, "If I have cleansed someone and taken away their sins, and yet you continue to call them unholy, it's the same as denying Me." By the direction of the Holy Spirit, Peter went from there to preach the Gospel to Cornelius and his family. Peter said to them,

"In truth I perceive that God shows no partiality..." (Acts 10:35)

More On Paul's Rebuke of Peter

Reader Study Reference, Galatians 2:14-16

Through Peter the Lord began to break down some of the barriers between the Jews and Gentiles. Peter ate shrimp, lobster, and bacon with the Gentiles in his new-found freedom! However, when the Judaizers showed up, Peter was intimidated. Peter wanted to convince these guys that he was keeping the law, but to do that he had to withdraw from being with the Gentiles. The love feasts were becoming unloving! Peter, an apostle with great influence, succumbed to pressure, separated himself from those who didn't keep the law, and attracted other Jewish Christians (including Barnabas) to separate themselves as well, thus causing division in the body.

> *But when I saw that they were not straightforward about the truth of the gospel, I said to Peter before them all, "If you, being a Jew, live in the manner of Gentiles and not as the Jews, why do you compel Gentiles to live as Jews? (Galatians 2:14)*

Paul rebuked Peter "before them all." Paul is saying, "Peter! You yourself haven't been following the Jewish law, and now you're trying to force the Gentiles to live like the Jews? You're not practicing what you're preaching! That's hypocritical!" Hypocrisy is pretending to be what we're not. In this context, it's when Peter was free from the law, but he acted like he was still in bondage to it. He was under grace, but to please mere men, he acted like he was still under law.

Paul went on to plead with Peter by telling him that even though they were Jews by birth, they did not have an advantage over the Gentiles:

> *We who are Jews by nature, and not sinners of the Gentiles, knowing that a man is not justified by the works of the law but by faith in Jesus Christ, even we have believed in Christ Jesus, that we might be justified by faith in Christ and not by the works of the law; for by the works of the law no flesh shall be justified. (Galatians 2:15-16)*

The cross is offensive to the flesh. The reason people reject pure grace is because they have to check all their best efforts, their investment in self-righteousness, and their reputations at the door. All that work that they did to "get close to God" and "get right with God" and to appear righteous to other people is worthless! But often it's simply too costly for them.

Jesus, a Minister of Sin?

Reader Study Reference, Galatians 2:17-19

In Galatians 2:17, Paul made a bold statement that anyone who believed that right standing with God could be achieved by works agreed with the enemies of Jesus who accused Christ Himself of being promoter and encourager of sin!

> *But if, while we seek to be justified by Christ we ourselves also are found sinners is Christ therefor a minister of sin? Certainly not! (Galatians 2:17)*

For clarity, here is that verse in The Message paraphrase:

> *And are you ready to make the accusation that since people like me, who go through Christ in order to get things right with God, aren't perfectly virtuous, Christ must therefore be an accessory to sin? (Galatians 2:17, The Message)*

Paul was asking the question, "If Jesus removed the law, does that mean He's leading us into sin? Is Christ promoting sin?!" It puts the charge of heresy on Jesus Himself for anyone to say that we can lose our righteousness when we don't obey the law. If you are accused of saying that sin is okay when you say that you are justified (made right with God) by faith in Christ alone, then you can say, "Hey, Jesus was charged with the same thing! And so was Paul!" You're in good company!

> *For if I build again those things which I destroyed, I make myself a transgressor. For I through the law died to the law that I might live to God. (Galatians 2:18-19)*

On this side of the cross, we don't live by the external accountability of the law. We live by the inward promptings of the Holy Spirit in the newness of life.[266] Paul taught that the law only aroused sinful behavior and does nothing to curb it. Using himself as the example, he said that sin "taking opportunity by the commandment" produced in him all manner of evil desire.[267]

It's obvious in the world today that sin is rampant, but the answer isn't law. It's grace! Paul in no way excused sin and had high expectations that believers would live holy lives, but what was his solution? Grace!

Grace, the Answer To Sin

I'm going on a little rabbit trail here to illustrate the point. I counted the number of times the Greek word for grace is used in the New Testament, and I found one hundred forty-seven occurrences.[268] Do you know where "grace" occurs the most often? It's used twenty-six times in Paul's letters to the Corinthians who were the most immoral! To the Philippians he only used the word "grace" three times. In Colossians he used it five times. In the letter to the Galatians, he used the word seven times. Yet to the church that WE would think needed less grace and more tongue-lashing about obedience, Paul spoke to them more about grace!

Whenever Paul found sin in the church, he always reminded them of who they were in Christ. Paul was very passionate about the believers living holy lives that honored Jesus, but he always taught them through their identity in Christ. For example, some of the Corinthian church members were going to temple prostitutes. This is how he responded to them:

> *DO YOU NOT KNOW that your body is the temple of the Holy Spirit who IS in you? (1 Corinthians 6:19, emphasis added)*

He reminded them of who was living in them: the Holy Spirit. He said, "the Holy Spirit who IS in you." Present tense. The Holy Spirit was still in them even when they sinned! It would seem reasonable that the Holy Spirit would leave when they did such a horrendous thing as sleeping with a prostitute, but God's eyes are on the perfection of Jesus' work, not our sin. Can you comprehend a love that massive? The Corinthians' biggest problem was ignorance of God's love and what He had done for them. That's why Paul kept saying, "Do you not KNOW...?"

Other church members in Corinth were suing each other. Again, look at Paul's response:

> *DO YOU NOT KNOW that the saints will judge the world? And if the world will be judged by you, are you unworthy to judge the smallest matters? DO YOU NOT KNOW that we shall judge angels? How much more, things that pertain to this life? (1 Corinthians 6:2-3, emphasis added)*

His rebuke was to remind them that one day they will judge the world and angels! In another place, Paul tells the Corinthians to stop arguing over what leader they follow:

For all things are yours. (1 Corinthians 3:21)

Again, he used present tense: "All things ARE yours!" God did not take away His love or His fellowship or His blessing because they sinned. Yes, Paul gave lots of exhortation in his letters to the Corinthians with this appeal:

WE'RE ROOTING FOR TRUTH TO WIN OUT IN YOU. (2 Corinthians 13:8, The Message, emphasis added)

Not long ago, while spending time with a friend who had worked several years in ministry and who had struggled with serious bondages her whole life, my friend confessed to me that she was going back to her old life, and she was finished with the church. She had been very wounded by all of the attempts of her leaders to "fix" her by casting out demons in long deliverance sessions, instructing her to fast and pray in order to cleanse herself, get accountability partners, and do better. I understood her hurt and her anger completely, and felt partly responsible because of my participation in pushing her to "get free." All these exercises served to condemn her and only drove her sin further into the dark. When she told me she was throwing in the towel, I felt prompted to ask her this question: "Have you ever had a real encounter with Jesus, or have you always piggy-backed off the experiences of others?" She didn't hesitate with her answer: "I piggy-backed off of others. I have never had a real encounter with God." This answer told me that she did not know Jesus for herself. We can't always know the condition of a person's heart and whether they are dead or alive. Some people are really well-behaved and yet don't know God, while others behave terribly, but have just forgotten who they are. However, her response that she had never known God gave me some direction in how to be her friend.

Paul made a distinction concerning how to relate to unbelievers and believers (or those who claim to be):

When I wrote to you before, I told you not to associate with people who indulge in sexual sin. But I wasn't talking about unbelievers who indulge in sexual sin, or are greedy, or cheat people, or worship idols. You would have to leave this world to avoid people like that. (1 Corinthians 5:9-10, NLT)

When Paul told them "not to associate" with people indulging in sexual sin, I do not believe he was talking about immature believers who were growing in their understanding of grace and their identity in Christ. I also do not believe that Paul was telling the Corinthians to sever their relationships with any believer who had fallen into sexual sin. That word "associate" is actually stronger in the original Greek than just casual association. It "strictly denotes living in an intimate and continuous relation with one."[269] In others words, Paul was warning them that there is a certain level of closeness in relationship that we can't go beyond with someone who indulges in sexual sin or else we'll fall into the same trap. It's called "putting confidence in the flesh." And we also can't just sit back and be flippant when people who claim to be Christians have no scruples about sin. These are people who believe that grace gives a license to sin. Grace does not condone sin.

However, when it comes to dealing with unbelievers, the instruction is different. How will they ever know the love of God if we separate ourselves from them? And it's not our job to fix people. It's our job to share the Gospel with them. In 2 Corinthians 5, Paul called us "ambassadors for Christ." It's as if God is pleading through us to our lost friends:

We implore you on Christ's behalf, be reconciled to God. For He made Him who knew no sin to be sin for us, that we might become the righteousness of God in Him. (2 Corinthians 5:20-21)

How could grace ever be used as a license to sin when we tell people that? Do you know when the grace of God gets twisted into a license to sin? It's when it's replaced with "different gospel."[270]

For certain men have crept in unnoticed, who long ago were marked out for this condemnation, ungodly men, who turn the grace of our God into lewdness and DENY the only Lord God and our Lord Jesus Christ. (Jude 1:4, emphasis added)

That word "turn" is the Greek word "metatithemi." It's the same word used in Galatians 1:6 for "turning away...to a different gospel," and again, it means to replace one thing with another. In other words, when grace is replaced with another doctrine in the church, immoral living will be the result! And if we replace grace, it's the same as denying the Lord Jesus!

Accountability?

Having good friends to encourage us and build us up in our faith and remind us that we are righteous is very healthy. We were created to be interrelated in a community of faith. Good friends inspire others to good works and to love one another. Although the goal of biblical church life is not to get people to stop sinning, they will sin less in a community that stands on the foundation of the Gospel of grace.

However, the "accountability" that I see advocated in the church today is more like having a spiritual parole officer. People in the church talk a lot about the need for everyone to have "accountability" so that we won't sin. If no one is watching out for us, there's no telling what we might do!

A motto I used to teach was this: "There should be at least one person in your life who knows everything about you." So here's how it would work: whenever someone was tempted to "take another cookie out of the cookie jar," he would imagine having to confess his sin to his accountability partner. The threat of shame and rejection would be the force that kept his hands tied safely behind his back when temptation would come... unless the temptation overtook him. What would he do then? For a time he would confess his sin after succumbing, but in a religious setting where righteousness is not understood and taught, he will eventually begin to keep his sin secret because of the condemnation. My experience with this type of accountability is that people will work very hard to give the impression that they are living holy lives, but their sin goes underground.

In an environment where pure grace is taught and lived, people feel the security to come out in the open and be transparent. Grace creates an atmosphere of safety in the church where it's alright to be weak. It's alright to have failures and to admit our struggles. People don't feel stripped of their dignity, dishonored, or gossiped about when they "confess their sins one to another" as James instructs us.[271] It's in that honesty that friends who walk in grace can encourage and build up others who are struggling. When there is a revelation of grace, the Holy Spirit speaks through believers to remind fellow believers that they haven't lost their righteousness. Sin will have no power over them because they are not under law, but under grace.[272] Sin won't go underground, it will be overcome by grace as the person rises up in their identity, takes authority over the flesh, and says no to sin.

All of this is a demonstration of the internal motivation of love by the Holy Spirit rather than the external motivation of fear that comes from legalism.

Perfect Love Casts Out Fear

The law used the external motivation of fear, and it had it's purpose. The law was given through Moses to natural, fallen men whose identity was in the flesh with a soul that did not have the life of God inside. The law was an exterior standard that demanded perfection and provided the accountability through the Aaronic priesthood with punishments, even death. The modus operandi of the law was fear of punishment.

When the Mosaic law was given on Mount Sinai, Moses said,

"God has come to test you, and that His fear may be before you, so that you may not sin." (Exodus 20:20)

However, the law was not made for a righteous man![273] The law — the external demands for righteousness on the flesh — was not made for the righteous person. It was not made for those who have been justified by Christ through faith in HIS finished work and filled with the Holy Spirit.

Does this mean that there are no consequences for sin? Of course not. There are natural consequences to sin. What I am talking about is a spiritual truth concerning being IN the world, but not OF it. It's about an inner transformation which has made us holy that results in an outward manifestation of holy living. The law of God given to

Moses was removed by the cross and replaced with something FAR superior: the Spirit of God inside! Love replaces law.

The religious are scared to death of this! Releasing people the fear of punishment gives the religious no foundation for control! The whole multi-million dollar business of sin management and how-to-be-a-better-Christian-by-getting-rid-of-sin conferences, books, sermon series, etc., etc., etc., would go bankrupt if believers started believing they are righteous.

Those who fear grace are sounding the age old alarms by screaming, "If you remove the fear of punishment, Christians will sin more! Yes, we are saved by grace, but we need the safety net of the truth (their way of saying "law") to give us the balance! We need more of the 'fear of God'!" They redefine the fear of the Lord to make it the FEAR OF PUNISHMENT. But under the New Covenant of grace, there is no longer fear of punishment or judgment from God! There is no fear in perfect love!

> *By this, love is perfected with us, so that we may have confidence in the day of judgment; because as He is, so also are we in this world. There is no fear in love; but perfect love casts out fear, because fear involves punishment, and the one who fears is not perfected in love. (1 John 4:17-18, NASB)*

The fear of the Lord under the New Covenant of grace is the worship and honor of Him and His word above all other. His word is Jesus. His word is that He has removed our sin and joined Himself to us. His word is "Fear not! I am WITH you! Come to ME! Come boldly to My throne of mercy and grace as My very own dear children! I will never leave you nor forsake you! I am near! You are in Me and I am in you."

If we, the righteous, keep the "safety net" of the law, it is sin for us![274] Living by the law as a new creation in Christ is not of faith. It is sin!

> *Yet the law is not of faith... (Galatians 3:12)*

> *...for whatever is not from faith is sin. (Romans 14:23)*

That "safety net" must be cast out! It must be replaced with reliance and utter dependance on the Holy Spirit from within! Today, our safety net is GRACE! When our flesh fails us by sinning, we look to Him, and He whispers, "I love you. You are My beloved child. You are holy and set apart unto Me. Let Me help you walk through this situation in wisdom." Then we see the lie of the power of sin that operates in our flesh for what it is and, we repent. We change our minds by setting them on things above where Christ is and where we are hidden in Him, and we walk in newness of life, bearing fruit to God.

It's No Longer I Who Live

Reader Study Reference, Galatians 2:20-21

Every time I read Galatians 2:20, I feel like exhaling and saying, "Thank you, Jesus." It's impossible for me to read it and not feel burdens instantly lifted. How much easier can it get than Jesus living His life through me?

> *I have been crucified with Christ; it is no longer I who live, but Christ lives in me; and the life which I now live in the flesh I live by faith in the Son of God, who loved me and gave Himself for me. I do not set aside the grace of God; for if righteousness comes through the law, then Christ died in vain. (Galatians 2:20-21)*

I like to take this passage and read it in The Message Paraphrase and make Paul's plea my own:

> *What actually took place is this: I tried keeping rules and working my head off to please God, and it didn't work. So I quit being a "law man" so that I could be God's man. Christ's life showed me how, and enabled me to do it. I identified myself completely with him. Indeed, I have been crucified with Christ. My ego is no longer central. It is no longer important that I appear righteous before you or have your good opinion, and I am no longer driven to impress God. Christ lives in me. The life you see me living is not "mine," but it is lived by faith in the Son of God, who loved me and gave himself for me. I am not going to go back on that. Is it not clear to you that to go back to that old rule-keeping, peer-pleasing religion would be an abandonment of everything personal and free in my relationship with God? I refuse to do that, to repudiate God's grace. If a*

living relationship with God could come by rule-keeping, then Christ died unnecessarily. (Galatians 2:19-21, The Message)

May it never be that Christ died unnecessarily! When we believe the Gospel of grace, we are exalting Jesus. Any other message points to man, and it is man-centered religion. May we never ever set aside the grace of God again!

Foolish Galatians

Reader Study Reference, Galatians 3:1-4

Next we have Paul's greatest recorded rebuke in the scriptures:

O foolish Galatians! Who has bewitched you that you should not obey the truth,[275] *before whose eyes Jesus Christ was clearly portrayed among you as crucified? (Galatians 3:1)*

If we use the law today on believers, it leads to control and manipulation which is nothing less than witchcraft. Paul was outraged with the Galatians for succumbing to it. He pleaded with them to return to the true Gospel that they received from him. He went on to say,

This only I want to learn from you: Did you receive the Spirit by the works of the law, or by the hearing of faith? (Galatians 3:2)

He's asking, "Did you receive the Holy Spirit because you kept the Ten Commandments? Or did your receive the Spirit by faith in Jesus Christ alone?"

Are you so foolish? Having begun in the Spirit, are you now being made perfect by the flesh? (Galatians 3:3)

Recall from our study of Romans 7 that "flesh" is the Greek word "sarx" and is speaking of self-effort. He's asking, "Do you think you can add to the righteousness of Jesus?! Is there anything in your flesh that can make you righteous?" The religious mindset is that we start by faith, but then we have to keep our end of the bargain. This is the sentiment:

"Lord, I promise this next week I am going to faithfully pray an hour each morning. And, Lord, I believe on the basis of ME keeping my promise to You, YOU are going to bless me. I believe that after all that prayer, I am going to be SO righteous by the end of this week that the windows of heaven are just going to open right up over me!"

Praying is good, but believers don't pray to BE righteous. We pray because we ARE righteous. "Thank you Lord that You have already blessed me with every spiritual blessing in heavenly places. I lack nothing. You have given me everything I need for life and godliness. You have not withheld any good thing from me! I am under grace!"

The next verse in Galatians 3 says:

Have you suffered so many things in vain—if indeed it was in vain? (Galatians 3:4)

These Galatians had suffered great reproach and persecution for the sake of the Gospel. They had suffered "so many things" to believe the pure Gospel, and now they were caving in.

Miracles and the Righteousness of Faith

Reader Study Reference, Galatians 3:5-6

Paul continues the thoughts from verses 2 and 3 of Galatians 3 concerning the entrance of the Holy Spirit into the hearts of the Galatians believers by telling them the resulting effect of the power of Spirit of God in their lives.

Therefore He who supplies the Spirit to you and works miracles among you... (Galatians 3:5)

The word "supplies" is the word Greek word "epichoregeo" which means "to supply abundantly or bountifully."[276] The verb tense for the verbs "supplies" and "works" here is the present active participle which means there was an active continuous flow of the supply of the Spirit and the working of miracles.[277] Paul was saying that even though the false teachers had come in and were making inroads, miracles were still happening. However, the church was slowly turning away from grace to self-effort, and it would hinder the flow of the miraculous in the church.

God's abundant supply of the Spirit and the grace for the working of miracles never stops flowing. This is what God intended for the church, but why don't we see it? Paul's next question answers that question:

> *...does He do it by the works of the law, or by the hearing of faith?...* *(Galatians 3:5, cont.)*

We don't get miracles by DOING anything! Miracles flow from the Spirit by the hearing of faith! It's so simple!

Many of us learned steps to "earn" miracles through our words of "faith." But so often nothing happened. Why? Because our faith was in our faith. Faith became a work. Yes, we talked about Jesus and His blood, but only in the context of our formulas of faith. Our faith became our law. We were toiling, sometimes even travailing, to earn miracles by our obedience, but the Scriptures say that God does miracles by the "hearing of faith." Here is a liberating truth about faith: faith isn't a bridge to Jesus; JESUS is the bridge! It's HIS righteousness, not ours!

God Preached the Gospel To Abraham

Reader Study Reference, Galatians 3:7-8

Do you know what the basis for receiving ANYTHING from the Lord is? It's simply believing we are qualified to receive it. This is the way Abraham received from the Lord. God told him He was going to bless him, and Abraham believed it, no questions asked.

But there is actually more to it than that...Abraham believed the same Gospel that you and I believe. God declared the Gospel to Abraham in a very creative way, and in that display of creativity He promised Abraham that you and I would be blessed today because of the coming Messiah.

> *...just as Abraham "believed God, and it was accounted to him for righteousness. Therefore know that only those who are of faith are sons of Abraham. And the Scripture, foreseeing that God would justify the Gentiles by faith, preached the gospel to Abraham beforehand, saying, "In you all the nations shall be blessed." (Galatians 3:6-8)*

If we look back in Genesis, we will see that God gave the Gospel story to Abraham when He told Him to look towards the skies:

> *He brought him outside and said, "Look now toward heaven, and count the stars if you are able to number them." And He said to him, "So shall your descendants be." And he believed in the LORD, and He accounted it to him for righteousness. (Genesis 15:5-6)*

The word translated in the New Kings James for "count" and "number" is the Hebrew word "caphar" which means "to count, to recount, to relate."[278] The King James Version translates it this way: "Look now toward the heaven and TELL the stars if thou be able to number them, and he said unto him, So shall thy seed be." God was telling Abraham that he would have as many descendants as the stars in the sky, but He was saying much more than that. The "Seed" of Abraham is Jesus Himself.[279] God was telling Abraham to look in the sky and see the story of Jesus. Before the Bible was even written, God put the Gospel story in the sky in the constellations, beginning with Virgo, the virgin, and then ending with Leo, the Lion of the Tribe of Judah, Jesus![280] Today the occult has perverted the meaning of the arrangement of the stars into astrology, but God is the one who arranged the stars in the sky to tell the story of redemption.[281] And Abraham looked at it and believed the same Gospel that you and I believe.

The stars in the constellations are all the spiritual descendants of Abraham. That includes you and me. Think of it: we are written in the story of the Gospel! His story is our story! We were baptized into His death and raised to new life in His resurrection![282] It's too awesome to get our minds around, but when we look up at the stars we should feel the extravagant love of God for us!

"Of the works of the law" Or "of faith"?

Reader Study Reference, Galatians 3:9-14

> *So then those who are of faith are blessed with believing Abraham. For as many as are of the works of the law are under the curse; for it is written, "Cursed is everyone who does not continue in all things which are written in the book of the law, to do them." But that no one is justified by the law in the sight of God is evident, for "the just shall live by faith." Yet*

the law is not of faith, but "the man who does them shall live by them."
(Galatians 3:9-12)

My friend, faith and rule-keeping as a means to relate to God are in direct opposition to each other. They are mutually exclusive. If we choose the rule route, we have to do it 100% or else!

I love the wording that Paul used when he says "those who are of faith are blessed with BELIEVING Abraham." It's like a title added to his name. I could say, "Hi, I'm BELIEVING Tricia and I am blessed!" Those who are OF FAITH are blessed. However, those who are OF THE WORKS of the law are under the curse. Paul didn't say we are cursed because we break the law. He said those "OF the law" are under a curse.

Paul said that "the man who does them shall live by them." We know that the covenant of law has been fulfilled in Christ and does not apply to us in any way. Yet, even though I am a Christian, my life will reflect what I believe about the place of the law in my life. If we believe we are under the law, we will believe we are under a curse. Every lie of satan we believe has ramifications in this life.

Several years ago at the birthday party for my son, one of my daughters had a stomach ache. A mom who had stayed at the party with her son was an influential leader in a local church, and she took my daughter aside (without my knowledge) and began to try to cast demons out of her. She told my daughter that her stomach ache was because of a generational curse on my husband's side of the family. Thankfully my daughter had a level head (and still does) and wasn't traumatized by the experience. But this is the kind of nonsense that goes on in the name of Christianity because people don't realize that Christ became a curse so that we don't have to be cursed!

For years I heard, "Speak words of life!" And if I didn't, I'd be under a curse. What happens if I admit I have a headache? Am I doomed to suffer consequences for making a "negative confession?" It's superstition that has taken verses like the following and made them a law to keep instead of a spiritual principle to bring us life:

Death and life are in the power of the tongue, and those who love it will eat its fruit. (Proverbs 18:21)

If we see that scripture through the eyes of law, we will believe that our words will be more powerful than what Christ has done! It's still the merit system. Am I blessed because I have made a positive confession, or am I blessed because Christ has redeemed me from the curse? When I believe that Christ has redeemed me from the curse, I will speak what I believe with authority and power! We believe and therefore we speak![283]

When we take our ground for blessing under the merit system, we're buying into the "karma" life: do good, get good; do bad get bad. It's amazing that people who call themselves Christians have bought into this type of mindset. It's actually the doctrine of Buddhism and other religions. Karma literally means "to do." It's the belief that we create our happiness and our misery; and therefore, we are the designers of our own destiny. It's said that a young buddhist disciple seeking truth asked Buddha this question:

"What is the cause, what is the reason, O Lord, that we find amongst mankind the short-lived and long-lived, the healthy and the diseased, the ugly and beautiful, those lacking influence and the powerful, the poor and the rich, the low-born and the high-born, and the ignorant and the wise?"

And here was Buddha's reply:

"All living beings have actions (Karma) as their own, their inheritance, their congenital cause, their kinsman, their refuge. It is Karma that differentiates beings into low and high states."[284]

In other words, we get what we deserve and inherit what our parents deserved. Is that the life we want?! Paul is saying that it's all about what we believe! Are we "of faith"? Or are we "of the works of the law"? Has the Father qualified us or not?

Christ has redeemed us from the curse of the law, having become a curse for us (for it is written, "Cursed is everyone who hangs on a tree"), that the blessing of Abraham might come upon the Gentiles in Christ Jesus, that we might receive the promise of the Spirit through faith. (Galatians 3:13-14)

God gave the law to show that religion doesn't work. No religion in this world has a Savior. They all expect you to save yourself by behaving yourself. Only the true God of heaven provided a Savior who could redeem us from every curse so that we could be blessed by simply receiving His grace.

CHAPTER SIXTEEN

Sonship

Key scriptures:
Galatians 3:15-4:7, Galatians 4:21-5:1

The idea of being a son verses being a servant in our relationship with the Lord under the New Covenant is a theme woven throughout Paul's writings. There is no more comforting thought than knowing that our Daddy is the creator and owner of the entire universe and beyond.

> *"Moses was faithful as a servant in all God's house, testifying to what would be said in the future. But Christ is faithful as a son over God's house." (Hebrews 3:5-6)*

Moses was a servant, and those who were under the law were servants.

Christ is the Son, and those who are in Christ are sons of God.

Once we understand the meaning of sonship, we will walk in the love and authority of our Father. His mission, vision, and heart will be our very own. However, before we can truly function as a family in the body of Christ in those horizontal relationships with honor, respect, submission, and love, we must understand the vertical love relationship of spiritual sonship with our heavenly Father.

I heard a teaching once in a leadership seminar based on the scripture above from Hebrews 3. This influential speaker taught on church leadership using the analogy of servants and sons in the house. Yet in the analogy, instead of teaching from the perspective of God being our Father and we being His sons, he likened the pastor of a church to the "father" and the leadership structure under him was made up of the "sons." This teaching was a part of the broader perspective where the pastor of the church provides a "covering" for all those submitted under his leadership. Those who come out from under the "covering" are in rebellion to the "father of the house" and susceptible to attack from demonic forces. Here are notes from that seminar taken directly from the speaker's comments (in the notes "father" refers to the pastor, "sons" refer to the leaders under him in the church structure):

- God builds His kingdom relationally in families. There is a "father" and there are "sons." In the same way, the pastor builds his house on sons.
- Christ is a Son. He took a position, in attitude and spirit, subservient to the Father. In the same way, the sons in the house are subservient to the father of the house (the pastor).
- The sons are faithful to the father's work (the pastor) and hold the father's heart and the success of his work as their own.
- Sons bond new people to the family and to the father (the pastor). Sons have no agenda, but the agenda of the father (the pastor).
- Sons share their inner conversations with their father (the pastor).
- Sons can handle correction, discipline and change. If you are a pastor, the way you know if someone is with you is if they stay with you after correction.

Throughout the seminar the thread of control was woven in every teaching. If the "father of the house" said it, it was the truth. Anyone who disagreed was "in rebellion."

There is certainly a place for teamwork and respect for the leadership roles in the local church. God gave some to be elders and deacons, and we have a common vision to share the Good News of the Gospel of Jesus Christ to the world in a strategic manner, as well as build up the local body of believers with encouragement, fellowship, and teaching. However, misapplications of Scripture and the use of the "father and son" relationship as an analogy for the relationship between a pastor and his staff is religion gone amuck! It's a serious diversion from the biblical truth of our sonship. Because we are sons, we can talk to and hear directly from our Father, and any good pastor will make one of his main objectives raising up a mature congregation who knows the voice of the Lord. No one stands between us and God. We are no longer under the Old Covenant system where we are dependent on a priest to represent us before God or a prophet to speak for God to us. We have our own personal, intimate relationship as sons and daughters with our Father.

Sadly, many who have come out of abusive church situations will adapt an attitude that even though they love God, they don't need church. There is a growing sentiment in Christianity: "I'm the church and you're the church. We don't need meetings or structure or pastors. Let's just BE the church." Abuse causes an anti-church attitude, but we need to remember that if we decide to ignore the portions of scripture that describe God's intent for the local church, then we're ignoring a part of the same Bible that tells us we are righteous, holy, redeemed, and loved.

In the New Covenant of grace, the first thing we need to know as sons of God is that our Father will never, ever, ever, ever break His covenant with us. We will forever be sons in His house and loved by Him. Once we know that, we'll walk as sons and find it easy to serve one another in humility.

God has put all things under the authority of Christ and has made him head over all things for the benefit of the church. (Ephesians 1:22, NLT)

In this chapter we will cover several passages in Galatians to drive home this point and hopefully bring great assurance to your heart.

Can't Annul Or Add To It

Reader Study Reference, Galatians 3:15-18

The covenant that God made on behalf of Abraham was an irrevocable covenant. That means it couldn't be changed. It was final. In Galatians 3:15, Paul illustrates the nature of covenants and how they work by using the example of human covenants. When someone enters covenant, he obligates himself to it unto his death.

> *Brethren, I speak in the manner of men: Though it is only a man's covenant, yet if it is confirmed, no one annuls or adds to it. (Galatians 3:15)*

The verb "confirmed" is in the perfect tense meaning it is a done deal and will not be done again.[285] It cannot be annulled or added to or it will be invalid — not worth the paper it is written on. With a covenant there are two ways to make it invalid: annul it directly or add to its conditions.

In the context of Paul's letter, he is saying that at first glance these seemingly "harmless" new conditions the Judaizers were bringing alongside grace would actually invalidate the covenant if what they were teaching was true! We know that we are righteous in Christ, and nothing can annul the covenant God made in Christ's blood for us. However, we can believe the lie that there are conditions to the covenant, and it will ruin the experience of the life of faith and intimacy with God. Any dependency on works is an abandonment of faith. Can you see the black and white of it?

Paul goes on to say,

> *Now to Abraham and his Seed were the promises made. He does not say, "And to seeds," as of many, but as of one, "And to your Seed," who is Christ. (Galatians 3:16)*

Where Paul says, "and to your Seed," he is talking about Jesus. The Good News is that we are descendants of this Seed! He was the firstborn of many brethren. If we are in Christ we are Abraham's seed and heirs according the promise.[286]

> *And this I say, that the law, which was four hundred and thirty years later, cannot annul the covenant that was confirmed before by God in Christ,*

that it should make the promise of no effect. For if the inheritance is of the law, it is no longer of promise; but God gave it to Abraham by promise. (Galatians 3:17-18)

The law covenant was revoked, but the covenant that God made with Abraham was an everlasting covenant. The law was given to Moses at Mount Sinai four hundred thirty years AFTER the Abrahamic covenant. It was supplementary to God's covenant of grace and was therefore secondary to it. The law came in alongside the Abrahamic covenant of grace, but this covenant of grace was never annulled!

Unlike the Mosaic covenant of law, Paul doesn't say that the Abrahamic covenant was FULFILLED in Christ; he says it was CONFIRMED by God in Christ. It confirms that God has always been a God of grace, and grace has always been His main agenda and His heart for us!

Purpose of the Law

Reader Study Reference, Galatians 3:19

> *What purpose then does the law serve? It was added because of transgressions, till the Seed should come to whom the promise was made;... (Galatians 3:19)*

If the law couldn't earn us the inheritance, what was it for? The law entered that sin might increase.[287] The law entered that sin might be exceedingly sinful.[288] The law was given to show the sinner that he needed a Savior and was only given until the Seed, Jesus, would come. It was designed to govern them until Jesus came, and they accepted the New Covenant. The people before the cross looked FORWARD to Christ's sacrifice for them. All of us since the cross look BACK at the accomplishment of our salvation. The law has no place in God's dealings with His people under grace. When the Seed came, His purpose was to close every door of access to God, but one: Jesus Christ.

Jesus, Our Mediator

Reader Study Reference, Galatians 3:19-20

The law says, "draw back." Grace says, "draw near."

...and it [the law] was appointed through angels by the hand of a mediator. Now a mediator does not mediate for one only, but God is one. (Galatians 3:19-20, brackets added for emphasis)

In the Old Covenant of law, Moses and the angels were mediators between the people and God because the people could not come near God in that covenant. In the New Covenant God Himself mediated the covenant with Himself so that man could draw near to Him.

Jesus Christ is the one and only meeting ground between God and man. Through the cross of Jesus,

Mercy and truth have met together; righteousness and peace have kissed. (Psalm 85:10)

Even to this day, the Man, Jesus Christ, intercedes for us with His blood that declares us cleansed and righteous.

There is a fountain filled with blood drawn from Emmanuel's veins
And sinners plunged beneath that flood lose all their guilty stains.[289]

It takes revelation to understand that Christ has done it all for us and continues to mediate the New Covenant on our behalf.[290] The mixture of law and grace is so appealing because it is easy to preach and easy to understand: "You are saved by faith, and the 'good news' is that you now have your part to play! You will be so fulfilled as you keep your end of the bargain. And you'll find your purpose in life!" Sounds like a great deal! But it's man-centered, and it will wear you out.

My seventeen-year-old daughter recently told me that the grace life is the hardest in one sense: we can't DO anything to be right with God. She said, "Mom, people want to DO something. They want to feel like they have accomplished something and that they have something to add. It's the hardest thing in the world to do nothing." What insight. Wish I had been that smart at seventeen.

The Law Is Not Opposed To Grace

Reader Study Reference, Galatians 3:21

Is the law then against the promises of God? Certainly not! For if there had been a law given which could have given life, truly righteousness would have been by the law. (Galatians 3:21)

Paul asked the question "is the law then against the promises of God?" because he had said just a couple of verses back that the law was added to bring out the sinfulness of sin and the guilt of man. Wouldn't that make it impossible for man to ever be right with God?

The law isn't a negation of God's promises because it actually had a purpose to lead us to the promises of God. Law and grace are not in conflict because they function in different realms. The law is the "ministry of condemnation"[291] and judges a man based on his obedience. The law operates in the seen, natural realm bringing condemnation in order to LEAD ONE TO FAITH. Faith and grace operate in the spiritual realm and bring complete union with God through the "ministry of righteousness."[292] Grace doesn't take into account obedience to laws, but assesses a man based on his faith in the finished work of Jesus.

Grace is and always has been God's heart for man! The law isn't opposed to grace because it was never intended to express God's approach towards a relationship with man. The law is NOT the basis of God's assessment of man. Faith is. A sinner who rejects Jesus is alienated from the life of God, not because he has been disobedient — his sin has been paid for and is not counted against him! Sin isn't the issue. He is alienated from the life of God because he rejects God's grace.

Is Sin the Central Issue of Life?

...so also Christ was offered once for all time as a sacrifice to take away the sins of many people. He will come again, NOT TO DEAL WITH OUR SINS, but to bring salvation to all who are eagerly waiting for him. (Hebrews 9:28, NLT, emphasis added)

Do you know why Jesus is not coming back to deal with sins? Because He already dealt with them 2000 years ago!

The challenge for people is that they can't see beyond sin. They think God assesses people based on sin, so they think it is the central issue of life. If sin were the issue for righteousness, then we would only have two options: try not to sin or say that sin isn't sin. Most of the church would never go the direction of condoning sin, so the answer is to just do better so God will be pleased with us. However, there is a growing trend towards re-interpreting scriptures to somehow prove that particular sins aren't really sins. In other words, we just misunderstood God in a few places. Under the banner of "grace" and with the intention of being inclusive and loving, some are redefining certain sins to take them out of the category of sin and put them in the category of non-sin. What would be the motivation to redefine sin? It's the same EXACT motivation as trying not to sin: to make oneself acceptable to God. Either way it's still legalism! It's what the Pharisees did. They just moved the bar so they could reach it.

We don't have anything to lose by letting sin be sin. Why? Because the Lamb of God has taken it away! The more people focus on sin or "non-sin," the more they are going to sin, and the more miserable they are going to be. Any time we focus on sin, we're back to the law. We don't have to rewrite the Bible so that people will "feel" loved. They will know and believe they are loved when they look at Jesus and see what He did for them.

The legalistic church has really found herself between a rock and a hard place as the Gospel of grace is spreading like wildfire across the globe because they don't want to disenfranchise a culture of people who have been burned by the mixture. They want to appear gracious and welcoming, so many pastors are beginning to preach, "Your sins are forgiven, past, present, and future!" But then in the next breath they talk about how serving God and not sinning will make you closer to God. It is true that a mind occupied with sin will callous our hearts toward God and make us feel like He is far away, but it doesn't ever harden His heart towards us or change the way He sees us.

As far as true righteousness is concerned, whether an action or thought is sin is completely beside the point! God doesn't determine whether He is okay with me based on whether or not I am straight or gay, healthy or gluttonous, whether I smoke, drink, chew, or hang with those who do. God is okay with me because He took all my sin away, and I BELIEVE it! He's okay with me BECAUSE OF JE-

SUS! Only when people realize this will they know how MUCH God loves them! Only when Jesus is unveiled through the preaching of the Good News will people receive the free gift of righteousness. And the more grace we hear, see, and believe, the more the sap of His love will rise up in us and sin will fall off like dried leaves.

> *He died for our sins and rose again to make us right with God, filling us with God's goodness. (Romans 4:25, The Living Bible)*

Some time ago a young man who was struggling with homosexuality reached out to me. As I was driving up to the coffee shop where we were meeting, I asked the Lord what He wanted me to say, and He only gave me one thing: ask the young man whether he believed that he was saved. After we had gotten to know each other, I asked him that simple question, and he answered that he knew that Jesus was his Savior and had died for him. After we discussed his life as a Christian, he began to share with me the torment that he was under. My heart was broken as he described the details. I sensed that the Holy Spirit's heart was broken, too, and then I heard a strong word: "Tell him he isn't going to hell." I repeated that sentence just as I heard it, and the young man broke down and bawled. He had been so desperate to hear those words! The enemy had tormented him for years with the lie that he was headed for hell. I told him that he was righteous before the Father. I unveiled Jesus to him and watched his hope return.

Whatever the sin is, the answer is to turn our focus OFF of it and ONTO Jesus. It would behoove all of us if we would refuse to be drawn into discussions about sin and only discuss the remedy. We are not required to get into endless discourse on all of the nuances of sin. If someone wants to theorize about sin, end of discussion. If somebody wants to talk about Jesus, let's talk all night!

If a believer is struggling with sin, the best thing we can do is remind him of who he is in Christ.

> *Or do you not know that the unrighteous will not inherit the kingdom of God? Do not be deceived; neither fornicators, nor idolaters, nor adulterers, nor effeminate, nor homosexuals, nor thieves, nor the covetous, nor drunkards, nor revilers, nor swindlers, will inherit the kingdom of God. Such WERE some of you; but you WERE WASHED, but you WERE SANCTIFIED, but you WERE JUSTIFIED in the name of the*

Lord Jesus Christ and in the Spirit of our God. (1 Corinthians 6:9-11, NASB)

Back to Galatians...

The Tutor

Reader Study Reference, Galatians 3:22-26

> *But the Scripture[293] has confined all under sin, that the promise by faith in Jesus Christ might be given to those who believe. But before faith came, we were kept under guard by the law, kept for the faith which would afterward be revealed. Therefore the law was our TUTOR to bring us to Christ, that we might be justified by faith. But after faith has come, we are NO LONGER UNDER THE TUTOR. For you are all sons of God through faith in Christ Jesus. (Galatians 3:22-26, emphasis added)*

Paul likened the law to a "tutor." The word translated "tutor" is the Greek word "paidagogos."[294] A "paidagogos" was a slave employed in the culture of that day who was given the responsibility of the moral supervision of a boy who was between the ages of six and sixteen. This guardian watched over the boy's behavior and made sure he followed the rules.[295] What is Paul talking about here? He's talking about the Israelites under the Ten Commandments and the rest of the law. The law was like a guardian whose job it was to make sure they obeyed. But Paul says that after faith in Christ has been revealed, we are no longer under an outward guardian to make sure we are minding our "p's and q's" because the only One who could keep the law perfectly lives in us and through us.

Heirs According to the Promise

Reader Study Reference, Galatians 3:27 - 4:3

> *For as many of you as were baptized into Christ have put on Christ. There is neither Jew nor Greek, there is neither slave nor free, there is neither male nor female; for you are all one in Christ Jesus. And if you are Christ's, then you are Abraham's seed, and heirs according to the promise. (Galatians 3:27-29)*

Think about this: an heir inherits right now. Contrast this with the "heir-apparent." For example, Prince Charles is an heir apparent. One day he will be the heir to the throne, but not until his mother dies. In fact, Prince Charles has been the heir apparent longer than any other heir in British history, having assumed that position when his mother inherited the throne in 1952.[296] That's a long time to be a prince-in-waiting. However, OUR King of kings has died and risen again, making us heirs with Him right now!

In Galatians 4, Paul uses the symbolism of being a child, unable to inherit, verses being a mature son, ready to inherit. Here are a couple of words that he uses:

- A full mature son is the Greek word "huios."[297]
- A baby, an infant, a minor is "nepios."[298]

Now I say that the heir, as long as he is a child [nepios], does not differ at all from a slave, though he is master of all but is under guardians and stewards until the time appointed by the father. (Galatians 4:1-2, brackets added for emphasis)

A child (nepios) is someone who is immature, both intellectually and morally. He's not old enough to govern his own actions. The "guardians" were the overseers of the child's person, and the "stewards" were the overseers of the child's property.[299] In other words, even though a child might be the richest little kid in the country, because of his age, he's no more privileged than the slaves. He can't enjoy his position, can't drive his dad's car, write a check, or even make a decision for himself. However, when the father dies and he leaves his inheritance, he'll leave it to his son even if an employee is more deserving.

This passage is talking about the children of Israel when they were under law in the Old Testament, and they were "nepios" (infants, not ready to inherit) until the time appointed by our heavenly Father when Jesus would come to bring all of us into sonship, "huios" (full, mature sons, ready to inherit NOW).

Even so we, when we were children, were in bondage under the elements of the world. (Galatians 4:3)

When Paul said "we," he was referring to himself and the Jewish people when they were under the law. The word "elements" is referring to the law. It's the Greek word, "stoicheion," which refers to the first principles of something.[300] It's used to refer to things in a series, such as the alphabet. In other words, the law was the "ABC's." When they came out of Egypt and made it to the foot of Mount Sinai, God gave them the Ten Commandments because they were babies. At the appointed time, Jesus would come to bring grace so that they could graduate. The law was given through Moses, but grace and truth came through Jesus Christ.[301]

The law is for "infants," not for sons who are ready to inherit. The law is for "toddlers" who can't make a decision on their own. The law is for "kindergarteners" who are learning the alphabet but can't put two letters together to make a word yet. Can you see what Paul is saying? If we lived in the confinement to external oversight of the law, we'll never walk in our inheritance as sons in grace. Law is for babies. Grace is for sons.

Adoption As Sons

Reader Study Reference, Galatians 4:4-5

> *But when the fullness of the time had come, God sent forth His Son, born of a woman, born under the law, to redeem those who were under the law, that we might receive the adoption as sons. (Galatians 4:4-5)*

The word translated "adoption" is the Greek word "huiothesia" which means "adult son-placing."[302] We have been redeemed from the slavery of the law in order that we might be placed as adult sons! That is our status under grace as opposed to the status of the Israelites under law.

The idea of "adoption" in this passage doesn't really express the depth of the word's meaning. Many of us think of adoption as taking in someone else's child as your own. That means the genetics of the child is from another set of parents, not your own. But that is not what this passage is saying. We are actually born of God as a new creation with His very own spiritual DNA. What is translated "adoption as sons" is one Greek word — "huiothesia" from the word "huios" which means full grown, mature son.

The Spirit of Sonship

Reader Study Reference, Galatians 4:6-7

> *And because you are sons [huois], God has sent forth the Spirit of His Son into your hearts, crying out, "Abba, Father!" Therefore you are no longer a slave but a son, and if a son, then an heir of God through Christ. (Galatians 4:6-7, brackets added for emphasis)*

This verse is saying that the Holy Spirit Himself cries out of our hearts, "Daddy!" It's an earnest, intense declaration of our belonging and our intimacy in the family. The presence of the Spirit of God inside proves that we are sons and daughters of God. The spirit of sonship brings with it a sense that we are right with God. The spirit of a slave brings with it the sense that we need to perform to earn the right to be in God's presence. There is no way to be at ease in the presence of our heavenly Daddy if we feel undeserving.

Under law, God was the Judge. Under grace, God is our Father. As sons we do not need to fear judgment from God.

> *For you did not receive a spirit of bondage again to fear, but you received the spirit of sonship by which we cry out Abba Father. (Romans 8:15)*

"Abba" is Aramaic for Daddy. It's the word Jesus Himself used for His Father.[303] God does not want us to have a formal uncomfortable relationship with Him that is based on fear. He wants us to have the spirit of sonship which gives us the freedom and privilege to call Him "Daddy."

Our sonship comes from three things[304]:

- It's our sense of identity.
- It's our sense of acceptance.
- It's our sense of approval.

Every human being was created to need those three things, and without them we are cannot function as healthy people. However, no human being is designed to meet our deepest need for these things. Only God can give us a true and lasting sense of belonging.

People under the performance based system of this world don't walk in the inheritance and heritage as sons of God. They don't walk with a sense of identity, approval, and acceptance released through grace. Today people are driven to gain their identities by the money they make, their appearance, their education, the achievements of their children, where they go on vacation, where they go to church, and even their ministries. Being driven by these things is a sign of religion because the law makes people insecure, always aspiring to BECOME, instead of resting in who they ARE.

Before Jesus went out into His public ministry and before He performed a single miracle or preached a sermon, the Holy Spirit came on Him and the Father said these words:

"This is my Son [identity], whom I love [acceptance]; with Him I am well pleased [approval]." (Matthew 3:17, NIV, brackets added for emphasis)

We get our identity, acceptance, and approval from being IN CHRIST. As Jesus is, so are we. As much as He is loved and accepted, so are we.

When I encountered the Spirit of Grace a few years ago on the beach, one of the greatest shifts in my paradigm was the sense of identity I received from just being God's beloved. In the ministry that I led at the time, I had a very strong identity in my role. When my mother became ill, it became necessary for me to resign my position in the ministry to care for her. My identity in that role was so deeply ingrained that it took over a year after I resigned for it to unravel. For those of us who were steeped in performance based ministry, there are no short cuts. Understanding righteousness as sons of God and gaining 100% security in our identity in Christ can take years. For me, I was too desperate and burned out to hang on to anything that had given me a sense of security outside of Christ. I felt like the woman who poured out the alabaster box at His feet. I saw what He had done for me, the extent of His forgiveness, and the unfairness of His sacrifice for me. And mostly, I saw His love. I am His beloved and He is mine. No other identity or position or title or role touches it. Now I know: I am loved. I am accepted. I am approved of.

Sarah and Hagar

Reader Study Reference, Galatians 4:21-22

To wrap up our brief study of Galatians, we'll jump down to verse 21 of Galatians 4 where Paul basically asks the Galatians, "Do you really understand what you are agreeing to by going along with these people who are trying to remove the Gospel by bringing the law back? Do you really want to go back to a legal relationship with God?"

> *Tell me, you who desire to be under the law, do you not hear the law? For it is written that Abraham had two sons: the one by a bondwoman, [Hagar, Sarah's slave] the other by a freewoman. [Sarah] (Galatians 4:21-22, brackets added for emphasis)*

If you recall, God had promised Abraham that he would be the father of many nations and that the whole world would be blessed by his Seed, Jesus. Yet nothing was happening, so when Abraham was age eighty-six, Sarah told him to bear a child with her slave, Hagar, and Abraham complied! Shortly thereafter, Abraham and Hagar brought forth Ishmael.

Ishmael and Isaac

Reader Study Reference, Galatians 4:23

> *But he who was of the bondwoman [Ishmael] was born according to the flesh, and he of the freewoman [Isaac] through promise... (Galatians 4:23, brackets added for emphasis)*

Ishmael is described by Paul as the son "born according to the flesh." This means that Ishmael was born out of Abraham's self-effort. Even at his age, Abraham was still able to father children naturally and was still "fruitful," although it was by his own self-effort. The lesson for us: don't ever fall for the lie that "success" means we are walking in God's plan! What some people call "fruit" could be the result of striving. If our success is born out of self-effort, we will have to maintain it by self-effort.

However, Isaac was described as the son of "promise." He was the fruit born out of faith. The lesson for us: every true success is birthed by grace through faith in God's promises to us. And the great news is that any fruit gained by grace is maintained by grace! The unearned favor of God will flow when we live by faith.

I have seen the deception of "success" born out of the flesh over and over in the church. The best example I have witnessed is the focus on numbers. How many are attending the services? How many are being saved? How many "re-dedicated" their lives? How many are being baptized? How many are in small groups? How many are being trained as leaders? How do we grow the church? How can we use business models to attract people? This all speaks of self-effort and a focus on the flesh rather than Jesus. Yes, there are places in the New Testament where we are given numbers of salvations, such as on the Day of Pentecost when three thousand people were saved.[305] But there are no instructions on HOW they strategized in long planning meetings to launch the church or grow the church. The Holy Spirit fell on the day of Pentecost, Peter preached about Jesus, and the church was born. Then they simply gathered to eat, fellowship, pray, hear the word being taught, and they grew in numbers daily! What attracted the people? 1) The preaching of the Gospel of the grace of Jesus Christ and 2) the resulting manifestation of the Holy Spirit in changed and healed lives.

Under grace, work is not a burden, but a joy. Under grace, we work, but as Paul said,

By the grace of God I am what I am, and His grace toward me was not in vain; but I labored more abundantly than they all, yet not I, but the grace of God which was with me. (1 Corinthians 15:10)

The sad thing about living in the sufficiency of our own effort is that we only get what we earn. The "fruit" is only the fruit of our own labor — there's no grace, no favor, except the favor we deserve. My experience with working "more abundantly than they all" under performance-based religion was that the harder I worked, the madder I got at others who didn't understand the sacrifices I was making. Everything in life became about the work. No joy, no laughter. Just a list of tasks. And when I got to the end of my strength, and I was living on fumes, I wondered what the original purpose was. Vision was sapped away. I was told that the reason I was so successful was my "stinkin tenacity," but all that produced in me was disillusionment!

Sometimes our biggest problem is our own strength. We are too smart or too strong in the flesh, and it's keeping us from our breakthrough or the manifestation of God's promise. Think about Abraham. He took matters in his own hands and had to live with his "mistake" (Ishmael) for fourteen years. Sometimes God waits to fulfill His promise to us until we have exhausted all our natural abilities and resources so there can be no mistake in recognizing "Who" is responsible. In His mercy, He closes all doors but the one of faith.

Sarah Is the Mother of Us All

Reader Study Reference, Galatians 4:24-29

Paul tells us in the next verse that these two ladies and these two sons represent the two covenants — law and grace. The Old Covenant and the New Covenant.

> *...which things are symbolic. For these are the two covenants: the one from Mount Sinai which gives birth to bondage, which is Hagar— for this Hagar is Mount Sinai in Arabia [where the law was given!], and corresponds to Jerusalem which now is, and is in bondage with her children (Galatians 4:24-25, brackets added for emphasis)*

Hagar, the slave girl, represents the bondage under the law which was given at Mount Sinai. The earthly Jerusalem of our time is still in bondage to the law. They have a zeal for God, but not according to knowledge. They are still working to establish their own righteousness and have not submitted to the gift of righteousness.[306]

> *...but the Jerusalem above is free, which is the mother of us all. For it is written: "Rejoice, O barren, You who do not bear! Break forth and shout, You who are not in labor! For the desolate has many more children than she who has a husband." (Galatians 4:26-27)*

In other words, if you are a person of grace, it might be for a moment that you don't see any results like Sarah who was barren for many years, but keep on rejoicing and keep on shouting because you will bring forth more fruit than the person of law! Remember "Sarah is the mother of us all!" Grace is our mother! Grace will be fruitful and multiply! Everything comes by promise under grace. Nothing under grace is achieved. It's only received.

> *Now we, brethren, as Isaac was, are children of promise. But, as he who was born according to the flesh [Ishmael, self-effort] then persecuted him who was born according to the Spirit [Isaac, grace through faith], even so it is now. (Galatians 4:28-29, brackets added for emphasis)*

Even so it is now... Ishmael is still persecuting Isaac. Ishmael and Isaac have the same father, but not the same mother. People of self-effort will always persecute those who preach grace and live by grace. And those who are doing the persecuting are not those outside the church. They have the same father of the faith.

What is our response? Love and grace. If we are truly of grace, we will respond with kindness to every criticism and misunderstanding. Like Jesus said of those who crucified Him,

> *"Father, forgive them, for they do not know what they do."(Luke 23:34)*

If you know who you are in Christ and the great eternal riches of His grace, you have nothing to lose by turning the other cheek. Your peace is of more value than winning an argument.

Cast her out!

Reader Study Reference, Galatians 4:30 - 5:1

> *Nevertheless what does the Scripture say? "Cast out the bondwoman and her son, for the son of the bondwoman shall not be heir with the son of the freewoman." (Galatians 4:30)*

Can you imagine the mistress living with the wife and raising the wife's child? There came a time when Sarah had to cast the bondwoman out. There comes a time when we have to stop compromising and cast the law out of our lives and our churches.

Hagar and Ishmael lived in the house with Sarah for several years. The symbolism: the law came alongside the Abrahamic Covenant of grace. However, once the promised child was born, the bondwoman and her child had to be cast out. The symbolism: when Christ came, the law was obsolete! Grace and law cannot co-exist anymore after the cross!

It seems like the body of Christ loves to talk about casting out demons, but why is it that we don't understand casting out the bond-woman? "Throw her out!" No mixture. It's all Jesus.

Some in the body of Christ today have bought into the lie that Hagar is better at raising Isaac than Sarah is. In other words, the law will do a better job at creating well-behaved sons and daughters than grace will. What are we saying to God with that mentality? We are saying that Jesus isn't enough. We are saying that His life in us won't cut it. The truth is that Sarah (grace) is fully equipped to raise her own child.

So then, brethren, we are not children of the bondwoman but of the free. Stand fast therefore in the liberty by which Christ has made us free, and do not be entangled again with a yoke of bondage. (Galatians 4:31-5:1)

We are children of the free! Free to love, free to forgive, free to inherit, free to give, free to do good works, free to bear fruit, free from sin, and free to enjoy the presence of our God!

17

The Eternal Blood of Jesus

Key scriptures:
Hebrews 8:7-13; Hebrews 9:9, 13-14, 22; Hebrews 10:1-4

A few years ago, my husband, Mark, asked a pastor if he believed that a Christian could lose his salvation. The pastor responded quickly saying, "I think it's a bad question."

Because skirting the issue by not answering it wasn't acceptable to Mark, he pressed the issue by asking the question a second time, this time in a slightly different way. "So you're saying that someone who once believed in Jesus can lose his salvation?"

The pastor was irritated and then made the age-old text book argument, "Are you trying to say that someone who says they were once a Christian and then becomes a satan worshipper is still saved?"

Mark didn't take the bait. He simply presented the question a third time, "My question is this: do you believe that a Christian who was once counted righteous by God can lose his righteousness by sinning and then have to earn back his righteousness for God to accept him?" I was present in this meeting, and it seemed to me like God

Himself was speaking through my husband — as if God had brought this man to a crossroads and was giving him an opportunity to make the right choice.

An indescribable sense of seriousness and heaviness fell in that room. That solemn moment is etched in my memory. It was as if angels were standing in attention at the utterance of this question and the gravity of it. In the brief pause while we were waiting on this man's answer, I became extremely aware of the unseen realm, and I heard the voice of the God in my spirit as clearly as I had ever heard it: "This man WILL NOT EXALT MY SON." It was as if a mighty wind blew through my spirit, taking my breath away as I felt the awesomeness of the sacrifice of Jesus. The fear of the Lord gripped me. It was not a terror that made me want to flea, but an utmost consciousness of His majesty, honor, and holiness.

In a very exasperated and deliberate tone, the pastor said, "I told you — it's a bad question and I'm not going to answer it." He then changed the subject to attempt to relieve the pressure in the room. He may have moved on, but I continued to be stunned. I had heard that doctrine espoused in one way or another my whole life; yet my awareness of the eternal blood of Jesus was so heightened at that moment that my spirit was deeply and intensely grieved.

When we believe that we can break the covenant of grace by our works, we have counted the blood of Jesus as a common thing. It is the greatest insult against the Son of God that we can make.

Overview of the Book of Hebrews

There is no more significant book than Hebrews in discovering the meaning behind the sacrificial death of Jesus.

In this brief study from the book of Hebrews, we will focus on just a few passages in Hebrews 8, 9, and 10. For context, we will begin with a very brief overview of all 13 chapters.

The book of Hebrews was written to Jewish people. Some of them were Christians, and some were on the brink of receiving Jesus as their Messiah and the final sacrifice for their sins. The entire book of Hebrews is about "better things." Each chapter contrasts Jesus in some respect with something inferior.

- **Chapters 1 and 2, Jesus is superior to the angels.** Chapters 1 and 2 contrast Jesus with the angels. Jesus is the only begotten Son of God and the third Person of the Trinity. No angel compares to Him, and no angel is a son of God.

- **Chapter 3, Jesus is superior to Moses.** Chapter 3 contrasts Moses, a faithful servant, with Jesus, the Son of God. The Son is greater than the servant. Grace is higher than law.

- **Chapter 4, Jesus is superior to Joshua.** Chapter 4 contrasts the Promised Land of rest we have in the finished work of the cross with the Promised Land that Joshua led the Israelites into. That promised land was just an earthly inheritance filled with enemies who had to be defeated. Possessing that Promised Land was dependent on their own faithfulness. The Promised Land of rest that Jesus brought to us is an unhindered, perpetual rest to be enjoyed by every believer, based on His faithfulness, not ours.

- **Chapter 5, Jesus is superior to Aaron.** Chapter 5 contrasts Jesus our High Priest in heaven with Aaron, the first high priest of Israel. The high priest stood before God on behalf of the people as their representative. If God accepted him and his sacrifice, then the people were accepted before God. Their spiritual standing depended upon his success in performing his duties as high priest. If he performed his duties according to God's instructions, the nation would be blessed; but if he failed, whether in his duties as a priest or in his morals, the nation would be cursed. Even if the high priest performed his duties perfectly his entire life, there was still no lasting value in the work of an earthly high priest because Aaron and every high priest after him were sinners by nature, and each would eventually die. Jesus, on the other hand, having died once and risen again, will NEVER die again. He is our perfect, sinless High Priest representing us before God. His perfect work has removed our sins forever!

- **Chapter 6, Jesus is the superior (and final) sacrifice** compared to all of the sacrifices of the Old Covenant. Chapter 6 contrasts the perfect hope that we can have in Jesus as the final offering with the impossibility of the Old Covenant sacrifices to save us. For those who embrace Jesus, God promises on oath: God says, "Surely blessing I will bless you, and multiplying I will multiply you." This hope is the "anchor for our soul, both sure and steadfast."

- **Chapter 7, The priesthood of Jesus is superior to the Levitical priesthood of the Old Covenant.** The priesthood of Jesus came "according to the order of Melchizedek" who was a king-priest with no record of a beginning or an end, unlike the levitical priesthood that was wrapped up in the priest's earthly genealogy. Melchizedek appears in only two verses in the entire Old Testament[307] and was a type and shadow of Jesus as the Son of God, rather than the Son of Man. He was "king of righteousness" and the "king of peace." Jesus is FOREVER the King whose word has all authority and our High Priest who lives according the power of an endless life. The levitical priesthood could only bless the people when they were faithful and curse them when they weren't. However, our King-Priest Jesus only blesses! We, the lesser, are always blessed by the Better.

- **Chapter 8, Grace is superior to the law.** Chapter 8 contrasts the Old Covenant of law with the New Covenant of grace. It's all about a better covenant based on better promises!

- **Chapter 9, Heaven is superior to the Holy of Holies of the tabernacle of Moses.** Chapter 9 contrasts the earthly man-made tabernacle of Moses with the heavenly sanctuary made without hands that was not of this creation. Jesus entered this superior sanctuary to appear in the presence of God for us; not with the blood of another, but with His own blood to forever put away sins.

- **Chapter 10, The blood of Jesus is superior to the blood of bulls and goats.** Chapter 10 contrasts the eternal efficacy of the blood of Jesus with the blood of bulls and goats which only offered temporary forgiveness.

- **Chapter 11, God provided something better for us.** Chapter 11 is the renowned "hall of fame of faith" of all the heroes from the Old Testament. These heroes looked down the corridors of time to a better resurrection than even being raised from the dead in this life. They achieved great feats of faith to see the promise of the New Covenant come to pass. They all died in faith, believing the promise that God would send salvation through a Savior. Today God has "provided something better for us." The promises have been fulfilled through Jesus, and when we are born again, we enter His heavenly kingdom immediately by the spirit and are seated in Christ at the Father's right hand.

- **Chapter 12, The "great cloud of witnesses" cheer us on.** Those heroes of the Old Testament who have gone before us join in one heavenly voice declaring our victory as they witness from the heavenly perspective. This should bring great encouragement to us to keep on keeping on and to fix our eyes on Jesus, "the author and finisher of our faith." Jesus endured persecution unto death. The writer exhorts the readers in light of the heavy persecution they faced to throw off the sin of unbelief which so easily entangles. Chapter 12 also contrasts the mountain of the law, Mount Sinai, with the mountain of the Lord, Mount Zion, the heavenly Jerusalem, where our spirits are right now!

- **Chapter 13, Concluding instructions, a benediction, and farewell.**

That's a brief overview of the main ideas of each chapter. Now we'll look at a few passages in detail.

A Better Covenant

Reader Study Reference, Hebrews 8:7-11

In Hebrews 8 the writer contrasts the Old Covenant of law with the New Covenant of grace.

For if that first covenant had been faultless, then no place would have been sought for a second. (Hebrews 8:7)

Think about what this verse is saying: if the Ten Commandments had worked to make man righteous, then there would have been no reason for the New Covenant. Jesus would not have needed to die.

Next in Hebrews 8:10-13 the writer gives the Old Testament prophecy from Jeremiah 31:31-34 about the coming New Covenant now revealed in Christ:

For this is the covenant that I will make with the house of Israel after those days, says the Lord: I will put My laws in their mind and write them on their hearts; and I will be their God, and they shall be My people. None of them shall teach his neighbor, and none his brother, saying, 'Know the Lord,' for all shall know Me, from the least of them to the greatest of them. (Hebrews 8:10-11)

Let's look at verses 10 and 11 to see what happens with this New Covenant.

"I will put My laws in their mind and write them on their hearts"
Reader Study Reference, Hebrews 8:10

Hebrews 8:10 tells us that God puts His laws in our minds, and He writes them on our hearts. What are these new laws? Are they the Ten Commandments re-stated in a kinder, gentler, more gracious manner? Absolutely not!

When Jesus taught the people before He went to the cross, He said some pretty harsh and straightforward things regarding keeping the law, such as:

If your right eye causes you to sin, pluck it out and cast it from you; for it is more profitable for you that one of your members perish, than for your whole body to be cast into hell. And if your right hand causes you to sin, cut it off and cast it from you... (Matthew 5:29-30)

Did Jesus really intend for people to start plucking out eyeballs and cutting off limbs? Most of us look at that passage and say, "No, that's just symbolism. Jesus didn't really mean that." Really?

Throughout the all of the years of Hebrew history under the law, no one had been able to keep the law completely. If under the New Covenant we are to believe that the laws He puts on our hearts are actually the Ten Commandments, we would need to decide what to do with His teachings in the four Gospels. There are basically three choices: 1) He's instructing us to pluck out our eyeballs and cut off our limbs to keep us from sinning, or 2) He's exaggerating to make a point and simply intends to help us when we try our hardest (God helps those who help themselves), or 3) Jesus was speaking to people who were under the law at that time (the Jewish people) to show them their inability to keep it.

Jesus meant what He said. Pluck them out and cut them off. The Pharisees had watered down the law and tinkered with it so they could give the appearance that they were keeping it and were superior to the people, and Jesus exposed their hypocrisy. Jesus did not come to be another, better, superior Moses with a new improved set of stones. Those stones could not be more perfect than when God wrote on them with His own finger. Jesus didn't raise the bar of the law with His standards. He raised the bar from where the legalists (the Pharisees) had lowered it so that they could appear righteous BACK to where it was intended to be. However, He did not restore the unbending standard of the law so that the we could reach it, but in order to show us that we couldn't! He wants us to receive righteousness as a gift, by faith!

Here's what Grace (from the inside) will do that the law (from the outside) never could:[308]

First commandment: The law will command you "Thou shalt have NO other gods before Me," but only Grace will give you a heart of worship for your King springing forth from a revelation of His amazing unmerited favor and extravagant love.

Second commandment: The law will command you "Thou shalt NOT make unto thee any graven image," but only Grace can capture your heart's desires more than the things of the world as your eyes are opened to the wealth of your inheritance in Christ and every spiritual blessing stored up for you in heavenly places.

Third commandment: The law will command you "Thou shalt NOT take the name of the Lord thy God in vain," but only Grace will inspire words of praise and honor from a heart overflowing with gratitude.

Fourth commandment: The law will command you "Remember the sabbath day, to keep it holy," but only Grace gives you uninterrupted rest in perpetual fellowship with the Father, Son, and Holy Spirit.

Fifth commandment: The law will command you "Honor thy father and thy mother," but only Grace opens your ears to hear your parents' heart of love for you and the ability to love them back. Where there has been abuse and neglect, Grace releases your heavenly Father's heart for restoration, commitment to healing, and the ability to forgive just as you have been forgiven.

Sixth commandment: The law will command you "Thou shalt NOT kill," but only Grace will give you a love that will cover over a multitude of sins.

Seventh commandment: The law will command you "Thou shalt NOT commit adultery," but only Grace will give you passion for our spouse.

Eighth commandment: The law will command you "Thou shalt NOT steal," but only Grace gives you a heart that trusts the Lord to provide.

Ninth commandment: The law will command you "Thou shalt NOT bear false witness against thy neighbor," but only Grace will give you the security that comes from knowing that if God is for you, who can be against you?

Tenth commandment: The law will command you "Thou shalt NOT covet," but only Grace will give you contentment with what you have.

God found fault with the old system of dependence on the flesh of man. Under the New Covenant we have NEW commandments in a new system of dependence on the Holy Spirit! We love today because He has first loved us.[309] We forgive today because we have been forgiven — past tense.[310] Jesus gave us a new commandment to love one another AS He has loved us.[311] The order has been completely flipped. We don't give to get; we give because we have everything as sons and daughters of God.

The Old Covenant law was so burdensome that the people begged that the words not be spoken to them. The writer of Hebrews says "they could not endure what was commanded."[312] In Acts 15, Peter argued with those who wanted to bring the law back into the early church:

> *Now therefore, why do you test God by putting a yoke on the neck of the disciples which neither our fathers nor we were able to bear? (Acts 15:10)*

In Matthew 11, Jesus was speaking to people who were heavy laden under the bondage of the law when He said:

> *Are you tired? Worn out? Burned out on religion? Come to Me. Get away with Me and you'll recover your life. I'll show you how to take a real rest. Walk with Me and work with Me—watch how I do it. Learn the unforced rhythms of grace. I won't lay anything heavy or ill-fitting on you. Keep company with Me and you'll learn to live freely and lightly. (Matthew 11:28-30, The Message)*

Jesus came to do away with the whole system of the law. He replaced the relationship based on law with the relationship based on faith:

- He replaced labor with rest.
- He replaced fear of punishment with perfect love.
- He replaced separation with union with Him.

John compared the new commandments of Jesus with the oppressive commandments of the law:

> *For this is the love of God, that we keep His commandments. And His commandments ARE NOT BURDENSOME. (1 John 5:3, emphasis added)*

Imagine commandments with no burden! The "commandments" of Christ are not the Mosaic law or any aspect of the law. The law of Christ is not the law of Moses. It's not the ministry of death and condemnation.[313] It's the law of the Spirit of life in Christ Jesus![314] His laws are...

> *...the royal law of love... (James 2:8)*

> *...the perfect law of liberty... (James 1:25)*

And this is His commandment: that we should believe on the name of His Son Jesus Christ and love one another, as He gave us commandment. (1 John 3:23)

Bear one another's burdens, and so fulfill the law of Christ. (Galatians 6:2)

All of this is possible because in this New Covenant of grace we are in union with the Lord!

"I will be their God, and they shall be My people"

Reader Study Reference, Hebrews 8:10

I will be their God, and they shall be My people. (Hebrews 8:10)

Under the New Covenant God says He will be our God, and we will be His people. Whenever God said that phrase in the Old Testament, it was related to a miraculous intervention on His part. If the people heard that statement, they knew they could expect supernatural signs and wonders directly from God Himself.

If you are sick, hear God say to you, "I am your Healer."

By His stripes you WERE healed. (1 Peter 2:24, emphasis added)

If you are suffering financially, hear God say to you, "I am your Provider."

For you know the GRACE of our Lord Jesus Christ, that though He was rich, yet for your sakes He became poor, that you through His poverty might become rich. (2 Corinthians 8:9, emphasis added)

If you are lacking peace in your life, hear God say to you, "I am your everlasting Peace."

Peace I leave with you, My peace I give to you; not as the world gives do I give to you. Let not your heart be troubled, neither let it be afraid. (John 14:27)

"All shall know Me, from the least of them to the greatest of them"

Reader Study Reference, Hebrews 8:11

> *None of them shall teach his neighbor, and none his brother, saying, 'Know the Lord,' for all shall know Me, from the least of them to the greatest of them. (Hebrews 8:11)*

God says no one will need to teach his neighbor saying, "Know the Lord." Why? Because all will know Him! The first time the word "know" is used in verse 11 ("Know the Lord"), it's the Greek word "ginosko," and it means "to learn to know, come to know, get a knowledge of."[315] Someone would need to tell you this type of knowledge for you to know it. It's the kind of knowledge that someone would give to another who was ignorant of God. Under the Old Covenant the priest was the intermediary between the people and God, and he gave them the knowledge of God and the law.

The second time the word "know" is used in verse 11 ("all shall know Me"), it's a DIFFERENT Greek word, "oida," which speaks of an absolute knowledge of something.[316] Under the New Covenant, we do not have someone standing between us and God. The Holy Spirit lives inside of us, and we have a personal, direct relationship with God. All will intimately know Him from the least to the greatest in the New Covenant by the Holy Spirit who lives inside of us! There is no more hierarchy!

> *[Jesus said] "the Helper, the Holy Spirit, whom the Father will send in My name, He will teach you all things, and bring to your remembrance all things that I said to you." (John 14:26, brackets added for emphasis)*

Knowing that the Spirit lives in us and will guide us into all truth should bring great peace and confidence. However, when we don't believe that we can hear Him, fear will creep in. Religion teaches that only "men of God" hear from the Lord, and we must be dependent on them. Legalism has convinced people that only certain men have the anointing of God and speak for Him. Even with good intentions, leaders often abuse their spiritual authority and cause great insecurity in the body of Christ. Under religion we were programmed to be spoon fed by men, so that when our eyes are opened to grace, we might find it very uncomfortable to listen to the voice of the anointing within for ourselves. We ask, "What if I'm wrong?" There is a witness of truth in our spirit, but our flesh is fearful. Good leaders will encourage other believers to listen to the voice of the Spirit and trust it. Good leaders will encourage other believers to grow in the maturity and security in their identity in Christ.

> *But the anointing which you have received from Him abides in you, and you do not need that anyone teach you; but as the same anointing teaches you concerning all things, and is true, and is not a lie, and just as it has taught you, you will abide in Him. (1 John 2:27)*

Officer Hiroo Onoda

People who lean on other people to speak for God are easily deceived. A great illustration of this can be seen in the story of a Japanese army officer in World War II.[317]

In 1944 a young Japanese intelligence officer named Hiroo Onoda was sent to the Philippines to go behind enemy lines during the war to gather intelligence and conduct guerrilla warfare. His orders from his commanding officers were simple: "You are absolutely forbidden to die by your own hand. It may take three years, it may take five, but whatever happens, we'll come back for you. Until then, so long as you have one soldier, you are to continue to lead him. You may have to live on coconuts. If that's the case, live on coconuts! Under no circumstances are you to give up your life voluntarily."

He and three other men comprised a small cell gathering intelligence and conducting guerrilla warfare in the jungles of the Philippines. In August of 1945, Japan surrendered to the Allies, ending the war, but Onoda was so deep in the jungle that he was unaware of it. A couple of months later Onoda and his guys came across a paper flyer saying "The war ended August 15th. Come down from the mountains!" They decided that it was Allied propaganda, so they continued to fight the war following the instructions they had been given. The people on the island became fed up with being shot at by Onoda and his men so they hired a plane to drop flyers all over the jungle instructing them to surrender because the war was over. Once again the guys believed it was the Allies trying to trick them.

More flyers and photos of other soldiers with the families back home were dropped in an effort to convince Onoda that the war was over. There were even pleas from loudspeakers begging them to give up, but Onoda maintained that it was all just a hoax. His cell continued to perform their sworn duty, but they became very paranoid and isolated themselves even more. Over the course of time, Onoda's three comrades died, and he was left alone.

Thousands of people over the years attempted to find Onoda, but he masterfully hid himself. After Onoda was hold up in the jungles of the Philippians for twenty-nine years, a college student on a world tour decided that one of the things on his travel agenda would be to find Onoda. Low and behold, he was successful! Once again, however, Onoda did not believe that Japan could have surrendered. He was still waiting for his commanding officer to come and get him. So the college student went out and found Onoda's former commander who was now retired and working in a book store, and brought him from Japan to Onoda. The old man told Onoda the war was over and to come on home. This, of course, came as a crushing blow to Onoda who had wasted most of his life believing a lie!

There is freedom in grace. We are no longer under the bondage of the priestly system where only one man can hear from God. Under the New Covenant all will know Him, from the least to the greatest.

"I will remember their sins no more"

Reader Study Reference, Hebrews 8:12-13

Let's continue in the next verse in Hebrews 8:

For I will be merciful to their unrighteousness, and their sins and their lawless deeds I will remember no more." In that He says, "A new covenant," He has made the first obsolete. (Hebrews 8:12-13)

That last statement is what makes everything else happen. God says, "I will put My laws on their mind, I will be their God, all will know Me... BECAUSE "I will be merciful to their unrighteousness." God has already "remembered" all of our sins when Jesus bore them on the cross and was punished in our place. Our response is simply to believe it.

The Blood

Reader Study Reference, Hebrews 9:22

The writer of Hebrews continues into chapter 9 with the theme of chapter 8 by contrasting the Old Covenant of law and the New Covenant of grace. To understand the book of Hebrews, context is helpful. In Hebrews 9 we find the reference to the tabernacle "made with hands."[318] This was the portable temple that God told Moses to build after He gave the law, and it was the place where the blood sacrifices of spotless animals would be made to atone for the sins of the people. Each part of the tabernacle was a "shadow" of the better things to come under the New Covenant. In Hebrews 9 and 10 the high priest is a central figure because he was a shadow of our High Priest, Jesus. The sacrifices made by the priests were also shadows of the Lamb of God who would shed His blood to remove the sins of the world forever.

The importance of the blood sacrifice cannot be overstated in our study of the scriptures.

For without the shedding of blood, there is no forgiveness. (Hebrews 9:22, NLT)

Sin is lethal and has contaminated every human being since Adam. The holiness and justice of God requires that sin must be punished by death.

The soul who sins shall die. (Ezekiel 18:4)

Blood signifies death. When we see blood, we know that someone has either been injured or has died. Blood is supposed to stay IN-SIDE the body because the life is in the blood.

For the life of the flesh is in the blood, and I have given it to you upon the altar to make atonement for your souls; for it is the blood that makes atonement for the soul. (Leviticus 17:11)

Sin and death are represented by the shedding of blood.

For the wages of sin is death, but the gift of God is eternal life in Christ Jesus our Lord. (Romans 6:23)

For as in Adam all die, even so in Christ all shall be made alive. (1 Corinthians 15:22)

The Day of Atonement

In the Old Covenant system, God gave instructions to Moses to assign each of the tribes of Israel roles and duties to be carried out in the building, assembling, and offerings of the tabernacle. The tribe of Levi was given the role of the priesthood who would administer the offerings of animal sacrifices to cover the sins of the people. One Levite from the line of Aaron (Moses' brother) would be the high priest over Israel.[319]

In the outer court of the tabernacle, the priests would sacrifice various offerings to God for their own sins as well as for the sins of the people. There were five kinds of offerings: the burnt offering, the grain offering, the peace offering, the sin offering, and the trespass offering. There were daily sacrifices, weekly sacrifices on the Sabbath, sacrifices associated with each of the seven feasts of Israel, and the sacrifices on the Day of Atonement. Can you imagine the carnage and the bloodiness of tabernacle?

Hebrews 9 and 10 speak specifically about the Day of Atonement. On the Day of Atonement once a year, the high priest would make the regular daily offerings, but he would also make additional sacrifices of a bull and TWO goats.

In the tabernacle was a tent which had two parts, the Holy Place and the Most Holy Place, also called the Holy of Holies. The Holy of Holies was the "earthly sanctuary" where God's presence would dwell.[320] Only the high priest could stand in the presence of God, and only once a year on the Day of Atonement did the high priest enter in order to sprinkle the blood of the bull and ONE of the goats on the Mercy Seat of the Ark of the Covenant which containing the two stones on which were etched the Ten Commandments. This was so that the sins of entire nation of Israel would be covered, and the people would be blessed for another year. As long as the Old Covenant tabernacle system (or later on, the temple system) was in place, the Holy of Holies was closed to anyone but the high priest. In other words, God was INAPPROACHABLE. No one else in all of Israel could enter the Holy of Holies and live. Even the high priest himself would drop dead if he failed to perform every ritual perfectly.

If the sacrifice of the blood of the bull and the goat was acceptable, and the high priest came out alive with his hands raised pronouncing a blessing on the nation, everyone would cheer because they knew that this meant their harvests would be plentiful, and they would be victorious over their enemies. However, if the sacrifice was not acceptable or the high priest did not perform his duty perfectly, he would not come out of the Holy of Holies alive, and all of Israel would know that they would be under a curse that year.

The Scapegoat

As I mentioned, there were two goats sacrificed on the Day of Atonement. The other goat would be the "scapegoat."[321] The high priest would lay both of his hands on the head of the goat and confess all of the sins of the people, and all of those sins would be transferred to the goat. The "scapegoat" would then be driven into the wilderness carrying[322] the sins of the people "as far as the east is from the west."[323]

As the goat goes into the wilderness, it will carry all the people's sins upon itself into a desolate land. (Leviticus 16:22, NLT)

This scapegoat is a shadow of Jesus, our Scapegoat. All of our sins were laid upon Him, and He was led away to be crucified outside the gate of the city because all of our uncleanness was imputed to Him. He became our sin that we might become His righteousness.[324] We were all like sheep who had gone astray, but all of our iniquity was laid on Jesus.[325] He was despised and rejected as the sinner of all sinners as He made intercession for us.[326]

Jesus is the superior substance of every inferior shadow. Sadly, people today are still living in the shadows of Old Covenant thinking as if Jesus has not removed our sin.

With that context, we will see how the shadows of the Old Covenant system could never truly fix the problem of sin or the consciousness of it.

A Perfect Conscience

Reader Study Reference, Hebrews 9:9

> *It was symbolic for the present time in which both gifts and sacrifices are offered which cannot make him who performed the service perfect in regard to the conscience... (Hebrews 9:9)*

Even with all of the daily, weekly, and annual sacrifices of the Old Covenant system, the conscience of the offerer would never be clean. The "shadows" could never permanently remove the guilt and stain of sin. There was always a sense of incompleteness because the job of removing sin could never be finished with the inferior blood of animal sacrifices.

Today, however, we can have a perfect conscience. A perfect conscience says to us we are complete in Christ. The moment we receive Jesus, in God's eyes we are perfect in Him. There is a progressive discovery for us of the perfection of our new identity in Christ and a progressive maturity that will result, but more perfect we cannot be.

A Cleansed Conscience

Reader Study Reference, Hebrews 9:13-14

> *For if the blood of bulls and goats and the ashes of a heifer, sprinkling the unclean, sanctifies for the purifying of the flesh, how much more shall the blood of Christ, who through the eternal Spirit offered Himself without spot to God, cleanse your conscience from dead works to serve the living God? (Hebrews 9:13-14)*

The phrase in verse 14 that says "through the eternal SPIRIT offered HIMSELF without spot to GOD" has all three persons of the Trinity represented. This New Covenant was an intrinsic covenant that was made within the infallibility of the Trinity so there is nothing we can do to break it. The terms of the covenant are not dependent on our faithfulness to keep it because God keeps the covenant that He made within Himself. The only way that the covenant could be broken would be if Jesus sinned or Jesus died. Neither is possible! God is faithful in His integrity to judge Christ's righteousness as perfect and Christ's work of cleansing us from all unrighteousness as complete.

Not only does the blood of Jesus cleanse us from all unrighteousness, believing this truth should cleanse our conscience! If our conscience is cleansed, then we will be free from dead works. What are dead works? Dead works are "Christian" religious activities that we do, thinking that by doing them we will attain good standing before God. In other words, dead works are simply self-righteousness. We all fall into self-righteousness when we don't have a cleansed conscience, or a conscience that is free of guilt.

Have you ever felt shame or guilt and stayed in it for a period of time with your mind replaying your failure? Well, if we receive guilt, we will end up doing something to try to make ourselves right before God. For example, we'll try to make restitution, make resolutions to stop the bad behavior, pray harder, go to more church services, serve more… A conscience struggling with sins will sow the seeds of self-righteousness. The goal of self-righteousness is to atone for — COVER — sin.

Self-righteousness, the Door of the Works of the Flesh

Self-righteousness is the open door to the works of the flesh. Before the works of the flesh manifest (for example, adultery, fornication, selfish ambitions, heresies, envy, drunkenness[327]), guilt causes us to work on ourselves to clean up our act. Whenever we get into self-righteousness, in time sin will be the result. We sin, then we try to fix it, then we fail again, then we experience shame, then we sin again, attempt to fix it, fail, experience shame, and on it goes, like a vicious circle with no end.

Cycles of sin develop because of self-condemnation. And if we condemn ourselves, we cannot get out of the cycle of sin. Why? Because we have identified ourselves by our behavior instead of by our identity in Christ. It's an identity issue. We will act like what we believe we are.

The more people think that God demands righteousness by performance, the more they say, "I can't live this Christian life. It's just too hard for me!" But in reality, the Christian life is not too hard — it's impossible! There's only one Person who lived up to the standards that God's holiness requires, and His name is Jesus Christ. We simply allow Him to live through us by resting in Him. The first thing we need to know, though, is that we are holy and blameless at the core of who we are. There is no sin in our spirit!

The Old Covenant Could Never Make Us Perfect

Reader Study Reference, Hebrews 10:1

Now we'll move into Hebrews 10 where we'll see more confirmation that Jesus' blood has forever made us holy.

For the law, having a shadow of the good things to come, and not the very image of the things, can never with these same sacrifices, which they offer continually year by year, make those who approach perfect. (Hebrews 10:1)

The priests of the Old Covenant would offer the blood of bulls and goats and lambs to God continually year by year to cover the sins of the people, but these offerings could never make the people perfect. Perfect in what sense? In Hebrews 9:9 we saw what "perfect" means. In the context it means "perfect in regard to conscience."

The atonement of the priestly sacrifices was just a covering — like sweeping the sins of the people under the rug. Each year more would be swept under the rug, but it was still there. The rug would get thicker and thicker, looking clean on the outside, but in reality it was dirty on the inside. Atone is the Hebrew word "kaphar" which means "to cover."[328] Sins were covered, but still there. The Day of Atonement was a annual reminder that the Lamb of God had not yet come.

ONCE Purified

Reader Study Reference, Hebrews 10:2

For then would they not have ceased to be offered? For the worshipers, once purified, would have had no more consciousness of sins. (Hebrews 10:2)

Because the sacrifices never worked, the worshippers were never "once purified." This verb is in the perfect passive participle.[329] Perfect means it's one act that needs never be repeated. If the sinners had been ONCE purified then they would have had no reason to have sin on their conscience.

Hallelujah! The true Lamb came, lifted up the rug, and took away all of our sin by His blood. Now nothing is covered. Can I encourage you with a shocking truth? God doesn't see you covered in anything. He sees you — the real you — as completely righteous and holy and blameless.

Even as we begin to understand our righteousness as a new creation in Christ, often we still think of ourselves as being "sinners saved by grace." We think of God looking at us through the "filter" of the blood of Jesus. When He looks at us, He sees what APPEARS to be holy. In other words, we are only "covered" in the blood of Jesus, and what He is looking at is Jesus, not us. But the truth is that He IS looking at us! The truth is that we — the REAL you and I — are perfect! Our true selves have been completely severed from the flesh. The more we realize this, the more we will behave accordingly! WE HAVE BEEN ACCEPTED BY GOD BECAUSE WE HAVE NO SIN IN US!!

Come Boldly

We hear sometimes that we need to keep on asking Jesus to wash us with His blood. We don't realize that we are actually devaluing the blood of Christ in our minds by saying such things. The blood of Jesus has washed us once forever, and God wants us to have a clean conscience before Him so that we come boldly and confidently to His throne of grace.

Let us therefore come boldly to the throne of grace, that we may obtain mercy and find grace to help in time of need. (Hebrews 4:16)

The Greek word for boldly, "parresia," means "freedom in speaking, openly, without concealment, with free and fearless confidence!"[330] There is no need to fear in the presence of God! Many of us are afraid of the presence of God because we are afraid our sins will be exposed, and He will judge us, condemn us, and punish us. Yet His light only shows one thing: the excellent job that His Son did in removing those sins!

Sin Consciousness

Is it hard to believe that God doesn't want you to be conscious of sin? Isn't sin consciousness what we've been taught our whole lives? But think about what happens when we focus on our sin and our flesh. We feel unworthy in God's presence. We hesitate in awkwardness and struggle to spend ten minutes talking to Him. Usually it's all one-sided — we just mutter a few things and don't listen for a response, anxious to move on with our day.

For the mind set on the flesh is death, but the mind set on the Spirit is life and peace. (Romans 8:6, NASB)

It's so clear that God is not interested in us being self-occupied, introspective, and focused on the sins of the flesh. He wants our minds on Jesus and on others! But it seems like the very goal of Christianity is often the opposite. The thinking is that the more conscious we are of sin and our unworthiness before God, the more pleasing we are to Him. In fact, we're told we need to search our hearts and ask God to reveal any sinful ways in us before we can worship Him or take the Lord's Supper or pray for someone. However, the answer is not to focus on sin, but to turn to Jesus!

In the past I used to lead people in searching for sins. Don't let this startle you for I had good intentions because I believed that sin drove away the presence of God and caused Him to withdraw His fellowship with us. In training leaders I felt a responsibility to encourage them to go through a cleansing process regularly, and especially before they ministered to others. The problem with all of this is that it hinders God's grace from being received. The barrier of sin HAS BEEN removed by the cross! We have been cleansed. Jesus' blood either worked or it didn't!

Sin consciousness gives people the perception that the debt still exists. We think that we'll be forgiven if we daily confess all of our sins and repent and beg for forgiveness as if the debt hasn't already been paid. These "sacrifices" do nothing to cleanse the conscience. Like the Old Covenant sacrifices they present the idea that we're on credit with God, and we still owe Him. This is serious! If you owe someone, you won't be comfortable around them. This is the reason the enemy wants the veil of condemnation to remain over the eyes of the church. If we believed that we don't owe God anything, we would relax in His presence, enjoy Him, and hear His voice clearly.

If we feel an indebtedness towards God, we will try to compensate even though in our heart of hearts we know that there is nothing we can possibly do to truly relieve the debt. I can remember thinking that Jesus had done so much for me, and I was so undeserving that I should be His slave for life. It wasn't too much to ask, was it? I used to sit on the front row in church services with my hands held high, tears streaming down my cheeks, singing my heart out, "There's sooooo much more I could give..." I was consumed with my sense of indebtedness to God. I was so focused on works that I was getting only four or five hours of sleep at night, using the balance of the day trying to repay Jesus and attempting to find more to give Him because I so longed to please Him.

This line of thinking is completely contrary to the Gospel.

Insufficient Funds

Reader Study Reference, Hebrews 10:3-4

> *But in those sacrifices there is a reminder of sins every year. For it is not possible that the blood of bulls and goats could take away sins. (Hebrews 10:3-4)*

If we were indebted to God, it would be like having insufficient funds in the bank when we go to cash a check. I looked up the simple definition of "insufficient funds": "NSF occurs when an account cannot provide adequate funds to satisfy the demand of a payment."[331] Imagine you want to pay off a debt, and you give your creditor a check for the amount of the debt, but there aren't enough funds in your account. When the creditor goes to cash the check, the bank teller will get an error message that says "insufficient funds."

"A reminder of sins" is like the bank saying that the funds were insufficient to satisfy the demand of the payment, and the creditor isn't satisfied. It means the debt is still on the books. Consciousness of sins says that the cross of Jesus didn't pay the debt and the Father has rejected the blood of His Son. It's like saying the spotless Lamb of God was not perfect and still has a spot on Him! This disparages both Jesus and God the Father!

The blood of bulls and goats only offered short-term relief, but couldn't fix the problem. Many Christians today believe the blood of Jesus has only cleansed our past sins, and we must be forgiven as we go. However, that's no more effective than the blood of bulls and goats and will keep us constantly focused on the flesh.

The blood of Jesus gives us eternal redemption and the freedom to live with a perfect conscience before God. Yes, the news seems to good to be true, but it's true. He wants us to have a sin-free consciousness. When our minds aren't on sin, we might just find it easier to set our minds on things above.

One Sacrifice For Sins Forever

Key scriptures:

Hebrews 10:5-23, Hebrews 10:26-31, Hebrews 12:1-8

Since I encountered the Spirit of grace (a day I will never forget), my life has been marked with joy. I know what "joy inexpressible" is now. There are times that I just can't find words for the ecstasy I feel inside. It's like the people who were witnesses to the healing of the man lowered through the roof:

> *"And overwhelming astonishment and ecstasy seized them all, and they recognized and praised and thanked God; and they were filled with and controlled by reverential fear and kept saying, We have seen wonderful and strange and incredible and unthinkable things today!" (Luke 5:26, Amplified Bible, emphasis added)*

The heart of that story is the reason for my joy:

> *"Which is easier, to say, 'Your sins are forgiven you,' or to say, 'Rise up and walk'? But that you may know that the Son of Man has power on earth to forgive sins..." (Luke 5:23-24, emphasis added)*

My sins are forgiven. Sounds so simple. Have I not known that my whole life? I was raised in the church, but somehow I missed it all those years. Now there is "overwhelming astonishment and ecstasy" at the thought. It's what the prophets studied about salvation and the "grace that would come to you..."[332]

My Grace Journal

I want to share with you some "journal entries" from this glorious unfolding of the revelation of grace in my life. Several years ago during the first year of my ambush of Grace, one morning I wrote down a list of what brought me ecstasy, a river of grateful thoughts to our Lord:

- I am forgiven of my sins — past, present, and future. Not just of the sins I know of. Not just the sins that I have confessed. Not just my past sins. All of them.

- When God looks at me, He sees me as righteous, not sinful.

- God is happy with me, not mad at me.

- I don't have to prove anything to God. He is pleased with me.

- God isn't a nagger who convicts me of sin, always pointing out my faults. He's the one who convicts me of righteousness — His righteousness. He's the encouraging voice that says to me when I fall, "Tricia, get back up. That's not who you are. You aren't a sinner. You are the righteousness of God in Christ."

- God doesn't remember my sin. He only remembers the good that I do.

- When I look at Jesus, I am looking at God.

- Jesus healed everyone.

- Jesus smiles and laughs.

- Jesus is never in a hurry.

- His feet bring Good News. I am the lady who washed them and poured out her love on them. I am forgiven so much. Oh, how I love Him!

- The blood of Jesus perpetually cleanses. I sin, I'm clean. I sin, I'm clean. Grace is greater than all my sin.

- I don't want to sin anymore.

- God's demonstration of love overwhelms me. The blood trickling through the nail-piercings in His hands says, "My peace I leave you."

- The blood dripping from his head from the crown of thorns says, "You are whole."

- The blood gushing from His side says, "I love you."

- The stripes on His back say, "You are healed."

- His bruises, His face all torn up, His head hung low, His nakedness all says to me, "I became sin that you might become righteous."

- He was forsaken that I might be accepted.

- He became poor that I might become rich.

- He said, "My God, My God! Why have you forsaken Me?!" So that I might say, "My God, My God! Why have you so blessed me?!"

- He called God "God" that I might call Him "Father."

- I don't have to focus on my love for Him anymore. Now I just enjoy His love for me.

- No more work. Rest. Labor to enter the rest. Work at not working. Labor more abundantly — but not I, the grace of God in me.

- The power for my wholeness, healing, and peace is in the simplicity of the Gospel. Not in fasting. Not in prayer. Not in serving. All of that is good, but that's not where the power is. It's in the Gospel — Jesus Christ laid down His life for me.

- There is nothing standing between me and God anymore. Nothing. Not even my sin.

- I am the temple of the Holy Spirit. He will never leave me nor forsake me. He will abide with me forever and ever and ever. Even when I fail, He will not leave me.

- I am a prisoner of hope. Even if I tried to run, I couldn't get away from His love!

That was year one. Another year passed, and it was a year of trials and heartbreak, the most difficult year of my life. The deepest

310 • UNVEILING JESUS

heartbreak of that year was the loss of my mom to cancer. As I lay on the bed with my mom and best friend in her last days on the earth, I learned what it really meant to trust God. Through that year, in a way I have no words to explain, I still had the river of joy unspeakable. The other devastation of that year was a massive loss of friendship because of persecution from teaching this beautiful message of grace. Even with deep sadness from my mother's home-going and great suffering from rejection, my list of thoughts that brought heavenly ecstasy was growing, not diminishing. I learned to look at that which is UNSEEN, and I added some things to my list:

- The work is finished.
- His work is completely complete and perfectly perfect.
- His blood is sprinkled on the Mercy Seat....and I am beginning to understand what that means.
- He is the Mercy Seat.
- He is my High Priest seated there.
- His blood cries forgiveness, justification, acquittal, healing, wholeness, peace for me.
- He is completely glorified.
- His smile towards me is constant.
- At any given moment at any time of day, I can look straight into His face.
- His eyes are pools of love for me.
- I am a precious jewel in His heart that shimmers and shines with beauty.
- He is my Best Friend.
- He is my Lover.
- He is the One who sticks closer than a brother.
- I am His and He is mine.
- He feeds on HIS LOVE FOR ME.
- I feed on HIS LOVE FOR ME.
- I am in Him in the highest heaven.

- Nothing can ever separate us again.
- We are completely intertwined.
- We are one.
- Because of His blood, I am holy.
- Because of His blood, I am blameless.
- Because of His blood, I stand in the presence of God without a single fault.
- As He is, so am I in this world.
- There are no limits in the Spirit realm of heaven.
- All things are possible to Him [Jesus] who believes.
- I have the faith of God.
- Whatever He did on earth, I can do.
- Faith isn't the bridge. Jesus is the bridge.
- I am a new creation in Him. Nothing like the old.
- Because He obeyed, I am blessed.
- Because He obeyed, everything I touch is blessed.
- He is my King of kings. I am a king.
- He is my Lord of lords. I am a lord.
- He is my High Priest. I am a priest to God.
- He is the firstborn among many brethren. I am a daughter of the Most High God.
- My name is written in the book of life.
- The Good News is better than I thought.
- It gets better every day.

Another year passed… and wow! As I beheld the wonder of my God, I saw more and more… As I have experienced the joy of my salvation, I went from tears of healing and restoration that seemed like they would never end to an awe that absolutely overwhelmed me every single day, and then on to an insatiable desire to share this love and spread this Gospel to others! The river of joyful thoughts grew:

- He loves EVERYONE just like He loves me.

- He told me not to see anyone after the flesh — why? Because He sees no one after the flesh.[333]

- He told me not to call anyone unholy — why? Because no one is beyond the grip of His grace.[334]

- There are only two kinds of people: those who are in Him and those who are not....yet.

- His heart of love burns for those who are not in Him....yet.

- My heart of love burns for those who are not in Him....yet.

- He did NOT come to condemn the world, but to save it.

- He loved me while I was still in my sin, darkened in my understanding.

- He loves EVERYONE that way.

- His love knows no boundaries.

- His love is in me...my love knows no boundaries.

- There is only one thing that can penetrate a heart of stone: His love.

- The world is dying because they don't know His love.

- The world will know His love because He Himself will flow through me in rivers of living water, and the world will be drenched in pools of affection and forgiveness and acceptance and joy.

- In Christ there is no condemnation. He took care of sin. He took it away. What the law couldn't do, He did. HE DID IT! HE REALLY DID IT!

- When God looks at me, He sees ME and He likes what He sees.

- This news is too good to keep to myself.

Yes, the news is too good to just enjoy for myself. We must tell the world that Jesus loves them. Today, the truth that I ponder most is the fact that Jesus chose to die for me. Some days when I am contemplating this truth, I come close to going beneath the surface into the meaning of it, and I find myself unable to contain even the slightest revelation of it. It's too wonderful for me to handle! But in my spirit

I desire to go there even if it's by one glimpse at a time, and even if it takes all of eternity to grasp the depth of what He chose to do for me.

He Chose To Come For Us

Reader Study Reference, Hebrews 10:5

In Hebrews 12 we find a familiar verse that we often quote: "for the joy that was set before Him [Jesus] endured the cross."[335] The idea is that the Lord Jesus endured the sufferings of the cross because there was a reward of joy set before Him. This interpretation is based on the use of the word "for." He endured suffering "for" the joy that He would receive. However, the word translated "for" in most English translations is the Greek preposition "anti," and it actually means "instead of."[336] In other words, Jesus traded the joy and the glory that He already possessed in the bosom of the Father before the world was even created for the shame He would endure on the cross when He received all of our sin. The reason He is our great Hero is because "instead of" the joy He already had in the Father, He received the humiliation and death that we deserved. It was His choice to die for us!

Therefore, when He came into the world, He said: "Sacrifice and offering You did not desire, but a body You have prepared for Me." (Hebrews 10:5)

Jesus became human. Why? Because as God He could not die. Jesus was born as a human the same way we are born, however, instead of being conceived by the seed of a mortal man with sinful flesh, He was conceived by the Holy Spirit and born of a virgin. Jesus' blood came straight from heaven from His Father. His blood was holy, royal, sinless, and divine. That's why His blood can save us and wash our sins whiter than snow.

Jesus came in a real body prepared for Him. He shed real blood, experienced real pain, cried real tears, and died a real death.

[Jesus] made Himself of no reputation, taking the form of a bondservant, and coming in the likeness of men. And being found in appearance as a man, He humbled Himself and became obedient to the point of

death, even the death of the cross. (Philippians 2:7-8, brackets added for emphasis)

In the garden of Gethsemane Jesus struggled with extreme pressure and even sweat drops of blood, but not because He didn't want to endure the physical sufferings for us. He knew why He came and He was willing. No one murdered Him because it was His choice to lay down His life for us. The Father, the Son, and the Holy Spirit were all in agreement: this suffering must take place for it to be possible for us to be sinless and reconciled to the Trinity.

"Therefore My Father loves Me, because I lay down My life that I may take it again. No one takes it from Me, but I lay it down of Myself. I have power to lay it down, and I have power to take it again." (John 10:17-18)

"O My Father, if it is possible, let this cup pass from Me; nevertheless, not as I will, but as You will." (Matthew 26:39)

Aren't you glad He said "nevertheless"? It shows the nature of love. Love is a choice. That word "nevertheless" is shocking if you think of its implications. It means that Jesus could have chosen to go back to heaven without us. All of our blessed assurance is hinged on that word! He drank the cup of suffering and sin and sorrow and pain and sickness and shame and condemnation and wrath. All for us. But none of that was the worst part of taking that cup. Do you know why He asked God to let the cup pass from Him if it were possible? It wasn't because of the physical suffering. It was because of the inevitable separation from His Father that He would have to endure because of our sin. He was saying to God, "Father, is there any other way We can do this?" The answer: "No, Son. This is the only way."

As our sins were put on Him, He cried out in deep anguish,

"My God, My God, why have you forsaken Me?" (Matthew 27:46)

Jesus came from the Father, not as the Son of God, but as the Son of man. He became us, laden with all the effects of sin and the curse. God was not angry with His Son — ever. Jesus experienced separation from the Father on the cross — not because God was angry with Him, but because that's what SIN demanded. You'll never know how much God loves you until you know how much He loves His Son. Why? Because He gave His Son for you. Jesus received the full force of God's uncompromising wrath FOR THE SIN of mankind because the uncompromising love of the Trinity for us. Jesus experienced forsakenness so that we wouldn't have to. Today we hear the Father say, "I will never leave you, nor forsake you."[337] When we think of the cross, we might imagine scenes like in the graphic depiction of the crucifixion in the movie *The Passion of the Christ* where Jesus was beaten mercilessly at the whipping post, spit upon by the soldiers, hung by the nails hammered through His hands and feet. Or we might envision the devastating image of His last breath and last words. However, these scenes that we are privy to from the scriptures, only skim the surface of the sufferings that were not described in the Gospels. When Jesus gave up His Spirit, darkness covered the earth, and God shielded from our eyes the absolute humiliation of His Son as all of the eternal condemnation and punishment for all sin for all time was somehow compressed in time and poured upon the Lamb of God.

Why does the Father love the Son so much?

"My Father loves Me, because I lay down My life that I may take it again." (John 10:17)

Christ also has loved us and given Himself for us, an offering and a sacrifice to God for a sweet-smelling aroma. (Ephesians 5:2)

He Came To Do God's Will

Reader Study Reference, Hebrews 10:6-10

In burnt offerings and sacrifices for sin You had no pleasure. Then I said, 'Behold, I have come—In the volume of the book it is written of Me— To do Your will, O God.'" Previously saying, "Sacrifice and offering, burnt offerings, and offerings for sin You did not desire, nor had pleasure in them" (which are offered according to the law), then He said, "Behold, I have come to DO YOUR WILL, O God." He takes away the first that He may establish the second. (Hebrews 10:6-9, emphasis added)

Christians often wonder what the will of God is. The will of God is that He doesn't want His people under law. So Jesus took away the first covenant of law that He could establish the New Covenant of grace.

> *By that will we have been sanctified through the offering of the body of Jesus Christ once for all. (Hebrews 10:10)*

We've been sanctified. Past tense. "Sanctified" means "to separate from profane things and dedicate to God."[338] We have been separated from every profane thing in this world and have been dedicated to God. We have been separated from every curse of darkness to every blessing of light. This verb "sanctified" is in the perfect tense meaning one time, never to be repeated.[339] We have been made holy "once for all!" And it's "by that will" that we have been made holy, not by our performance, but through His blood!

One Sacrifice For Sins Forever

Reader Study Reference, Hebrews 10:11-12

> *Every priest stands ministering daily and offering repeatedly. But this Man, after He had offered one sacrifice for sins forever, sat down at the right hand of God. (Hebrews 10:11-12)*

Here are a few things to take note of in this passage:

- "Every priest stands." The only seat in the Holy of Holies was the Mercy Seat, and that was reserved for the blood of the sacrifice. The priest could not sit because the work was never finished.

- "Offering repeatedly." Why? Because the offerings only worked temporarily.

- "One sacrifice." Jesus offered ONE sacrifice for sins because the first time worked!

- "Forever." How long did the sacrifice of Jesus work? Eternally.

- He "sat down." After He offered the sacrifice, Jesus sat down because the work was finished!

- "At the right hand of God." He sat down at the right hand of God because that is the position of honor, power, acquittal, blessing, righteousness, and AUTHORITY.

Stop for a minute and recall the meaning of this truth for us today: no amount of confessing sin, promising to do better, praying, fasting, serving, giving, or any other work can add to what Jesus did! Anything good that we do should be IN RESPONSE to this great act of love! IT IS FINISHED!

> *...when He had by Himself purged our sins, sat down at the right hand of the Majesty on high. (Hebrews 1:3)*

Jesus BY HIMSELF purged our sins without any help from us!

In Hebrews 10:12, it says that Jesus sat down at the right hand of God as "this Man."

> *For there is one God and one Mediator between God and men, the MAN Christ Jesus, who gave Himself a ransom for all... (1 Timothy 2:5-6, emphasis added)*

Although Jesus is eternally God, it was as the "Man Christ Jesus" that He died for us. It was as the "Man Christ Jesus" that He rose for us. It is as the "Man Christ Jesus" that mediates for us at the right hand of God the Father.

Footstool

Reader Study Reference, Hebrews 10:13

While Jesus is seated at the right hand of the Father, having finished the work for our redemption, there is still activity at His throne:

> *...from that time waiting till His enemies are made His footstool. (Hebrews 10:13)*

Here's the reality for us as believers today: the devil has been disarmed and triumphed over. He is defeated! When demonic forces come against our minds today to lie to us, we must believe that they are already conquered and are being drug in chains one by one and made to be a footstool for our Lord.

> *...even when we were dead in trespasses, made us alive together with Christ (by grace you have been saved), and raised us up together, and MADE*

US TO SIT together in the heavenly places in Christ Jesus... (Ephesians 2:5-6, emphasis added)

Every enemy is also being made our footstool because we are in Christ seated in heavenly places far above all dominion and power.

Why did the writer of Hebrews use the analogy of the footstool? It was the custom of ancient warriors to stand on the necks of vanquished kings to celebrate their triumph. After being defeated, these humiliated kings would have to get on all fours in shame before the people and in subjection to the victorious king.[340] In the same way, Jesus has conquered the enemies of sin, depression, poverty, disease, premature death, and all of the other curses that came with falling short of the standards of the law. When were they conquered? At the cross.

He must reign till He has put all enemies under His feet. The last enemy that will be destroyed is death. For "He has put all things under His feet." (1 Corinthians 15:25-27)

Our posture is Jesus' posture: seated, resting, trusting, so that when evil voices speak words of doubt and fear, we declare that we are in Christ and every enemy has already been defeated and is under our feet. No matter what our circumstances are screaming at us, we declare the FINISHED work. We're not trying to defeat the devil by "warring" against him. When we fight to defeat the enemy, we are revealing our disbelief in what Jesus has already accomplished. We don't fight the devil; we resist him with all the authority and dominion of heaven, and he will flee in utter fear.[341] The adversary has been disarmed of the weapon of the law, and he's nothing more than a public spectacle hoping to convince us that we deserve whatever is coming our way, and we have no power over him.

These principles work because they are based on the incorruptible word of God. We don't have to ask God for authority because we already have it in Jesus — in fact, it's HIS authority given to us. Jesus demonstrated this authority when He told the demons to leave the Gadarene demoniac: "Come out of the man, unclean spirit!"[342] They left and went into the swine. With the woman bowed down with the spirit of infirmity He didn't even speak to the spirit. He spoke to the woman: "Woman, you are loosed from your infirmity."[343] She was im-mediately made straight. Often He cast out spirits with a single word!

In Acts 16, Paul became greatly annoyed with a girl possessed by a demon who was following him around for days. He turned to her and said,

> *"I command you in the name of Jesus Christ to come out of her!" And it came out at that very moment. (Acts 16:18, NASB)*

I can tell you after being in ministry for years, I have seen all sorts of "deliverance" sessions that didn't even resemble biblical authority. Once I attended a meeting where the leader, a very respected older man who had led this particular ministry for decades, along with a team of about five other people, attempted for an hour to cast a de-mon out of a twelve-year-old little girl, sadly with no success. They were hovering over this child, laying their hands on her and praying loudly. The girl writhed on the ground making terrible sounds. I was shocked to find that the parents had brought this little girl to this meeting several times in the past, and the scene was the same each time. I call that insanity: doing the same thing over and over, but ex-pecting a different result. This should not be!

The devil is Christ's footstool. We are in Him, therefore, the devil is our footstool. The work is finished and our job is to enforce the victory. Period.

Perfected Forever

Reader Study Reference, Hebrews 10:14-17

> *For by one offering He has PERFECTED FOREVER those who are being sanctified. But the Holy Spirit also witnesses to us; for after He had said before, "This is the covenant that I will make with them after those days, says the LORD: I will put My laws into their hearts, and in their minds I will write them," then He adds, "Their sins and their lawless deeds I will remember no more." (Hebrews 10:14-17, emphasis added)*

Did you hear that? We have been perfected forever! We have been sanctified (past tense) and we are being (even now) continually set apart unto God. In other words, living in this fallen world in these earthen vessels of flesh, we are still sanctified. Nothing can change it. It's a permanent state that we live in. It's New Covenant reality. The writer reiterates the witness of the Holy Spirit in this New Covenant as the reason we have been forever made holy: "Their sins and their lawless deeds I will remember no more."

A New and Living Way

Reader Study Reference, Hebrews 10:18-20

> *NOW where there is remission of these [sins and lawless deeds], there is no longer an offering for sin. Therefore, brethren, having boldness to enter the Holiest by the blood of Jesus by a new and living way which He consecrated for us, through the veil, that is, His flesh... (Hebrews 10:18-20, emphasis and brackets added for emphasis)*

Our sins have been remitted. In other words, they have been let go as if they had never been committed.[344] Therefore, there is nothing required of us to make ourselves accepted by God, and there is nothing else that we could do to add to our acceptance. We'll never be more accepted, and we'll never be less accepted. Given that fact, we can enjoy the Holy of Holies — the presence of God — with cheerful courage and no reservation. The Hebrews to whom this was originally written would know the scandal of this statement. How could anyone but the high priest go into the Holy of Holies and not be immediately exterminated by the judgment and righteousness of God? And furthermore, how could anyone go into the presence of God without the offering? Even the high priest wouldn't make it inside the curtain empty handed!

The old way was deadly. The new way is a living way. Jesus' flesh — the body prepared for Him — was torn for us so that the way to the presence of God was opened forever. Today the more we enjoy the Presence, the more our minds and our bodies are renewed and refreshed. It's a fresh and life-giving way!

Even when we sin, we are still the temple of the Holy Spirit. We are still holy. NOW we are in the presence of God. NOW God lives in us. God cannot be in an unholy place. He has found a permanent dwelling place in His new creation! And, by the way, God will not share His permanent holy dwelling with a demon. This is why a believer cannot be possessed by a demon. Jesus has taken possession of His home in us!

Sprinkled from an Evil Conscience

Reader Study Reference, Hebrews 10:21-22

Although we are near to God, so close that He is in us and we are in Him, there are times when we draw near in the sense that we intentionally worship Him, talk to Him, and ask Him questions. We don't have to worry that He will condemn us for our sin. In fact, He's there to help us by reminding us that we are still holy, righteous, and redeemed.

> *...and having a High Priest over the house of God, let us draw near with a true heart in full assurance of faith, having our hearts sprinkled from an evil conscience. (Hebrews 10:21-22)*

An "evil conscience" will give us the sense that we aren't worthy to be near Him. Take those thoughts captive![345] Never fear that God is angry with you or that He would ever leave you.[346] He will never leave you nor forsake you.[347] He will abide with you forever.[348] The word "evil" is the Greek word "poneros," and it means "full of labors, annoyances, hardships, pressed and harassed by labors."[349] An evil conscience is one that is full of displeasure, adversity, oppression, and worn out from self-effort because faith has not yet come or faith has been clouded by unbelief. An evil conscience is one that will keep us from drawing near to God until we somehow clean up our lives. But now that we can enter the Holiest by the blood, we should have a debt-free, labor-free, hardship-free, hassle-free, guilt-free righteousness-conscience born out of rest in His righteousness given to us as a free gift.

Our Confession of Hope

Reader Study Reference, Hebrews 10:23

> *Let us hold fast the confession of our hope without wavering, for He who promised is faithful. (Hebrews 10:23)*

The writer is encouraging the listeners — those Jewish people who were abandoning the Old Covenant system — not to waver in declaring their faith in Jesus as the final sacrifice. For us today, this would be the encouragement to stand firm in our faith in the pure unmixed grace of our Lord Jesus Christ. We hold fast and earnestly contend for the faith![350]

The word "confession" is from the Greek word "homologeo" which means, "to say the same thing with."[351] Who are we to agree with? Jesus Himself! What is the confession of our hope, our confident expectation of good? We declare nothing lies between us and God! Now we can agree with Jesus that His prayers have been answered. The night He was betrayed, Jesus prayed for us:

"I do not pray for these alone, but also for those who will believe in Me through their word [that's us!]; that they all may be one, as You, Father, are in Me, and I in You; that they also may be one in Us, that the world may believe that You sent Me. And the glory which You gave Me I have given them, that they may be one just as We are one: I in them, and You in Me; that they may be made perfect in one, and that the world may know that You have sent Me, and have loved them as You have loved Me." *(John 17:20-23, brackets added for emphasis)*

What is our Father's response? "Come visit with Me. Talk to Me. Draw near to Me. All that I have is Yours. Come share in your inheritance. Come and receive!" Name a promise, for He who promised is forever faithful!

Sinning Willfully

Reader Study Reference, Hebrews 10:26-31

To end this chapter we will briefly look at a few passages that have been taken out of context in the body of Christ. The first passage is Hebrews 10:26-31 which contains a verse that has been misinterpreted in many Christian circles, bringing great insecurity to believers:

For if we sin willfully after we have received the knowledge of the truth, there no longer remains a sacrifice for sins, but a certain fearful expectation of judgment, and fiery indignation which will devour the adversaries. Anyone who has rejected Moses' law dies without mercy on the testimo-

ny of two or three witnesses. Of how much worse punishment, do you suppose, will he be thought worthy who has trampled the Son of God underfoot, counted the blood of the covenant by which he was sanctified a common thing, and insulted the Spirit of grace? For we know Him who said, "Vengeance is Mine, I will repay," says the Lord. And again, "The Lord will judge His people." It is a fearful thing to fall into the hands of the living God. (Hebrews 10:26-31)

Many people have lived in fear of judgment because of wrong interpretations of Hebrews 10:26. The reason is that they have been taught that there is a line in sinning that we can cross that will cause us to lose our salvation. Nothing could be further from the truth. As we have learned in the book of Hebrews, the blood of Jesus is eternal! It has forever removed our sins from us.

The misinterpretation of "willfully sinning" is the reason for the fear of judgment that some believers are tormented with. Haven't we all sinned willfully? In fact, isn't most sin willful? In the context of the entire book of Hebrews, it is clear that to "sin willfully" was to continue to believe that the blood of bulls and goats could atone for sins after the blood of Jesus had been shed. At its basic core, "sinning willfully" is the rejection of the blood of Jesus to save us and cleanse us.

In Chapter 6, the writer of Hebrews contrasts the sure hope that we have in Jesus as the final offering with impossibility of the Old Covenant sacrifices to save us. At the time of the writing of the book of Hebrews, many of these Jews were still sacrificing animals on the altar to atone for sins. This practice among Jews who had rejected Jesus as the Messiah went on for some forty years after the resurrection until the temple was destroyed in 70 AD.[352]

The writer is pleading with those who were on the brink of receiving Jesus as the final sacrifice. He begs them not to turn back.

For it is impossible for those who were once enlightened, and have tasted the heavenly gift, and have become partakers of the Holy Spirit, and have tasted the good word of God and the powers of the age to come, if they fall away, to renew them again to repentance, since they crucify again for themselves the Son of God, and put Him to an open shame. (Hebrews 6:4-6)

They had been enlightened, tasted of the heavenly gift, had partaken of the Holy Spirit, and tasted of the good word, but had not been born again. The disciples before the cross were in this category and had experienced all of these things. None of them were born again because the blood had not been shed. All but one were born again after the resurrection. Many think that Judas, the disciple who betrayed Jesus, "lost his salvation," but he never had it in the first place. He killed himself before the cross.

The warnings of Hebrews 6 and Hebrews 10 are for those who continually reject Jesus and never receive the free gift of righteousness. For them, it is impossible to renew them to repentance.

Today if we are in Christ, we are forever in Him. However, if we believe lies about the gift of righteousness and the eternal efficacy of the blood of Jesus, we will fall prey to erroneous teachings that will lead us to self-righteous acts that frustrate the grace of God in our lives. Just as throwing another bull on the altar would be a dead work for those that the writer of Hebrews was pleading with, we can perform "dead works" in a foolish attempt to achieve righteousness apart from faith in Jesus. Righteousness cannot be attained by works, but it can be obtained through faith.

We as believers in the Lord Jesus Christ, washed in the blood, raised to new life and seated in Him, never need to fear judgment. We do not need to fear Judgment Day or any day of judgment when fiery darts of condemnation from the enemy pummel our minds. ALL OUR JUDGMENT was received by our Lord. It is finished.

Love has been perfected among us in this: that we may have boldness in the day of judgment; because as He is, so are we in this world. (1 John 4:17)

However, for those who consistently and persistently reject the blood of Jesus their entire lives, there no longer remains a sacrifice for them. Jesus was our one sacrifice for sins forever. The sin of unbelief is no less than trampling underfoot the Son of God, counting His precious blood as common as the blood of bulls and goats, and insulting to the Spirit of grace. Yes, there is judgment for those who reject Jesus.

However, never forget these all powerful truths:

The Lord is not slow about His promise, as some count slowness, but is patient toward you, not wishing for any to perish but for all to come to repentance. (2 Peter 3:9, NASB)

For God so loved the world that He gave His only begotten Son, that whoever believes in Him should not perish but have everlasting life. For God did not send His Son into the world to condemn the world, but that the world through Him might be saved. (John 3:16-17)

The Discipline of the Lord

Reader Study Reference, Hebrews 12:1-8

In Hebrews 12 we find a passage of scripture that has been used by many to warn us against sins of the flesh that "so easily entangle," and if we refuse to do so, then God will punish us. When we look at the passage in its context in Hebrews 12 as well as in its context in the entire book of Hebrews, we will see that the writer's exhortation is not talking about staying away from sex, drugs, and rock-n-roll. He's talking about something that most modern day Christians know very little about: the temptation to give up in the face of persecution.

The letter to the Hebrews was written to believing Christians and unbelievers who were on the brink of receiving Christ as the final sacrifice. Again, at the time the book was written, Jesus had died and risen again, but the temple had not yet been destroyed by Nero; therefore, unbelieving Jews were still sacrificing animals on the altar. Everyone in that day who identified themselves with the church endured persecution, whether they were believers in the fellowship of the church or unbelievers who had left the sacrificial system and were leaning towards accepting Jesus Christ as Savior. The writer of Hebrews encouraged the readers with these words:

Therefore we also, since we are surrounded by so great a cloud of witnesses, let us lay aside every weight, and the sin which so easily ensnares us, and let us run with endurance the race that is set before us, looking unto Jesus, the author and finisher of our faith, who for the joy that was set before Him endured the cross, despising the shame, and has sat down at the right hand of the throne of God. For consider Him who endured such hostility from sinners against Himself, lest you become weary and discouraged in your souls. You have not yet resisted to bloodshed, striving against sin. (Hebrews 12:1-4)

The readers are reminded of the saints of the Old Testament referred to in the preceding chapter in "the Hall of Fame of Faith" who endured persecution, but now are in the heavenly galleries cheering us on because they see the beginning from the end.

We can receive this encouraging word for ourselves as we face resistance to the pure Gospel of grace which we are believing, living, and preaching. The only solution to the temptation to throw in the towel and crumble under the pressure is to look to Jesus. The word "looking" is the Greek word "aphorao" which means "to turn the eyes away from other things and fix them on something."[353] It's a verb in the present active participle tense which means ALWAYS looking away from other things and fixing them on Jesus.[354] In other words, we don't just look to Jesus when we feel the pressure, we keep our eyes on Him all the time.

No amount of persecution or pressure to succumb compares to the sufferings of Jesus. He became the sin of the entire world, suffered separation from the Father on our behalf, and endured the cross. If we fix our eyes on Him, we will have the strength to endure any temptation that comes against the flesh. He purchased that strength for us. We have entered into His joy and the heart of the Father, and the joy of the Lord is our strength.[355] The pressures of the system of religion that woo us to rely on the flesh for our success will challenge us to turn our eyes away from Jesus. If we fall from grace back into performance, then we will experience the "chastening" of the Lord as true sons and daughters.

And you have forgotten the exhortation which speaks to you as to sons: "My son, do not despise the chastening of the Lord, Nor be discouraged when you are rebuked by Him; For whom the Lord loves He chastens, And scourges every son whom He receives." If you endure chastening, God deals with you as with sons; for what son is there whom a father does not chasten? But if you are without chastening, of which all have become partakers, then you are illegitimate and not sons. (Hebrews 12:5-8)

The word "chastening" is the Greek word "paideuo" and refers to training children.[356] This word does not mean punishment. It speaks of training and educating children in virtue by correcting mistakes and teaching them the truth. One of the main aspects of the Lord's chastening is to lead us in repentance (changing our minds) by renewing our minds to truth so that we will turn our eyes back to Jesus. We can endure anything because He endured everything for us.

The Jews at that time had been taught that anything they suffered, whether enemy attack or famine or hardship, was because of God's displeasure with them for their sins. The writer of Hebrews is letting these believers know that the persecution they are enduring is not a result of God's displeasure or an indication that they weren't "right with God." It was in fact the opposite. It was proof of their sonship, therefore they should regard His discipline (child training) as an honor and a privilege. Sons and daughters of God who embrace the child training of the Lord will yield a restful, peaceful existence of God's life flowing through us. Doesn't that sound like the life you want? The other option is allowing bitterness to defile us and others.

God's desire is for us to manifest the sweet aroma of His knowledge and His presence everywhere with everyone. If we keep our eyes on Jesus and have eyes to see the heavenly reality that the great cloud of witnesses see, then we would not succumb to the voices of men who tempt us to compromise, but we would embrace the voice of the Spirit of God who always leads us in triumph!

> *Now thanks be to God who always leads us in triumph in Christ, and through us diffuses the fragrance of His knowledge in every place. (2 Corinthians 2:14)*

CHAPTER NINETEEN

Rest

Key scriptures:
Genesis 1:5; Genesis 2:2-3; Hebrews 4:2-3, 9-11; Ephesians 1:3; Mark 9:22-24; James 5:14-16; Matthew 10:8; Luke 11:5-13

Spiritual rest is the greatest result of the revelation of grace. Nothing has had a more practical effect on my life than knowing God is for me, God is smiling at me, God likes what He sees when He looks at me, and God is not counting my sins against me. And as a result, I would have to say that I am "gooder" than I've ever been. Grace truly is amazing. When Jesus is on my mind, sin isn't. Who has time for fear, doubt, anger, lust, jealousy, worry, and hatred when you've enjoying your salvation and sharing your joy with others?

Resting didn't come easy at first, though. We used to preach, "We'll rest when we get to heaven! We're serving God with all our hearts so one day we'll hear those words, 'Well done, My good and faithful servant.'" A servant's work is never done.

In the early days of my grace awakening, there was so much dismantling of a mindset of work. Once during those days I prayed,

"Lord, it seems to me that even believing is a work. It seems like the ONE thing we have to DO." He responded, "Believing is the choice to do nothing in your own strength. Rest, Tricia. Trust Me." Then He began to speak to me about my life. Maybe you can relate. He said:

- REST when you want to dredge up all your failures and get them off your back. I don't remember your sins. Trust Me.

- REST when people misunderstand you. I understand you better than you understand yourself. Trust Me.

- REST when untruths are spoken about you. I believe in you. Trust Me.

- REST when you mess up and you want to fix it. I can handle it all by Myself. Trust Me.

- REST when your flesh says, "DO SOMETHING!" It is finished. Trust Me.

- REST when logic tells you the exact opposite. My ways are not your ways. Trust Me.

- REST when people are screaming "GO!" and I am saying "stop." I know your future. Trust Me.

- REST when you have all the answers and they are on the tip of your tongue. I'll make sure everyone hears what they need to know when they need to know it. Trust Me.

- REST when you could fix it all. I gave you the fruit of self-control. Trust Me.

- REST when your dreams and visions have been etched in your heart for so long and people keep saying it's all just around the corner. I live outside of time. Live there with Me. It will all happen. I promise. Trust Me.

- REST when you are so stirred up you think you might just explode. Trust Me. I will still the storm in your soul.

- REST when there's so much to do. Through My strength only do what only you can do. Let other people do the rest. Trust Me.

- REST when you are burnt out. My grace will enable you to rise on wings with eagles and never get tired. Trust Me.

- REST when you have produced so much through DOING. I was pleased with you before you ever did anything for Me. Trust Me.

- REST when approval from others has come from DOING something. My approval of you comes through My approval of Jesus. You don't have to do anything. He already took care of it for you. I approve of you. Trust Me.

- REST when your value to men has been determined by what you do. Through the blood of My beloved Son you have been made perfect in My sight and can't do ANYTHING to be more valuable to Me. Trust Me.

- REST when DOING something ensured that you had friends. I AM your best friend and I will never, ever leave you. Trust Me.

- REST when others are having the time of their life doing what you think you want to do. My plans for you would blow your mind if I told you. The best is yet to come. Trust Me.

- REST while the clock ticks and you get older and older. I am renewing you. I will restore years! Trust Me.

- REST while your dreams fade. I gave you those dreams in the first place. I am faithful. Trust Me.

- REST and hear My voice. Trust Me.

The remainder of **Unveiling Jesus** is a series of "nuggets" on resting in the finished work of Jesus that have changed my life. I hope they change your life, too.

7th Day

Did you know that when God created the first day, He made the evening first? In the evening we rest. So rest comes first .... rest before work. God intended for everything in life to be initiated out of rest.

God called the light Day, and the darkness He called Night. So the evening and the morning were the first day. (Genesis 1:5)

God created everything by simply speaking the word, and then He rested. Does God get tired? No. He didn't rest because He was tired. He rested because His work was finished.

And on the seventh day God ended His work which He had done, and He rested on the seventh day from all His work which He had done. Then God blessed the seventh day and sanctified it. (Genesis 2:2-3)

God made Adam and Eve on the sixth day, the last day of creation. God made man last because man was the object of His affection and the recipient of all He had made. God put Adam and Eve in the beautiful Garden of Eden to enjoy it forever. "Eden" means pleasure,[357] and their job was to tend the garden of pleasure.[358] I've tried to imagine what tending a garden would be like with no weeds and no pests. Everything was in perfect balance in nature so there was no toil and no labor. I guess they just plucked the fruit and enjoyed it. Rest, enjoyment, and fellowship with God was their life!

New Covenant Rest

How much more today should we be resting in the presence of God! Today God's presence is within us because God Himself became man and dwelled among us, and then joined Himself to us and lives inside of us. This was not true of Adam and Eve. Although they were perfect and God was with them and His glory crowned them, His presence was outside. They were created in their own righteousness which they gave away. Now because of the eternal righteousness of Christ in us, the presence of God is inside giving us unending life and fellowship. Life in the New Covenant is resting in the finished work of Jesus.

He who dwells in the secret place of the Most High shall abide under the shadow of the Almighty. (Psalm 91:1)

The word "dwells" is the Hebrew word "yashab" which means to SIT down.[359] He who SITS down in God's presence abides under His protection. Jesus SAT down at the right hand of the Father when His work of redeeming us was finished. Sitting = resting. To rest is to be spiritually minded and to see the invisible by faith with our spiritual eyes. When we aren't resting, it's because we're focusing on what is visible.

...while we do not look at the things which are seen, but at the things which are not seen. For the things which are seen are temporary, but the things which are not seen are eternal. (2 Corinthians 4:18)

But the natural man does not receive the things of the Spirit of God, for they are foolishness to him; nor can he know them, because they are spiritually discerned. (1 Corinthians 2:14)

We live in parallel realms. We walk in this earth while we dwell (rest) in heavenly places.

If then you were raised with Christ, seek those things which are above, where Christ is, sitting at the right hand of God. Set your mind on things above, not on things on the earth. For you died, and your life is hidden with Christ in God. (Colossians 3:1-3)

We are born from above and are blessed with every spiritual blessing:

Blessed be the God and Father of our Lord Jesus Christ, who has blessed us with every spiritual blessing in the heavenly places in Christ... (Ephesians 1:3)

We have been blessed, past tense. Those who are in Christ have the awesome privilege of receiving unlimited blessings that are stored up for us in heavenly places. "All I have needed Thy hand hath provided..."

God Defeated Amalek

Remember the two month period of grace in the dessert described in Exodus between the Red Sea and Mount Sinai from our study of 2 Corinthians 3? Even though the children of Israel complained against God, He showered them with grace. There was only one battle fought during that time period of pure grace: the battle with the Amalekites. No Israelite died, and when God defeated the Amalekites, He declared His name: Jehovah Nissi. It was another fresh demonstration of the Lord's grace.

Here is that account from Exodus 17:

Now Amalek came and fought with Israel in Rephidim. And Moses said to Joshua, "Choose us some men and go out, fight with Amalek. Tomorrow I will stand on the top of the hill with the rod of God in my hand." So Joshua did as Moses said to him, and fought with Amalek. And Moses, Aaron, and Hur went up to the top of the hill. And so it was, when

Moses held up his hand, that Israel prevailed; and when he let down his hand, Amalek prevailed. But Moses' hands became heavy; so they took a stone and put it under him, and he sat on it. And Aaron and Hur supported his hands, one on one side, and the other on the other side; and his hands were steady until the going down of the sun. So Joshua defeated Amalek and his people with the edge of the sword. Then the LORD said to Moses, "Write this for a memorial in the book and recount it in the hearing of Joshua, that I will utterly blot out the remembrance of Amalek from under heaven." And Moses built an altar and called its name, The-LORD-Is-My-Banner [Jehovah Nissi]; for he said, "Because the LORD has sworn: the LORD will have war with Amalek from generation to generation." (Exodus 17:8-16, brackets added for emphasis)

Every detail is important, and this story is loaded with symbolism for us! The Israelites were camped at Rephidim by the direction of God's presence.[360] When they first reached Rephidim, if you recall, there was no water, so God gave them water from the rock.[361] "Rephidim" literally means "rests or resting places."[362] They were living life and not looking for a fight when all of a sudden the enemy Amalek came against them. "Amalek" comes from the Hebrew word "amal" which means "trouble, labor, toil."[363] Think about it — they were resting in Rephidim when trouble, labor, and toil attacked them. In fact, in Deuteronomy there is a reference to this event where we learn that Amalek attacked the weak stragglers in the rear ranks first while Israel was weary from their journey.[364] Can you see the symbolism for us? When we're resting and weary from the journey, the enemy sends trouble, labor and toil our way. He sneaks up from behind when we least expect it. What should our response be? Let's look at the story again to find out.

While Israel was on the field in the battle, Moses was on the hill with his hands raised. As long as his hands were in the air, Israel prevailed in the battle. When Moses became weary and his hands went down because he was tired, Amalek gained an advantage in combat with them. His friends came, made Moses sit on a rock, and they held his hands up to keep them steady. Meanwhile, Joshua, which means "Yahweh (Jesus) is deliverance," defeated the enemy!

The word "steady" is the Hebrew word "emuwnah" which is also translated faith or faithfulness.[365] The use of this word is the first time

FAITH is mentioned in the Bible — in the context of the enemy coming against our REST!

So what does all this say to us? When the enemy attacks with trouble, labor, or toil, we sit down in rest and raise our hands in faith. Faith is our response! Others come along beside us to encourage us, and we all declare the finished work of our Jehovah Nissi, our heavenly Joshua. Through the cross and resurrection, Jesus has blotted out the remembrance of trouble, labor, and toil so that we can rest in Him, even while enduring the most difficult circumstances. We can set our minds on things above, feasting on God's love and peace in the presence of our enemies.[366]

God has given us the ability by His Spirit to live the stress-free life of unending supply and protection. He wants us to sit down and rest.

REST is our warfare.
REST is our obedience.
REST is our faith.

Grasshoppers in Our Own Sight

Two years after the Israelites were delivered from the hand of the Egyptians, they reached an area called Kadesh-Barnea.[367] God told Moses to send out twelve spies from there to check out the Promised Land. When the twelve spies returned after forty days of investigation, they brought a sample of giant grapes from the land strung on a long pole. The grapes were so magnificent in size that it took two men to carry them! The Promised Land was glorious! However, when they came back, ten of the spies were the bearers of bad news and two (Caleb and Joshua) brought good news and rejoiced over what they had seen. How could they have brought back such contrasting reports? It's not because of what they saw with their natural eyes. It's because of what they believed in their heart: some saw with eyes of fear and some saw with eyes of faith based on whether they trusted God enough to believe that He had given them the land.

Caleb declared:

"Let us go up at once and take possession, for we are well able to overcome it." (Numbers 13:30)

The naysayers whined,

"We are not able to go up against the people, for they are stronger than we." And they gave the children of Israel a bad report of the land which they had spied out, saying, "The land through which we have gone as spies is a land that devours its inhabitants, and all the people whom we saw in it are men of great stature. There we SAW the giants (the descendants of Anak came from the giants); and we were like grasshoppers IN OUR OWN SIGHT, and SO WE WERE IN THEIR SIGHT." (Numbers 13:31-33, emphasis added)

Ten spies FIRST saw themselves as grasshoppers, and THEN they appeared as grasshoppers to the giants! Actually, the giants were all terrified of the children of Israel because they had heard how the God of Israel had opened up the Red Sea and delivered His people.[368]

Joshua and Caleb saw the giants for what they were:

"The land we passed through to spy out is an exceedingly good land. If the Lord delights in us, then He will bring us into this land and give it to us, 'a land which flows with milk and honey.' Only do not rebel against the Lord, nor fear the people of the land, for THEY ARE OUR BREAD; their protection has departed from them, and the Lord is with us. DO NOT FEAR THEM." (Numbers 14:7-9, emphasis added)

How did Joshua and Caleb perceive the giants? As bread! And not only that, God had removed the protection of the giants so that all the Israelites had to do was go in and take the land. God was on their side! Joshua and Caleb said, "Do not fear them," but unfortunately, here was Israel's response:

And all the congregation said to stone them [Joshua and Caleb] with stones. (Numbers 14:10, brackets added for emphasis)

Two years before, God had delivered the Israelites from the Egyptians to bring them into the Promised Land, and it was not His desire nor His plan for it to take forty years for them to reach it. It was because of their lack of trust and their rebellion that they wandered for forty years.

According to the number of the days in which you spied out the land, forty days, for each day you shall bear your guilt one year, namely forty years, and you shall know My rejection. (Numbers 14:34)

A trip that should have taken eleven days,[369] took forty years because they would not do one simple thing: trust God by taking the land by faith in His promise. If God says something, there is enough power in those words to make it happen!

Because of their unbelief, every man of fighting age would die in the desert, except for Joshua and Caleb.[370] About two and a half million people had come through the Red Sea (six hundred thousand men, not including woman and children[371]), but because they did not trust the Lord, only TWO men out of all of the men who had crossed the Red Sea actually entered the Promised Land. The Promised Land that God had told them to enter into and take was already theirs! Yet they chose to believe what their natural eyes told them: that they were grasshoppers compared to the might and strength of their enemies. A whole new generation joined Joshua and Caleb as they crossed over the River Jordan to possess the land, but because of unbelief, they left a whole generation of corpses in the desert.

What does this mean for us today? Are you a grasshopper in your own sight? Or are your enemies bread for you? Are you facing giants? Or is your God all powerful? Will the enemies of fear, depression, sickness, financial ruin, and relational difficulty overtake you? Or are you well able to overtake them through the power of the Holy Spirit within you?

Promised Land of Rest

The writer of Hebrews speaks of that great tragedy in the desert:

...they could not enter in [the Promised Land] because of unbelief. Therefore, since a promise remains of entering His rest, let us fear lest any of you seem to have come short of it." (Hebrews 3:19 - 4:1, brackets added for emphasis)

Today our Promised Land is the realm of RESTING in the finished work of Jesus. We can rest in every word that God has spoken. We can rest in everything provided in the great exchange at the cross.

Our obedience of faith is simply to trust and obey the Spirit of God as He orchestrates and directs our path through life. Every enemy that resists us is "bread" for us. We are well able to overcome them because Jesus has already overcome them.

There is only ONE thing we are to fear: that we aren't at rest. It seems like the very thing we're supposed to fear is the thing we're hanging on to. For many of us, fear is a crutch that we have leaned on. For some of us fear has even become our "friend" because we wouldn't know how to live without it. There is fear of not having enough and fear of the future. Our emotions cry, "If I don't do it, who will?! If I don't think about my problems, who will?!" There's fear of failure, fear of rejection, fear of sickness, fear of man, fear of death, and the list goes on.

Fear and rest cannot co-exist.

Think about Jesus as our Overcomer of fear. He's our heavy-weight champion. He went into the ring heavy-ladened with all of our sin, all of the hand-writing against us, all of the curse of the law, and all of our punishment. He stepped up to the adversary, and it looked like all odds were against Him. Before the first punch was thrown, the enemy watched Jesus die right before his eyes. He thought he had won before the bell even rang. Yet in a shocking turn of events, the bell sounded and as Jesus was rising from the dead, He used all the weight of His glory and threw the first (and only!) knockout punch. Satan was slammed flat on his back never to recover, and all the hosts of heaven rejoiced!

Imagine that this Victor is our Husband, and we are the Bride who gets to take home the prize check: all of the riches of His grace. He was the Conqueror, but we are MORE than conquerors because of His love!

Yet in all these things we are more than conquerors through Him who loved us. (Romans 8:37)

Why don't we believe it? The Israelites in the desert are like many today who set their minds on flesh rather than the promises of God.

For indeed the gospel was preached to us as well as to them; but the word which they heard did not profit them, not being mixed with faith in those who heard it. For we who have believed DO enter that rest. "So I swore in My wrath they shall not enter My rest," [speaking of the Israelites in the dessert who did not trust God] although the works were finished from the FOUNDATION OF THE WORLD. (Hebrews 4:2-3)

Think of it: the works were finished before the foundation of the world! Before Adam and Eve even sinned and forfeited the glory of the Lord, God had the provision.

...the Lamb slain from the foundation of the world. (Revelation 13:8)

While Jesus walked the earth, He lived in the finished work. Look at the way He lived and moved and related to people in the four Gospels. Look at HIM because AS HE IS SO ARE YOU IN THIS WORLD![372]

There's nothing left for God to do. It's all finished. While we are praying and begging and pleading, God sits on His throne and says, "Hey, it's done." We fear when we lose sight of the finished work. Even our praying will become a heavy burden when we are in fear. Faith is no longer faith in Jesus, but faith IN OUR OWN FAITH worked up from self-effort. Self-dependency replaces dependency on Him.

What is life supposed to look like for us?

There remains therefore a rest for the people of God. (Hebrews 4:9)

That word "rest" is the Greek word "sabbatismos" from which we get our word sabbath. This word literally means "perpetual sabbath rest to be enjoyed uninterruptedly by believers in their fellowship with the Father and the Son."[373] Our rest today is a perpetual sabbath rest to be enjoyed CONTINUOUSLY. The only thing God tells us to work at is to work at staying in rest. When the devil tempts us to become unrestful and messes with our minds to tell us to fight as if he hasn't been defeated, we tell him, "You are already defeated. Jesus has already conquered you."

For he who has entered His rest has himself also ceased from his works as God did from His. (Hebrews 4:10)

Resting in the Lord is not a lazy, passive existence. Christians who view spiritual rest as an excuse to be slothful have misunderstood what God's promised rest is meant to be. When we know that God has already provided everything we need, and we access His wisdom, provision, strength, and protection by faith, we'll be governed by the Holy Spirit in a highly strategic and active life. Rest is not an inactive lifestyle. It's a Spirit-led lifestyle where we flow in the good works that God planned for us long ago.[374]

Let us labor therefore to enter the rest lest any man fall after the same example of unbelief. (Hebrews 4:11, KJV)

The opposite of rest is unbelief! When we are restless or anxious, it's because there is something we are not believing about God. Remaining at rest means we are guarding our faith. What's the best way to do that? Faith comes by hearing the word of God,[375] and meditation on the word of God will strengthen our faith. If you can worry, you can meditate! Worry is taking a fear and thinking about it from every angle. Meditation is just worry in reverse. It's taking a scripture and thinking about it from every angle!

The Finished Work

In the Old Testament we see descriptions of the Promised Land that was prepared for God's people. These were shadows of the Promised Land for us today and the provision that flows from heaven:

So the LORD brought us out of Egypt with a mighty hand and with an outstretched arm, with great terror and with signs and wonders. He has brought us to this place and has given us this land, "a land flowing with milk and honey." (Deuteronomy 26:8-9)

...when the LORD your God brings you into the land of which He swore to your fathers, to Abraham, Isaac, and Jacob, to give you large and beautiful cities which YOU DID NOT BUILD, houses full of all good things, which YOU DID NOT FILL, hewn-out wells which YOU DID NOT DIG, vineyards and olive trees which YOU DID NOT PLANT... (Deuteronomy 6:10-11, emphasis added)

All of this means that they were walking right into a finished work!

Our promised land of rest is the place of God's rest, seated in the heavenlies. God has flung open the gates to the land of rest and said to us, "Come on in! It's a land flowing with milk and honey. There is endless supply of every provision!" Everything we will ever need has already been provided.

Blessed be the God and Father of our Lord Jesus Christ, who has blessed us with every spiritual blessing in the heavenly places in Christ... (Ephesians 1:3)

We often think of spiritual blessing as having nothing to do with physical blessing. We might think, "Well, it's great that one day I'll get to heaven and never have to worry about money or sickness or hardship or problems. But what good does that do me now?" What we aren't understanding when we think like that is that everything in the natural came forth from the Spirit. God is a Spirit. A Spirit created this natural world. A Spirit created you and me. Everything we will ever need in this life was provided for us at the cross and is simply accessed by faith. It doesn't mean we'll never have a problem in this fallen world, but it does mean that God has already provided.

The Greek verb tense Paul used in the verse above when he said "who has blessed us" is the aorist tense. This means that the action has already taken place in the past. God has already blessed us, and these spiritual blessings are to be discovered and enjoyed right now. God's provision is available to us now.

Faith OF God

The question we might have is "How do I get faith?" The answer is that you already have it if you are in Christ because it's actually the faith of God in you. In Galatians 2:20 Paul said this:

The life which I now live in the flesh I live BY FAITH IN THE SON OF GOD, who loved me and gave Himself for me. (Galatians 2:20, emphasis added)

However, the words in the original Greek text say it like this:

The life which I now live in the flesh I live by THE FAITH OF THE SON OF GOD, who loved me, and gave himself for me. (Galatians 2:20, KJV, emphasis added)

Switching "of" to "in" might not seem such a big deal, but actually it changes everything! When Christ lives His life through us, it means that we are living by HIS faith, not our own. Ride on His faith. If the voice comes saying to you, "Are you sure you have enough faith for this?" You say, "It's not my faith. I live by the faith OF THE SON OF GOD." Even if you think you don't have faith, just rest and see His faith. He's the faithful One. Jesus had faith that when He went to the cross for us, He purchased every spiritual blessing for us. Do you believe that HE believed? The answer to that question should settle the issue.

When you live by the faith OF the Son of God, the result will be rest.

Help Me with My Unbelief

In Mark 9 we find the story of a father coming to Jesus asking Him to heal his son who was possessed by an evil spirit that would cause him to convulse, foam at the mouth, and throw himself into the water and into the fire. The man had asked Jesus' disciples to cast the demon out, but they could not do it. This is interesting because the disciples certainly had experience with healing and deliverance, but this time they could not help the man and his son. The father said to Jesus,

"But if You can do anything, take pity on us and help us!" And Jesus said to him, "'If You can?' All things are possible to him who believes." Immediately the boy's father cried out and said, "I do believe; help my unbelief." (Mark 9:22-24, NASB)

Some versions of the Bible translate Jesus' question as a statement: "If you can BELIEVE, all things are possible to him who believes." This makes it sound like the burden is on us to heal ourselves or drum up faith. However, in the original Greek manuscript that word "believe" is not in Jesus' question. He simply said, "If You can?" The New Living Translation says it like this: " What do you mean, 'If I can'?'" Jesus was saying in effect, "What a ridiculous question! OF COURSE I CAN!"

When He said, "All things are possible to him who believes," I think that He is referring to HIMSELF! In the context, that's the only thing that makes sense. Who else was believing? Were the disciples? Was the father of the possessed child? Were the people? It looks to me like the only Person on the premises whose faith wasn't counteracted by unbelief was Jesus Himself. His disciples had faith to do miracles, but I believe that they saw this boy convulsing, and their faith was clouded by what their natural eyes were beholding.

Jesus is the One who never doubts. He's the One we need to be beholding. The father said, "Lord, I believe! Help me with my unbelief!" Jesus' response? He simply cast the demon out. We need to believe that with Jesus all things are possible. See Him and unbelief will flee!

When Jesus had first arrived on the scene, the man told Jesus that His disciples could not cast the demon out. Jesus then called them a "faithless generation."[376] Why? Because just prior to the healing of this boy, we see in Luke's account of that same event that Jesus had given His disciples authority to cast out demons.

Then He called His twelve disciples together and gave them power and authority over all demons, and to cure diseases. He sent them to preach the kingdom of God and to heal the sick. (Luke 9:1-2)

Think about this: how much more should we, this side of the cross today, walk in heaven's authority? The devil has been overcome by the blood of Jesus! I believe that the issue is not that we don't have enough faith. Honestly, we aren't faithLESS. We have the faith OF God because we have the Holy Spirit joined to our spirit. The issue is that our unbelief is overcoming the faith that we do have. In Matthew's account of this same miracle, the disciples asked Jesus why they couldn't cast the demon out. Here was His answer:

"Because of your UNBELIEF; for assuredly, I say to you, if you have faith as a mustard seed, you will say to this mountain, 'Move from here to there,' and it will move; and nothing will be impossible for you." (Matthew 17:20, emphasis added)

What was Jesus saying? He was saying that all you need is the mustard seed of faith: the incorruptible seed of the word of God. Jesus is the Word. The Word was standing in their midst. Jesus was revealing the Gospel when He performed this miracle. The Gospel is the power of God unto salvation — eternal life, wholeness, healing, deliverance, and provision — for all who believe.[377]

> But the Word of the Lord (divine instruction, the Gospel) endures forever. And this Word is the good news which was preached to you. (1 Peter 1:25, Amplified Bible)

Today, if you are born again, you have the seed within you. You have JESUS within you. His faith, His power, His life is joined to your spirit. All the potential for the release of every spiritual blessing in heavenly places is within you. When Jesus spoke of the mustard seed, He wasn't talking about something small. He was talking about a small seed that grows into a HUGE tree! He was talking about huge potential. Jesus said the Kingdom of God is like mustard seed that grows larger than all the other garden plants.[378] The mustard seed is one of the smallest seeds, but it grows into a treelike shrub that tends to grow out of control, spreading in every direction. It's been likened to the Kudzu vine that we deal with in the southern United States. It is a rapidly sprawling plant that climbs over trees or shrubs and grows so fast that it overcomes everything in sight.

Each one of us has the seed of potential for God's life to work in us and through us! The key is to see HIS faith working in us. Nothing is impossible to HIM who believes! Again, do you believe that HE believes?

Fear Not

In rest there is no fear. Over and over and over in the Gospels Jesus tells people to "fear not."

> But immediately Jesus spoke to them, saying, "Be of good cheer! It is I; DO NOT BE AFRAID." (Matthew 14:27, emphasis added)

I love that! If we know He is with us, fear should be replaced with good cheer. He spoke this to His disciples while their boat was being tossed by the waves in a violent storm! He's saying to us: "You can be of good cheer even in the middle of a storm if you know I am with you."

"DO NOT BE AFRAID; only believe, and she will be made well."
(Luke 8:50, emphasis added)

When fear is let go of, we can believe for miracles!

But the very hairs of your head are all numbered. DO NOT FEAR there-
fore; you are of more value than many sparrows. (Luke 12:7, emphasis
added)

Think about that: the fact that God knows everything about us is supposed to relieve our fears and give us a sense of value. That defies human logic. How many times have you thought, "Well, if they REALLY knew me..." But God knows everything about you, and He loves you anyway! Relax!

DO NOT FEAR, little flock, for it is your Father's good pleasure to give
you the kingdom. (Luke 12:32, emphasis added)

Our Father, ruler and owner of the universe, is pleased to give us the kingdom. So what do we have to worry about?

"Therefore I say to you, DO NOT WORRY about your life, what you
will eat or what you will drink; nor about your body, what you will put
on. Is not life more than food and the body more than clothing? Look at
the birds of the air, for they neither sow nor reap nor gather into barns;
yet your heavenly Father feeds them. Are you not of more value than they?
Which of you by worrying can add one cubit to his stature? "So why do
you worry about clothing? Consider the lilies of the field, how they grow:
they neither toil nor spin; and yet I say to you that even Solomon in all his
glory was not arrayed like one of these. Now if God so clothes the grass
of the field, which today is, and tomorrow is thrown into the oven, will
He not much more clothe you, O you of little faith?" (Matthew 6:25-30,
emphasis added)

Imagine that! God compares the lilies of the field to the glory of the wealthiest man who ever lived. He is saying to us that if we toiled and spun as hard as we could and amassed the greatest fortune known to man, it wouldn't even touch what God has done for us and what God has provided for us. But there's only one way to access it: by faith.

> *Therefore, having been justified by faith, we have peace with God through our Lord Jesus Christ, through whom also we have ACCESS BY FAITH INTO THIS GRACE in which we stand... (Romans 5:1-2, emphasis added)*

Justified through Jesus. Just as if I'd never sinned! That gives us the greatest peace that there is, and it gives us secret, private access by faith into His unlimited favor.

> *He who did not spare His own Son, but delivered Him up for us all, how shall He not with Him also FREELY GIVE US ALL THINGS? (Romans 8:32, emphasis added)*

Is anything more valuable than Jesus? If God gave us Jesus — His very best — how could He withhold anything good from us?!

Healing Testimony

Many years ago when my husband and I were newlyweds, he was stricken with a horrible disease that paralyzed most of his body and plagued him with many other symptoms. The prognosis was dire, and we had very little hope for a bright future. He improved somewhat over many months and was able to walk, but had attacks of the disease every few months so that he was under the constant care of doctors.

For eight years, we believed that this disease was God's punishment and His way of teaching us a lesson. When my husband was asked to speak in groups and give his "testimony," he would always say, "God put me on my back so that I would look up." We believed that God sent the disease. Of course, we didn't have a biblical foundation in the New Testament for that, but it was just the only thing that made sense to us. However, when you think about it, why do we go to doctors to get well if we believe that God made us sick? If we take that line of reasoning, we should stay home and let the sickness run its course and accomplish whatever God wanted to do with it. Trying to get well, taking medicine, surgery, and even having people pray for healing would be going against God's will if He gave us the sickness in the first place. Right?

So eight years into the disease, I was sitting on the couch in our den — the striped one with the hide-a-bed inside (you never forget the details of those Damascus Road experiences). I ran across a passage I had read many times before, but it was as if I had never seen it:

Is anyone among you sick? Let him call for the elders of the church, and let them pray over him, anointing him with oil in the name of the Lord. And the prayer of faith will save the sick, and the Lord will raise him up. (James 5:14-15)

My husband was sitting across the room in his leather chair, and I said to him, "We need to get the elders to pray for you." Prior to that time we had never heard about prayer for healing, even though we were active in church. However, from that point on we believed that it was God's will to heal my husband. We delved into the scriptures, had people lay hands on him, but mostly we looked to Jesus in the word, and we saw that He healed everybody that came to Him.

Of all the passages that opened my eyes to God's will concerning healing, Matthew 8:16-17 was the one that God used to completely solidify my unshakable belief that it is His will to heal:

Now when Jesus had come into Peter's house, He saw his wife's mother lying sick with a fever. So He touched her hand, and the fever left her. And she arose and served them. When evening came, they brought to Him many who were demon-possessed; and He cast out the spirits with a word, and healed all who were ill. This was to fulfill what was spoken through Isaiah the prophet: "HE HIMSELF TOOK OUR INFIRMITIES AND CARRIED AWAY OUR DISEASES." (Matthew 8:14-17, NASB, emphasis added)

Here is Jesus healing people to FULFILL the prophecy in Isaiah 53:5! I had always reasoned away God's promise of healing in Isaiah 53 by saying it referred to emotional healing or perhaps healing when we get to heaven. Yet the Bible clearly connects physical healing to Christ's atonement.

"Surely He has borne our griefs and carried our sorrows; yet we esteemed Him stricken, smitten by God, and afflicted. But He was wounded for our transgressions, He was bruised for our iniquities; the chastisement for our peace was upon Him, and by His stripes we are healed." (Isaiah 53:4-5)

End of story: Mark was gloriously healed, and Jesus got what He paid for.

Freely Give

Do you know why it's so important to receive what God has freely given? Because if we do not freely receive, we cannot freely give!

Heal the sick, cleanse the lepers, raise the dead, cast out demons. FREELY YOU HAVE RECEIVED, FREELY GIVE. (Matthew 10:8, emphasis added)

If we believe that anything stands in the way of God's grace in our lives, then we cannot freely receive. Is God's grace limited by natural circumstances? Is God's grace limited by sin? Is God's grace limited by demons? In the ministry I used to lead, we thought that we had to go through rituals of renouncing demons and all the powers of darkness before a person could experience the manifestation of God's power and grace. We thought that if a person could not forgive his father or his mother or his coach or his kindergarten teacher, he was stuck with the tormenters and on his way to hell until he forgave, FROM THE HEART! Yes, forgiveness is important, but until we freely receive God's forgiveness for ourselves, we have no lasting forgiveness to give! Freely receiving ANYTHING from God was nearly impossible in that environment. There were conditions to everything we were longing to receive.

When I look at the ministry of Jesus, I do not see Him requiring anything of anyone who came to Him. They simply came to Him in faith, and He healed them all![379] As many as touched Him were made completely whole.[380] I do not see Jesus questioning people when they came to Him for healing or deliverance. He didn't ask them, "Have you been taking your vitamins and laying off the soft drinks? If not, you can't expect anything from Me. Go home and clean up your act, and then we'll see what we can do." Or how about this one: "I noticed you arguing with your husband over there while you were waiting in the prayer line. I can tell that you are not a submissive wife and this is blocking your healing." You won't find Jesus ever saying to someone, "You have a generational curse. This is a tough one that will require a process of deliverance. Go repent of the sins of your forefathers and come back for your healing."

Once I shared this truth of the unconditional nature of Jesus' response to everyone who came to Him with a pastor whom I knew, and I could tell his blood pressure was rising. He said, "Tricia Gunn, you can't tell me that people can just go out and stuff their faces with donuts and smoke cigarettes and expect God to heal them!" I don't expect God to heal them. I believe He already did when Jesus received the stripes on His back and died on the cross two thousand years ago.

If people aren't asking us if we are saying that sin is ok, then we aren't preaching grace strong enough. Where sin abounds, grace abounds much more.[381] Jesus never condoned sin. Paul never condoned sin. But sin cannot stop God's grace. I cannot imagine anyone who has truly experienced the grace of God wanting to sin. It's just impossible. Grace is the answer to sin.

The people asked Jesus,

"What shall we do, that we may work the works of God?" (John 6:28)

Here was Jesus' answer:

"This is the work of God, that you BELIEVE in Him whom He sent." (John 6:29, emphasis added)

It's simple.

Begging God

Understanding the finished work of Jesus really takes the struggle out of faith. Faith is simply receiving what God has already provided through grace. Anything that Jesus died for is ours — and the list is long. Faith can't make God DO anything. Faith just receives what He's already DONE by His grace. It's just too simple for our brains to grab hold of. The natural mind can only understand deductive reasoning: do this, and you'll get that result. The things of God don't make any sense to the natural mind. My brain was blown some time ago by the idea that the work is finished. How can the work be finished if I haven't seen the answer to my need with my natural eyes? That's the way I used to look at. Yet, if we don't believe the work is finished, then faith is going to become a work. And from my experience, when faith becomes work, it's the worst taskmaster of all — untold hours of fasting and praying and crying out to God for Him to move, and the more people pleading with their faces on the floor before God, the better — as if God didn't care about or love people as much as we did. What nonsense.

Before I could be delivered from that mindset, I had to know what happened when Jesus said, "It is finished." More specifically, I had to know what happened TO ME when Jesus said, "It is finished." A few years ago, after being a Christian my whole life and working many years in ministry, I finally saw it! Jesus was unveiled to me. That day all the years of believing in an UNfinished work began to unravel. I learned what happened when I died with Him and rose again a new creation in Him. The result of all of this has been true REST. No more struggle to get God to do anything.

There are passages of scripture that I misinterpreted in the past and even taught others from my own lack of understanding. One of those passages is from Luke 11.

"Which of you shall have a friend, and go to him at midnight and say to him, 'Friend, lend me three loaves; for a friend of mine has come to me on his journey, and I have nothing to set before him'; and he will answer from within and say, 'Do not trouble me; the door is now shut, and my children are with me in bed; I cannot rise and give to you'? I say to you, though he will not rise and give to him because he is his friend, yet because of his persistence he will rise and give him as many as he needs." (Luke 11:5-8)

The misinterpretation that has been taught and believed by many Christians is that God is the so-called "friend" in that story, and we have to beg Him before He will give us what we are asking for.

What kind of "friend" would turn another friend away to go without food because he was tired and didn't want to be bothered? The point Jesus was making in this parable was the exact opposite of what many Christians think He was saying. Most Christians I know think He was saying that God is like that, and we need to persist and beg and plead with Him. Then, just to get us off His back, He'll give us what we're asking for. Once again, that's nonsense! The point Jesus was trying to make is that no true friend would treat another friend that way. It's evil! It follows that if a true friend who was merely human would never do that, then why in the world would we ever have to beg God for anything?

If you continue reading that passage in context, it's OBVIOUS what Jesus was saying about our Heavenly Father. So let's look at the very NEXT verse in Luke 11:

> *"So I say to you, ask, and it will be given to you; seek, and you will find; knock, and it will be opened to you. For everyone who asks receives, and he who seeks finds, and to him who knocks it will be opened. If a son asks for bread from any father among you, will he give him a stone? Or if he asks for a fish, will he give him a serpent instead of a fish? Or if he asks for an egg, will he offer him a scorpion? If YOU THEN, BEING EVIL, know how to give good gifts to your children, how much more will your heavenly Father give the Holy Spirit to those who ask Him!" (Luke 11:9-13, emphasis added)*

It's just plain dangerous to take passages out of context. On this particular mis-interpretation, millions of Christians have suffered unnecessarily. But the biggest problem with thinking we have to twist God's arm to get Him to do something for us, or use our "words of faith" to force Him to move on our behalf, is that it's a horrendous insult to God's character. It's saying that God doesn't want to help us!

The truth is that God loved us so much that He sent His only begotten Son for us, and He already provided everything we will ever need at the cross — way before we even needed it! There was a great, divine exchange that took place. For us, the greatest trade Jesus made with us was to become our sin so that we could become His righteousness. That made us sons and daughters of God and joint-heirs with Christ and heirs of God Himself. It couldn't get any better than that. We just need to believe it's true!

CHAPTER TWENTY

Peace

Key scriptures:
1 Peter 5:7-9; John 14:26-27; Mark 4:35-40; Mark 5:15, 18, 28-30, 33-36; Luke 10:38-42; Matthew 14:22-33

Did you know that your spirit is always at peace if you are a believer? It is never disturbed by outward circumstances. Just like God is not wringing His hands over the problems that we face, our spirit is in tune and in union with God and therefore undisturbed. This doesn't mean that we always feel at peace, though. Spiritual growth is a result of walking in the spirit and not after the flesh, and it will result in the manifestation of peace. Our emotions can be a means of expressing what is true in the spirit, or they can be a means of expressing what we see outwardly with our natural eyes. Whether we experience "peace that surpasses understanding" will depend on which eyes we are using.

You will keep him in perfect peace, whose mind is stayed on You, because he trusts in You. (Isaiah 26:3)

Even if the world is falling apart all around us, we can be filled with joy inexpressible. The key is keeping our eyes on Him.

Eternal life has already begun for those of us who are in Christ, so we can just believe: God's GOT IT because He already had it! He was and is and is to come. Living in His reality is where we need to live. The best thing we can do is live in this moment where heaven and earth meet. Eternity isn't time, and it isn't space. We can only access it in the present. We can't dwell in the past or worry about the future and still have our mind set on the spirit at the same time.

Casting Your Cares

This world and everything we face each day is in direct opposition to being at rest. It seems the enemy is on the prowl all the time. You've probably heard this verse:

Your adversary the devil walks about like a roaring lion, seeking whom he may devour. (1 Peter 5:8)

The devil is seeking people to devour through unbelief. That says to me that there are some that he can't find or if he finds them, he can't devour them. Now, we know he has been defeated and disarmed by the cross. He's been defanged, but he can still roar. If we read that verse in context, we'll see the key to keeping him seeking. The verse before that says,

...casting all your care upon Him, for He cares for you. (1 Peter 5:7)

The context is very clear: if we cast our cares on the Lord believing that He cares for us, the devil may sniff around like a lion looking for prey, but he won't be able to mess with us. We may see him coming, and even hear him roaring at us, but we just resist him and he has to flee.

Resist him, steadfast in the faith, knowing that the same sufferings are experienced by your brotherhood in the world. (1 Peter 5:9)

"Peace I leave with you"

Before Jesus went to the cross, He made a wonderful promise to His disciples. Because they would face tribulation in this world, He promised to leave them some help.

"But the Helper, the Holy Spirit, whom the Father will send in My name, He will teach you all things, and bring to your remembrance all things that I said to you. Peace I leave with you, My peace I give to you..." (John 14:26-27)

After three and a half years of watching Jesus teach, heal, deliver, and provide, the disciples were with Jesus on the last night before He would be taken from them. They didn't understand what was getting ready to happen, but Jesus did, and in John chapters 13-17 we have an absolute goldmine of encouraging words and promises that Jesus spoke to His disciples and to all who would believe in the ages to come. Whenever you feel hopeless or doubtful or persecuted, read through those chapters of John. I promise you will be strengthened in your faith.

In these final words to His disciples, Jesus promised that they would be severely persecuted for believing and spreading the Gospel, but He also promised to leave them with the most valuable and practical thing He could give them: PEACE. If believers could receive His peace, then they could walk in all of the other promises, such as the following:

Greater works will we do than even Jesus did. (John 14:12)
We can ask anything in His name and He will do it. (John 14:14)
We will bear much fruit. (John 15:8)
His joy will remain in us and be made full. (John 15:11)
We will love each other. (John 15:17)
We will be convinced of our righteousness. (John 16:10)
We will hear His voice. (John 16:13)
We will behold His glory. (John 17:24)
We will know His love. (John 17:26)

Jesus would have been speaking Hebrew to His disciples so He would have used the Hebrew word "shalom" for peace. According to Strong's concordance, "shalom" is completeness, soundness, welfare, safety, health, and prosperity.[382] It's more than just a peaceful, easy feeling. It's nothing broken and nothing missing. It's the kind of personal peace that He Himself had enjoyed here on earth. He was never ruffled or resistant to God's direction and voice. He displayed the peace that comes from unbroken communion with God. That's what He left us with!

"...not as the world gives do I give to you. Let not your heart be troubled, neither let it be afraid." (John 14:27, cont.)

The kind of peace Jesus left us with is not the kind the world can give us. It's not false and shallow and unsatisfying. The only requirement He gave us is to simply "let not our hearts be troubled." Being troubled comes first, then being afraid comes next. It's all about guarding our hearts. Because our spirit is at peace, our normal state as a believer is peace. It's a lot easier to maintain peace than to obtain it. If we don't ever let our hearts become troubled, we won't have to fight the battle of fear.

Throughout the years I have spoken Jesus' words to my own heart many times: "Tricia, let not your heart be troubled, neither let it be afraid." It's amazing what simply reciting that verse will do when the enemy fires his evil words of fear, doubt, condemnation, and pain to my mind. The voice of my Beloved speaks, and the devil flees.

A Restful Day in the Life of Jesus

In Mark 4-5 we see a day in the life of Jesus where we can witness firsthand this peace that He has given to us. Let's be a fly on the wall and behold Jesus on this "normal" day.

In Mark 4 we see Jesus start His day by preaching to multitudes from a boat in the water and then go off with His disciples to explain the parables He had just preached. Next, they got in a boat to go to the other side of the lake. Jesus knew the Gadarene demoniac would be on the other side, but his disciples were just along for the ride, clueless.

Storm at Sea

On the same day, when evening had come, He said to them, "Let us cross over to the other side." Now when they had left the multitude, they took Him along in the boat as He was. And a great windstorm arose, and the waves beat into the boat, so that it was already filling. But He was in the stern, asleep on a pillow. And they awoke Him and said to Him, "Teacher, do You not care that we are perishing?" Then He arose and rebuked the wind, and said to the sea, "Peace, be still!" And the wind ceased and there was a great calm. (Mark 4:35-39)

First, notice that Jesus said, "Let us cross over to the other side." If Jesus was in the boat, the One who spoke the world into existence, and He said "let's cross over," then nothing could possibly stand in the way!

The word "great" regarding the storm in the passage above indicates a violent, furious storm or hurricane.[383] While the waves were crashing against the boat, Jesus, worn out from the day, was resting His head on a pillow. Imagine that kind of peace: the noisiness of the storm, the tossing of the boat, and the splashing of the water into the boat did not wake Him up. He was awakened by the terrified cry of His disciples and their accusation that He did not care for them. He responded to their cry by commanding the storm, "Peace, be still." Be still literally means "to close the mouth with a muzzle."[384] I love that! When the tempests of life rage, we can speak out the words of the Master from within to every violent wind: "Be silent! I muzzle your mouth!" We speak to the mountain and it moves![385]

Next, Jesus said to His disciples,

"Why are you so fearful? How is it that you have no faith?" (Mark 4:40)

Jesus is saying, "How is it possible that you could be fearful and be in the boat with the One who created the universe and holds it all together?" These disciples believed that He was the Messiah. They had seen Him do miracles, but their lack of faith showed that they had a low estimation of Him.

What kind of estimation do we have of Jesus?

Gadarene Demoniac

When they arrived at the other side of the lake, only Jesus stepped out of the boat. He encountered the most demon-possessed man described in the Gospels, the Gadarene demoniac. This man was bound with chains, crying, and cutting himself. Jesus commanded the demons to come out of the man, and He cast them into a herd of swine.[386]

After the man was delivered of all the demons, Mark tells us in chapter 5 of four glorious results of this man's deliverance: 1) He was seated. 2) He was clothed. 3) He was in his right mind. 4) And the most beautiful of all: he wanted to be with Jesus.[387] These are the same results of deliverance for us: we're restful, we're self-controlled, our minds are sound, and we love to be with Jesus.

After this Jesus and His disciples got back in the boat and traveled back to the other side. A multitude gathered around Him again. This is when Jairus, a ruler of the synagogue, approached Him and begged Him to come and heal his twelve-year-old daughter. As Jesus was heading towards Jairus' house, He was touched by a woman who had been bleeding for twelve years.

Woman with the Issue of Blood

This woman was suffering from a blood disease and had spent all that she had on doctors. She was destitute and desperate, but she had heard about Jesus and believed in her heart that He could heal her.

"If only I may touch His clothes, I shall be made well." Immediately the fountain of her blood was dried up, and she felt in her body that she was healed of the affliction. (Mark 5:28-29)

Affliction is the Greek word "mastix" which means "a whip, scourge."[388] She had been whipped and scourged for twelve years by her disease, yet just by reaching out to Jesus, she was instantly relieved of this abuse from the enemy.

And Jesus, immediately knowing in Himself that power had gone out of Him, turned around in the crowd... (Mark 5:30)

Jesus stopped and turned around. Here He was on His way to heal a child who was at the point of death, but He stopped. Can you imagine having the presence of mind in an emergency situation to be aware of anything but the crisis at hand? Jairus' daughter died, by the way, before Jesus got there! But Jesus is never late even when the situation looks hopeless!

Jesus made time to pause for this woman. He said to her,

"Who touched My clothes?" ...the woman, fearing and trembling, knowing what had happened to her, came and fell down before Him and told Him the whole truth. And He said to her, "Daughter, your faith has made you well. Go in peace, and be healed of your affliction." (Mark 5:30, 33-34)

Why would Jesus say, "Your faith HAS MADE YOU WELL" and then say she would "BE HEALED" of her affliction? If she was well, why did she still need to be healed? Actually, the words "made well" and "healed" are two different Greek words.

The word "well" in the sentence "Your faith has made you WELL" is the Greek word "sozo." Sozo simply means healed.[389] But when He said "Be HEALED of your affliction" in verse 34 , it is the Greek word "hygies." What's the difference? "Sozo" meant that she was healed of the disease. The source of the disease was removed from her body so the bleeding stopped. But this did not mean that the effects of twelve years of the disease were restored. "Hygies" means to make whole, to restore.[390] Here is an example of "hygies":

...when they saw the mute speaking, the MAIMED MADE WHOLE, the lame walking, and the blind seeing; and they glorified the God of Israel. (Matthew 15:31, emphasis added)

Maimed means to lose a body part, literally to be crooked or mutilated.[391] In other words, where the maimed were crooked from the affects of diseases such as arthritis, they were made straight. Where the maimed were mutilated from events such as accidents, their flesh and bones were restored! What was Jesus saying to this woman? "Go into peace and you will be restored." The word "in" in the passage is actually the word "into," "eis" in the Greek.[392] Jesus was saying, "I've just opened a door for you to go INTO a place called 'peace.' Go and live there, and just watch what will happen to you. You will be restored!"[393] We should never underestimate the value of the peace that Jesus has given to us.

The Icing on the Cake of His Restful Day

After Jesus preached to multitudes, calmed the storm at sea, delivered the Gaderene demoniac, and traveled across the sea to meet multitudes again, the ruler of the synagogue, Jairus, met Him and begged Him to come to his house and heal his 12-year-old daughter who was dying. If you recall, it was while Jesus was walking towards the man's house that He stopped to heal the woman with the issue of blood.

Can you imagine stopping to talk to someone while you're headed to pray for a dying person? Wouldn't you call someone being on their death bed an emergency? If the woman had been bleeding for 12 years, what's a few more minutes going to matter? Why didn't Jesus rush to Jairus' home? What if the little girl died?

After Jesus had healed the woman with the issue of blood, and while He was still speaking to her, some people came from Jairus' house to tell him that his daughter had, in fact, died.

"Your daughter is dead. Why trouble the Teacher any further?" As soon as Jesus heard the word that was spoken, He said to the ruler of the synagogue, "Do not be afraid; only believe." (Mark 5:35-36)

Jesus said, "Only believe." In other words, "Put your confidence in Me, rely on Me, be persuaded that I can do this. Trust Me." Jesus went in with the parents and Peter, James, and John, passing friends and family who were wailing loudly. He touched the twelve-year-old girl and said, "Little girl, arise." And immediately she got up and walked.

Even when Jesus is late, it's not too late.

All of this in the course of a day!

His yoke is easy and His burden is light. The life of peace is the most exciting life. It's the life of the supernatural, and He's opened the door and invited us to live that life in Him.

The One Thing Needful

One of my favorite pictures of beholding Jesus is the story of His friend Mary sitting at His feet and listening to Him speak. I don't think this study would be complete without a glimpse into this revealing incident.

> *Martha welcomed Him [Jesus] into her house. And she had a sister called Mary, who also sat at Jesus' feet and heard His word. But Martha was distracted with much serving, and she approached Him and said, "Lord, do You not care that my sister has left me to serve alone? Therefore tell her to help me." And Jesus answered and said to her, "Martha, Martha, you are worried and troubled about many things. But one thing is needed, and Mary has chosen that good part, which will not be taken away from her."* (Luke 10:38-42)

Martha reminds me of my kids tattling on each other when they were little: "Mom! She's not helping us clean the kitchen!" Jesus responded to her, "Martha, I'm not going to tell her to help you. I like what she's doing." We get so offended when others don't work as hard as we do, and we miss the whole point that we are often making sacrifices that God never asked us to make! We beg God to make our husbands or our children or our co-workers help us. Sometimes He says, "Nope. I'm not going to do that. You need to learn how to rest and not be so dependent on others to change for you or to help you. And the way to do that is to HEAR MY WORD like Mary did."

Have you ever noticed that Martha didn't just blame Mary for not caring about her? She blamed Jesus, too! And notice that Jesus didn't chastise her for working too hard or even for accusing Him of not caring, He corrected her for not doing the ONE THING THAT WAS NEEDED. We don't need to reason this one away. Jesus doesn't lie! There's only ONE thing that is needed in this life, and it's what Mary was doing: sitting at His feet to hear His word. Where it says that Mary sat at His feet and "heard" His word, it's the Greek word "akouo." It means to attend to, to understand, to perceive.[394] Mary was attending to His word. She was perceiving what He was saying and understanding it. I'm sure Martha in all her busyness could hear what Jesus was saying; however, was she attending to it? Apparently not.

According to Jesus the one thing that is needful in this life is to attend to the word of God. That's probably the most important statement I have made in this entire book.

Walking on Water

The last picture of Jesus that I want to leave with you is the story of Jesus walking on the water in Matthew 14.

> *Immediately Jesus made His disciples get into the boat and go before Him to the other side, while He sent the multitudes away. And when He had sent the multitudes away, He went up on the mountain by Himself to pray. Now when evening came, He was alone there. But the boat was now in the middle of the sea, tossed by the waves, for the wind was contrary. (Matthew 14:22-24)*

Life can be like that. We can feel tossed by the waves with circumstances that seem beyond our control. Sickness, debt, and relational difficulties can make us feel like we're going down, and the waves are overcoming us. Whatever the storm is, I believe with all my heart that the answer is to see Jesus walking on top of it.

> *Now in the fourth watch of the night Jesus went to them, walking on the sea. (Matthew 14:25)*

The fourth watch was the last watch just before dawn. You know the old saying: "It's always darkest before the dawn." I don't know if that is literally true, but I know from experience that breakthrough often comes when everything in the natural goes against the promises of God in my heart. What I have learned is this: in my darkest hour, Jesus still has not abandoned me.

> *And when the disciples saw Him walking on the sea, they were troubled, saying, "It is a ghost!" And they cried out for fear. But immediately Jesus spoke to them, saying, "Be of good cheer! It is I; do not be afraid." And Peter answered Him and said, "Lord, if it is You, command me to come to You on the water." So He said, "Come." And when Peter had come down out of the boat, he walked on the water to go to Jesus. (Matthew 14:26-29)*

When Jesus said, "It is I," He literally said, "to be."[395] In other words, "You don't need to be afraid. I exist, and if I exist, I can walk on these waves. Nothing is impossible for Me." Peter wanted to believe it, but he had to throw out reason to do that. When Jesus told him to come, he came! Peter literally walked on the water as his eyes were fixed on the Author and Perfecter of faith.

Peter looked at Jesus, and he became like Jesus. It's the same for us!

But when he saw that the wind was boisterous, he was afraid,... (Matthew 14:30)

Peter took his eyes off Jesus. He looked at the circumstances, and fell from the supernatural into fleshly reasoning. Think about it this way: he fell from GRACE (receiving the undeserved favor of God) to LAW (believing that he was limited to the flesh).

Here's another question to ponder. What in the world does walking on water have to do with whether there are waves or not? If the water was perfectly peaceful without a ripple, can a person walk on it? Faith is drawing from something unseen and believing that nothing is impossible.

For we walk by faith, not by sight. (2 Corinthians 5:7)

Sometimes we have faith, but our unbelief comes and clouds it. When we look at Jesus, we have faith. When we take our eyes off of Him, we still believe He's there, but we begin to believe that the storm is bigger than He is. Unbelief rises up like waves that obstruct our view of Him.

...and beginning to sink he cried out, saying, "Lord, save me!" And immediately Jesus stretched out His hand and caught him, and said to him, "O you of little faith, why did you doubt?" (Matthew 14:30-31)

In Mark's account of this story, we see that not only did the disciples doubt, they were absolutely shocked and beside themselves with astonishment at this miracle of Jesus walking on the waves and then calming the storm. Mark gave us the reason that they were so astounded:

And they were greatly amazed in themselves beyond measure, and marveled. For they had not understood about the loaves, BECAUSE THEIR HEART WAS HARDENED. (Mark 6:51-52, emphasis added)

Mark was referring to a miracle from earlier in the day, the feeding of the five thousand. In Mark 6:52 where it says they had not "understood" about the loaves it's the Greek word "syniemi," and it means "to put the perception with the thing perceived."[396] In other words, they did not connect the miracle with the miracle Worker. They had just seen Jesus feed the five thousand, but even that amazing miracle did not penetrate their hearts enough to keep them from fearing the waves. Their hearts were hard to who He was (and is!) because they were more preoccupied with the waves than with the One who had authority over the waves.

The reason that they were so amazed that Jesus walked on the water is because they didn't expect Him to be able to do that. The disciples' "heart was hardened" because they did not consider — or connect the dots — that JESUS was the source of the miracle of the multiplication of the loaves and fish. They had seen Him solve an impossible problem (feeding the five thousand), but when they encountered another impossible situation just a short time later (the storm at sea), they were terrified. It wasn't until after the wind ceased and the power of God was displayed that they "were greatly amazed in themselves beyond measure, and marveled."

One day I pray that the body of Christ will get so accustomed to seeing the miraculous that nothing will shock us. We will praise Jesus in the middle of the storm, expecting a good outcome, instead of waiting until we see it to believe it.

In Mark's account of that day, we see the beautiful and powerful truth in the feeding of the five thousand that the disciples neglected to consider when the waves were crashing against them later in the day.

And when He had taken the five loaves and the two fish, He looked up to heaven, blessed and BROKE the loaves, and GAVE them to His disciples to set before them; and the two fish He divided among them all. (Mark 6:41, emphasis added)

In the past I used to teach that when the disciples distributed the loaves and fishes, it multiplied in their hands. But actually, that wasn't correct. If you look in the original Greek, you will see why.

Kenneth Wuest, a renowned Greek theologian, wrote in his commentary on the book of Mark the following note on Mark 6:41: "The verbs are in different tenses; the former ['broke'] in the aorist, the latter ['gave'] in the imperfect. The aorist implies instantaneous, the imperfect the continuous act."[397] Another important point about the aorist tense is that it's not only an instantaneous act, it's also an act that will never be repeated again. In other words, the BREAKING of the bread only happened once and was never repeated; however the GIVING of the bread was continuous.

Do you see what this means? The multiplication of the bread took place in JESUS' hands between the breaking and giving! Jesus was giving us a picture in this miracle of what happened when His body was broken at the cross. That one act would never be repeated, but the blessing flowing from that one act is continuous!

The picture I used to have was of Jesus carefully pinching off minuscule amounts of food giving each disciple a teeny tiny, almost microscopic, crumb of bread and morsel of fish the size of a granule of salt and telling them to go and feed the five thousand with it. It was all up to them. Now I picture the disciples running back and forth as fast as they can to catch the food multiplying from Jesus' hands. It's all about Jesus! It's all about His power and His provision.

All of Jesus. None of us.

What is the message here? May we consider Jesus in everything. May we remember the miracles we have seen in our lives and expect the same in the future. May we be less sensitive to the things of this world, and more sensitive to His presence with us!

Back to Matthew's account and the end of the story of Jesus walking on the water:

And when they got into the boat, the wind ceased. Then those who were in the boat came and worshiped Him, saying, "TRULY YOU ARE THE SON OF GOD." (Matthew 14:32-33, emphasis added)

Let this cause a joy explosion in your heart:

Truly, Jesus is the Son of God.

Truly, He has made you perfect and has come to make His home in you.

Truly, as He is so are you in this world.[398]

My friend, here is my last word to you: turn your eyes upon Jesus. Let peace reign in your hearts through faith, and may everything around you become dim in the light of His glory and grace.

Turn Your Eyes Upon Jesus

O soul are you weary and troubled?
No light in the darkness you see?
There's light for a look at the Savior,
And life more abundant and free:

Turn you eyes upon Jesus,
Look full in His wonderful face;
And the things of earth will grow strangely dim
In the light of His glory and grace.

Through death into life everlasting
He passed, and we follow Him there;
Over us sin no more hath dominion
For more than conqu'rors we are!

His word shall not fail you He promised;
Believe Him and all will be well.
Then go to a world that is dying,
His perfect salvation to tell![399]

Notes from Chapter 13, "Do You Trust Me?"

Following is a brief description of the eight covenants that God has made with man:

1. Edenic Covenant. This is the covenant that God made with Adam in the Garden of Eden. He gave man dominion over the earth and everything in it, with one stipulation: don't eat from the Tree of the Knowledge of Good and Evil. This covenant was broken when Adam and Eve ate from that tree. This covenant was fulfilled when Jesus became our righteousness through the cross, and restored authority to His body, the Church. (Genesis 1:26-30, 2:16-17)

2. Adamic Covenant. Because Adam and Eve ate from the Tree of the Knowledge of Good and Evil, these things would result: the ground would be cursed so that Adam would have to toil to get food, there would be enmity between satan and all of their descendants, there would be marital strife, thorns and thistles were introduced, the woman would be cursed in childbirth, and physical and spiritual death entered. However, the wonderful promise of a Savior was introduced in Genesis 3:15: "He [Jesus] shall bruise your head [satan's], and you shall bruise His heel." God promised that One born of the woman would be wounded in the process of destroying satan, but He

would crush satan's head. This curse was broken and this covenant was fulfilled when Christ became the curse for us. (Genesis 3:14-19)

3. The Noahic Covenant. This was an unconditional covenant between God and mankind. After the flood that destroyed the earth and everyone in it, God put a rainbow in the sky and promised that He would never again destroy the earth with a flood. He also promised prophetically through the prophet Isaiah that there would come a day when He would never be angry nor punish us again because of the atonement of Jesus. (Genesis 9; Isaiah 53-54)

4. Land Covenant with Israel, "The Promised Land." God made a covenant with Abraham concerning the promise of land for the people of Israel live in. This is a promise to Abraham's natural descendants. This is a covenant that still stands today. (Genesis 12:1-2, 13:14-17, 15:18-21, 17:8)

5. Abrahamic Covenant. This is the unconditional covenant of grace for all of Abraham's spiritual children, and that includes us as believers in Jesus Christ. This covenant promised that all of Abraham's descendants would be blessed on this earth, and benefactors of this covenant receive the Promised Land of eternal rest through the righteousness which comes by faith. This is the everlasting covenant of grace and was realized in the New Covenant of grace! (Genesis 12:3, 15:5-6, 17:1-6)

6. Mosaic Covenant. This covenant was made with Israel and consisted of the Ten Commandments, social judgments, and religious ordinances. It is also called "The Law." It was the covenant of works and the ministry of death and condemnation because of its impossible requirements. However, God called it good because it leads the sinner to redemption in Jesus. This covenant was fulfilled in Christ. (Exodus 20:1-31:18, 2 Corinthians 3:7-9)

7. Davidic Covenant. The unconditional kingdom covenant regulating the everlasting rule of David's future generations. God promised that the line of David would last forever and his kingdom would never pass away. From the line of David came Jesus Christ who would reign forever. This covenant was confirmed by divine oath in Psalm 89, renewed to Mary, and fulfilled in Christ as the Savior and Israel's coming King. (Psalm 89:34-37, Luke 1:31-33, Revelation 19:16)

8. New Covenant. This is the covenant of grace based upon the finished work of the cross of Jesus Christ. It flows from the Abrahamic covenant which was never annulled. This covenant promises eternal righteousness through the blood of Jesus for all who believe. It is unconditional and irreversible, and it is for all who are saved by faith in Jesus from Adam onward. (Jeremiah 31:31-33, Matthew 26:28, Hebrews 8:8-12, Romans 3:25)

Further study on the covenants will reveal differences of opinion on the specifics of all the covenants. My brief description of the eight covenants is my best synopsis from my own study of the Scriptures and other resources.

ENDNOTES

1 Keyes, Aaron. "Not Guilty Anymore." Revive. Integrity Music, 2009

2 Vine, W.E. "knowledge" (epignōsis), Vine's Expository Dictionary of New Testament Words, Minneapolis, MN, 1984. Print.

3 Hebrews 4:16

4 Revelation 22:1-2

5 Colossians 1:16-17

6 Hebrews 7:16

7 John 4:14

8 John 7:38

9 Albert Barnes, note on Matthew 5:40, Barnes' Notes on the Bible, Bible Hub, website: http://biblecommenter.com/matthew/ 5-40.htm, accessed 6-16-14

10 Kenneth S. Wuest, First Peter, Wm. B. Eerdmans Publishing Company, Grand Rapids, Michigan, 1942, p. 34 11 G3525 (nēphō), Thayer's Greek Lexicon, website: http://www.blueletterbible.org/lang/Lexicon/Lexicon.cfm?

11 G3525 (nēphō), Thayer's Greek Lexicon, website: http://www.blueletterbible.org/lang/Lexicon/Lexicon.cfm? strongs-G3525&t=KJV, accessed 5-17-14

12 G5342 (pherō), Thayer's Greek Lexicon, http://www.blueletterbible.org/lang/Lexicon/Lexicon.cfm?strongs=G1722&t=KJV http://www.blueletterbible.org/Bible.cfm?b=1Pe&c=1&t=KJV&ss=1#s=t_conc_1152013, accessed 5 17 14

13 apokalypsis, Holman Quick Source Bible Dictionary, Holman Bible Publishers, Nashville, TN, 2005, p. 19

14 revelation, "I. The Idea of Revelation," The New Bible Dictionary, Wm. B. Eerdmans Publishing Company, Grand Rapids, Michigan, 1975

15 Another small translation distinction is the use of the word "at" in the phrase "at the revelation of Jesus Christ." This word is the Greek word "en"8 and means "in" in English. Again, the word "at" would indicate something happening in the future.

16 euaggelion, Kittle, Theological Dictionary of the New Testament, Volume 2, Wm. B. Eerdmans Publishing Company, Grand Rapids, Michigan, 1966, p. 722

17 G1411 (dynamis), Thayer's Greek Lexicon, website: http://www.blueletterbible.org/lang/lexicon/lexicon.cfm? Strongs=G1411&t=KJV, accessed 5-17-14

18 1 Corinthians 13:1-3

19 G4991 (sōtēria), Thayer's Greek Lexicon, website: http://www.blueletterbible.org/lang/lexicon/lexicon.cfm? Strongs=G4991&t=KJV, accessed 5-17-14

20 Romans 8:17

21 Vine, W.E. "believe" (pisteuō), Vine's Expository Dictionary of New Testament Words, Minneapolis, MN, 1984. Print.

22 Galatians 3:13

23 2 Corinthians 4:18

24 John 19:30

25 Galatians 5:9

26 Andrew H. Trotter, Jr. "grace," Baker's Evangelical Dictionary of Biblical Theology, website: http://www.biblestudytools.com/ dictionary/grace/, accessed 6-12-14

27 G1411 (dynamis), Thayer's Greek Lexicon, website: http://www.blueletterbible.org/lang/lexicon/lexicon.cfm? Strongs=G1411&t=KJV, accessed 5-17-14

28 Vine, W.E. "truth" (alētheia), Vine's Expository Dictionary of New Testament Words, Minneapolis, MN, 1984. Print.

29 Colossians 2:14

30 G226 (hamartia), Thayer's Greek Lexicon, website: http://www.blueletterbible.org/lang/Lexicon/Lexicon.cfm? strongs=G266&t=KJV, accessed 5-17-14

31 Hebrews 7:25

32 John 3:18

33 Exodus 31:18

34 Romans 8:1

35 G2511 (katharizō), Thayer's Greek Lexicon, website: http://www.blueletterbible.org/Bible.cfm? b=1Jo&c=1&t=KJV&ss=1#s=t_conc_1160007, accessed 5-17-14

36 Leviticus 13:45-46

37 Romans 3:23

38 Revelation 4:3

39 H7107 (qatsaph), Gesenius' Hebrew-Chaldee Lexicon, website: http://www.blueletterbible.org/lang/Lexicon/Lexicon.cfm? strongs=H7107&t=KJV, accessed 5-18-14

40 H3559 (kuwn), Gesenius' Hebrew-Chaldee Lexicon, website: http://www.blueletterbible.org/lang/Lexicon/Lexicon.cfm? strongs=H3559&t=KJV, accessed 5-18-14

41 Vine, W.E. "convict" (elencho), Vine's Expository Dictionary of New Testament Words, Minneapolis, MN, 1984. Print.

42 2 Corinthians 10:5

43 Philippians 2:8

44 Isaiah 54:9

45 Hebrews 13:5

46 John 14:6

47 1 John 4:17-18

48 1 Corinthians 2:16

49 G5319 (phaneroō), Thayer's Greek Lexicon, website: http://www.blueletterbible.org/lang/Lexicon/Lexicon.cfm? strongs=G5319&t=KJV, accessed 5-18-14

50 Galatians 5:22-23

51 G3306 (menō), Thayer's Greek Lexicon, website: http://www.blueletterbible.org/lang/Lexicon/Lexicon.cfm? strongs=G3306&t=KJV, accessed 5-18-14

52 1 Corinthians 15:56)

53 Matthew 26:7, "Barnes Notes on the Bible", website: http://biblehub.com/commentaries/matthew/26-7.htm, accessed 7-2-14

54 Romans 8:19

55 2 Corinthians 4:16-18

56 Romans 8:11

57 H5849 (atar), Gesenius' Hebrew-Chaldee Lexicon, website: http://www.blueletterbible.org/lang/Lexicon/Lexicon.cfm? strongs=H5849&t=KJV, accessed 5-19-14

58 H1926 (hadar), Gesenius' Hebrew-Chaldee Lexicon, website: http://www.blueletterbible.org/lang/Lexicon/Lexicon.cfm? strongs=H1926&t=KJV, accessed 5-19-14

59 H3519 (kabowd), Gesenius' Hebrew-Chaldee Lexicon, website: http://www.blueletterbible.org/lang/Lexicon/Lexicon.cfm? strongs=H3519&t=KJV, accessed 5-19-14

60 H3515 (kabad), Gesenius' Hebrew-Chaldee Lexicon, website: http://www.blueletterbible.org/lang/Lexicon/lexicon.cfm? page=3&strongs=H3513&t=KJV, accessed on 6-13-14

61 Genesis 1

62 H430 (elohiym), Gesenius' Hebrew-Chaldee Lexicon, website: http://www.blueletterbible.org/lang/Lexicon/Lexicon.cfm? strongs=H130&t=KJV, accessed 5-19-14

63 Genesis 2:7, Blue Letter Bible (interlinear tab), website: http://www.blueletterbible.org/Bible.cfm? b=Gen&c=2&t=KJV&ss=1#s=t_conc_2007, accessed 6-21-14

64 H3068 (Yĕhovah), Gesenius' Hebrew-Chaldee Lexicon, website: http://www.blueletterbible.org/lang/Lexicon/Lexicon.cfm? strongs=H3068&t=KJV, accessed 5-19-14

65 S. Michael Houdmann, "What is YHWH? What is the tetragrammaton?" Got Questions?.org, http://www.gotquestions.org/ YHWH-tetragrammaton.html, accessed on 6-13-14

66 Adonai, "The Hebrew Names for the Lord," website: http://www.hebrew4christians.com/Names_of_G-d/Adonai/ adonai.html, accessed 5-19-14

67 H8432 (tavek), Gesenius' Hebrew-Chaldee Lexicon, website: http://www.blueletterbible.org/lang/Lexicon/Lexicon.cfm? strongs=H8432&t=KJV, accessed 5-19-14

68 Genesis 1:31

69 1 Corinthians 1:30

70 G3670 (homologeō), Thayer's Greek Lexicon, website: http://www.blueletterbible.org/lang/Lexicon/Lexicon.cfm? strongs=G3670&t=KJV, accessed 5-19-14

71 G3340 (metanoeō), Thayer's Greek Lexicon, website: http://www.blueletterbible.org/lang/Lexicon/Lexicon.cfm? strongs=G3340&t=KJV, accessed 5-19-14

72 G3340 (metanoeó), "HELPS Word-studies" Bible Hub, website: http://biblehub.com/greek/3340.htm, accessed on 6-13-14

73 G859 (aphesis), Thayer's Greek Lexicon, website: http://www.blueletterbible.org/lang/Lexicon/Lexicon.cfm? strongs=G859&t=KJV, accessed 5-19-14

74 John 16:33

75 1 John 4:4

76 Psalm 23:5

77 John 14:27

78 John 7:38-39

79 Colossians 2:13-15

80 Exodus 1:22

81 Matthew 2:16

82 Matthew 2:13

83 Matthew 27:46

84 Matthew 27:29

85 John 14:27

86 Matthew 6:34

87 Genesis 3:14

88 1 Corinthians 2:16

89 John 3:16

90 Exodus 25:17-22

91 John 20:12

92 1 Corinthians 15:45

93 Romans 8:21-23

94 2 Peter 1:4

95 Romans 8:16

96 2 Thessalonians 2:7

97 Colossians 3:5-7

98 Peter Toon, "Righteousness," BibleStudyTools.com, website: http://www.biblestudytools.com/dictionaries/bakers-evangelical- dictionary/righteousness.html, accessed 6-14-15

99 justification, "I. Meaning of the Word," The New Bible Dictionary, Wm. B. Eerdmans Publishing Company, Grand Rapids, Michigan, 1975

100 Romans 8:3

101 Derek Prince, Bought with Blood, Chosen Books, Grand Rapids, Michigan, 2007, p. 33

102 Romans 3:25

103 H1926 (hadar), Gesenius' Hebrew-Chaldee Lexicon, website: http://www.blueletterbible.org/lang/Lexicon/Lexicon.cfm? strongs=H1926&t=KJV, accessed 5-20-14

104 Isaiah 61:3

105 Genesis 3:11

106 The "much more's" listed come from the following scriptures: Matthew 6:30, Matthew 7:11, Luke 11:13, Luke 12:24, Romans 5:9-10, Romans 5:15, Romans 5:20, 2 Corinthians 3:9, 2 Corinthians 3:11, Hebrews 7:22, Hebrews 9:14

107 Revelation 13:8

108 G2983 (lambanō), Thayer's Greek Lexicon, website: http://www.blueletterbible.org/lang/Lexicon/Lexicon.cfm? strongs=G2983&t=KJV, accessed 5-22-14

109 Romans 5:17, Blue Letter Bible (interlinear tab), website: http://www.blueletterbible.org/Bible.cfm? b=Rom&c=5&t=KJV&ss=1#s=t_conc_1051017, accessed 6-14-14

110 G4050 (perisseia), Thayer's Greek Lexicon, website: http://www.blueletterbible.org/lang/Lexicon/Lexicon.cfm? strongs=G4050&t=KJV, accessed 5-22-14

111 Vine, W.E. "gift" (dōrea), Vine's Expository Dictionary of New Testament Words, Minneapolis, MN, 1984. Print.

112 G1343 (dikaiosynē), Thayer's Greek Lexicon, website: http://www.blueletterbible.org/lang/Lexicon/Lexicon.cfm? strongs=G1343&t=KJV, accessed 5-22-14

113 G936 (basileuō), Thayer's Greek Lexicon, website: http://www.blueletterbible.org/lang/Lexicon/Lexicon.cfm? strongs=G936&t=KJV, accessed 5-22-14

114 G2222 (zōē), Thayer's Greek Lexicon, website: http://www.blueletterbible.org/lang/Lexicon/Lexicon.cfm? strongs=G2222&t=KJV, accessed 5-22-14

115 Romans 5:19

116 H6495 (pĕqach-qowach), Gesenius' Hebrew-Chaldee Lexicon, website: http://www.blueletterbible.org/lang/Lexicon/Lexicon.cfm? strongs=H6495&t=KJV, accessed 5-22-14

117 G3922 (pareiserchomai), Thayer's Greek Lexicon, website: http://www.blueletterbible.org/lang/Lexicon/Lexicon.cfm? strongs=G3922&t=KJV, accessed 5-22-14

118 Romans 7:13

119 Galatians 3:17

120 G4121 (pleonazō), Thayer's Greek Lexicon, website: http://www.blueletterbible.org/lang/Lexicon/Lexicon.cfm? strongs=G4121&t=KJV, accessed 5-22-14

121 G5248 (hyperperisseuō), Thayer's Greek Lexicon, website: http://www.blueletterbible.org/lang/Lexicon/Lexicon.cfm? strongs=G5248&t=KJV, accessed 5-22-14

122 Kenneth S. Wuest, The New Testament, Wm. B. Eerdmans Publishing Company, Grand Rapids, Michigan, 1961, p. 360

123 John 6:63

124 Martyn Lloyd-Jones Romans, Exposition of Chapter 6, The Banner of Truth Trust, Carlisle, PA, 1989, pp. 8-9

125 G907 (baptizō), Thayer's Greek Lexicon, website: http://www.blueletterbible.org/lang/Lexicon/Lexicon.cfm? strongs=G907&t=KJV, accessed 5-22-14

126 Galatians 2:20, King James Version and Young's Literal Translation

127 1 John 4:17

128 Romans 14:23

129 G599 (apothnēskō), Thayer's Greek Lexicon, website: http://www.blueletterbible.org/lang/lexicon/lexicon.cfm? Strongs=G599&t=KJV, accessed 5-23-14

130 G226 (hamartia), Thayer's Greek Lexicon, website: http://www.blueletterbible.org/lang/Lexicon/Lexicon.cfm? strongs=G266&t=KJV, accessed 5-23-14

131 G264 (hamartanō), Thayer's Greek Lexicon, website: http://www.blueletterbible.org/lang/Lexicon/Lexicon.cfm? strongs=G264&t=KJV, accessed 5-23-14

132 G3049 (logizomai), Thayer's Greek Lexicon, website: http://www.blueletterbible.org/lang/Lexicon/Lexicon.cfm? strongs=G3049&t=KJV, accessed 5-23-14

133 1 John 3:5

134 G3985 (peirazō), Thayer's Greek Lexicon, website: http://www.blueletterbible.org/lang/Lexicon/Lexicon.cfm? strongs=G3985&t=KJV, accessed 5-23-14

135 This is the way that Jesus described the Pharisees in Matthew 23:27

136 G5219 (hypakouō), Thayer's Greek Lexicon, website: http://www.blueletterbible.org/lang/Lexicon/Lexicon.cfm? strongs=G5219&t=KJV. accessed 5-23-14

137 G1322 (didachē), Thayer's Greek Lexicon, website: http://www.blueletterbible.org/lang/Lexicon/Lexicon.cfm? strongs=G1322&t=KJV, accessed 5-23-14

138 1 Corinthians 2:16

139 Ezekiel 36:26

140 "Be Careful Little Eyes", author unknown

141 Tracey R. Rich, "Divorce", Judaism 101, http://www.jewfaq.org/divorce.htm, Copyright 5757-5771 (1996-2011), Tracey R. Rich, accessed on 5-24-14

142 Galatians 5:22-23

143 Philippians 4:13

144 Galatians 5:19-21

145 Romans 6:16

146 G4561 (sarx), Thayer's Greek Lexicon, website: http://www.blueletterbible.org/lang/Lexicon/Lexicon.cfm? strongs=G4561&t=KJV, accessed on 5-24-14

147 2 Peter 1:4

148 Romans 8:2

149 Romans 8:2

150 Kenneth S. Wuest, Romans, Wm. B. Eerdmans Publishing Company, Grand Rapids, Michigan, 1955, p. 127. My notes on the the Wuest commentary: The Bible translation in the text changes from NKJV to NASB as I move into Romans 8 because of the phrase "who do not walk according to the flesh, but according to the Spirit" in the NKJV

of verse 1. Many commentaries, including the commentary noted by Kenneth Wuest above, point out that this phrase was was not in the original manuscript for verse 1, but was added later.

151 G2631 (katakrima), Thayer's Greek Lexicon, website: http://www.blueletterbible.org/lang/Lexicon/Lexicon.cfm? strongs=G2631&t=KJV, accessed on 5-24-14

152 James 2:8

153 1 John 1:19

154 Ephesians 4:32

155 Colossians 2:10, Blue Letter Bible (interlinear tab), website: http://www.blueletterbible.org/Bible.cfm? b=Col&c=2&v=10&t=KJV#s=t_conc_1109010, accessed on 6-23-14

156 Kenneth S. Wuest, The New Testament, Wm. B. Eerdmans Publishing Company, Grand Rapids, Michigan, 1961, p. 472

157 Romans 4:3

158 Genesis 17:12

159 G2537, (kainos), Thayer's Greek Lexicon, website: http://www.blueletterbible.org/lang/Lexicon/Lexicon.cfm? strongs=G2537&t=KJV, accessed on 5-24-14

160 1 Corinthians 6:17

161 John 10:9

162 1 Corinthians 15:50-54

163 Psalm 103:12

164 Ephesians 2:5-6

165 1 Peter 1:23

166 Patricia Gunn, 2014, Life curriculum excerpts

167 G2222 (zōē), Thayer's Greek Lexicon, website: http://www.blueletterbible.org/lang/Lexicon/Lexicon.cfm? strongs=G2222&t=KJV, accessed 8-11-14

168 G5590 (psyche), Thayer's Greek Lexicon, website: http://www.blueletterbible.org/lang/Lexicon/Lexicon.cfm? strongs=G5590&t=KJV, accessed on 8-11-14

169 Exodus 12:12

170 apokalypsis, Holman Quick Source Bible Dictionary, Holman Bible Publishers, Nashville, TN, 2005, p. 19, accessed on 5-25-14

171 1 Peter 1:13

172 H3444 (yĕshuw`ah), Gesenius' Hebrew-Chaldee Lexicon, website: http://www.blueletterbible.org/lang/Lexicon/Lexicon.cfm? strongs=H3444&t=KJV, accessed on 5-25-14

173 Chris Poblete, "Yahweh Is Salvation," The BLB Blog, Blue Letter Bible, 1-31-12. website: http://blogs.blueletterbible.org/blb/ 2012/01/31/yahweh-is-salvation/, accessed on 5-25-14

174 Complaining, see Numbers 11:20

175 H4478 (manna), Gesenius' Hebrew-Chaldee Lexicon, website: http://www.blueletterbible.org/lang/Lexicon/Lexicon.cfm? strongs=H4478&t=KJV, accessed on 5-25-14

176 Psalm 105:37-41

177 Exodus 7:14-25

178 1 Corinthians 10:4

179 Colossians 2:14

180 Romans 5:20

181 Hebrews 8:5, Hebrews 9:23, Hebrews 10:1

182 Exodus 20:4

183 Exodus 32:19

184 John Darby, "2 Corinthians 3", (sixth paragraph), John Darby's Synopsis of the New Testament, BibleStudyTools.com, website: http://www.biblestudytools.com/commentaries/john-darbys-synopsis-of-the-new-testament/2-corinthians/2-corinthians-3.html, accessed on 5-26-14. Also see "2 Corinthians 3", Darby Translation, website: http://www.biblegateway.com/passage/?search=2+corinthians +3&version=DARBY, accessed on 5-27-14

185 Exodus 34:28

186 Exodus 24:4

187 Deuteronomy 31:24-26

188 Exodus 34:1

189 Exodus 33:1-3; Exodus 33:11; Exodus 33:15-17

190 Exodus 34:9, 29-35

191 Psalm 85:10

192 Exodus 25-27

193 Deuteronomy 10:5

194 Tracey R. Rich, "A List of the 613 Mitzvot (Commandments)", Judaism 101, website: http://www.jewfaq.org/613.htm, accessed on 6-2-14

195 G3954 (parrēsia), Thayer's Greek Lexicon, website: http://www.blueletterbible.org/lang/Lexicon/Lexicon.cfm? strongs=G3954&t=KJV, accessed on 6-2-14

196 H7759 (Shuwlammiyth), Gesenius' Hebrew-Chaldee Lexicon, website: http://www.blueletterbible.org/lang/lexicon/lexicon.cfm? Strongs=H7759&t=KJV, accessed on 5-24-14

197 Albert Barnes, "2 Corinthians 3:17," (see note on verse 17), Barnes' Notes, Bible Hub, website: http://biblehub.com/ commentaries/barnes/2_corinthians/3.htm, accessed on 5-26-14

198 H157 ('ahab), Gesenius' Hebrew-Chaldee Lexicon, website: http://www.blueletterbible.org/lang/Lexicon/Lexicon.cfm? strongs=H157&t=KJV, accessed on 6-2-14

199 James 1:17, Ephesians 1:3

200 St. Augustine of Hippo [354-430] is credited with this famous quote [Quaestiones in Heptateuchum 2.73]

201 G3339 (metamorphoō), Thayer's Greek Lexicon, website: http://www.blueletterbible. org/lang/Lexicon/Lexicon.cfm? strongs=G3339&t=KJV, accessed on 6-2-14

202 Exodus 33:18, 20

203 2 Corinthians 3:15-16

204 Romans 4:13, 16; Romans 9:8; Galatians 3:29; Galatians 4:28

205 Romans 7:18

206 Acts 8:3

207 Acts 9:4

208 Hebrews 13:8

209 John 8:32

210 Romans 4:3

211 Genesis 15:17: the smoking oven and burning torch also symbolized the coming afflictions that Abrahams descendant would suffer at the hands of the Egyptians, but God's glorious and joyful deliverance for them.

212 Hebrews 9:19-21

213 Genesis 17:5

214 Genesis 13:2; Genesis 24:35

215 For the entire story of Joseph, read Genesis, chapters 37-50

216 Galatians 4:21-31

217 Exodus 5:14

218 1 Corinthians 15:10

219 H1657 (Goshen), Gesenius' Hebrew-Chaldee Lexicon, website: http://www.blueletter-bible.org/lang/Lexicon/Lexicon.cfm? strongs=H1657&t=KJV, accessed on 6-11-14

220 Exodus 8:22 and 9:26

221 Galatians 3:17-18

222 Psalm 105:37

223 Exodus 16:20, NKJV

224 "Drug Abuse, Addiction, and the Brain," Substance Abuse and Addiction Health Center, WebMD, website: http://www.webmd.com/ mental-health/addiction/drug-abuse-addiction, accessed 6-15-14

225 John 8:36

226 H6213 (`asah), Gesenius' Hebrew-Chaldee Lexicon, website: http://www.blueletterbible.org/lang/Lexicon/Lexicon.cfm? strongs=H6213&t=KJV, accessed 7-5-14

227 Joshua 24:14

228 Romans 5:13

229 Genesis 15:1

230 Galatians 4:4-5

231 Vine, W.E. "redeem" (exagorazō), Vine's Expository Dictionary of New Testament Words, Minneapolis, MN, 1984. Print.

232 G1448 (eggizō), Thayer's Greek Lexicon, website: http://www.blueletterbible.org/lang/Lexicon/Lexicon.cfm? strongs=G1448&t=KJV, accessed 6-3-14

233 John 19:30

234 Romans 10:3

235 James 1:8

236 Genesis 12 and 20

237 James 2:23

238 Genesis 12-14, 20; Genesis 13:1 and 24:35

239 Hebrews 11:8-10, 17-19

240 G2889 (kosmos), Thayer's Greek Lexicon, website: http://www.blueletterbible.org/lang/Lexicon/Lexicon.cfm? strongs=G2889&t=KJV, accessed 6-3-14

241 John 13:3

242 Luke 12:32

243 G2758 (kenoō), Thayer's Greek Lexicon, website: http://www.blueletterbible.org/lang/Lexicon/Lexicon.cfm? strongs=G2758&t=KJV, accessed 6-17-14

244 G2673 (katargeō), Thayer's Greek Lexicon, website: http://www.blueletterbible.org/lang/Lexicon/Lexicon.cfm? strongs=G2673&t=KJV, accessed on 6-4-14

245 G1680 (elpis), Thayer's Greek Lexicon, website: http://www.blueletterbible.org/lang/Lexicon/Lexicon.cfm? strongs=G1680&t=KJV, accessed on 6-4-14

246 Hebrews 11:1

247 G1391 (doxa), Thayer's Greek Lexicon, website: http://www.blueletterbible.org/lang/Lexicon/Lexicon.cfm? strongs=G1391&t=KJV, accessed 6-4-14

248 2 Corinthians 4:13

249 G1252 (diakrinó), Thayer's Greek Lexicon, website: http://biblehub.com/greek/1252.htm, accessed 6-4-14

250 G1223 (dia), Thayer's Greek Lexicon, website: http://biblehub.com/greek/1223.htm, accessed, 6-4-14

251 G2919 (krinó), Thayer's Greek Lexicon, website: http://biblehub.com/greek/2919.htm, accessed, 6-4-14

252 Hebrews 12:2, Matthew 19:26

253 JewishAnswers.org, "Men and Women in the Synagogue," http://www.jewishanswers.org/ask-the-rabbi-category/womens- issues/women-and-prayer/?p=1003, accessed 6-4-14

254 Genesis 3:14

255 Revelation 13:18; 2 Thessalonians 2:3-4; 1 John 2:18, 22; 2 John 1:7; Daniel 7:8, 21

256 John 20:13

257 G3346 (metatithēmi), Thayer's Greek Lexicon, website: http://www.blueletterbible.org/lang/Lexicon/Lexicon.cfm? strongs=G3346&t=KJV, accessed 6-25-14

258 G331 (anathema), Thayer's Greek Lexicon, website: http://www.blueletterbible.org/lang/Lexicon/Lexicon.cfm? strongs=G331&t=KJV, accessed 6-4-14

259 Kenneth S. Wuest, Galatians, Wm. B. Eerdmans Publishing Company, Grand Rapids, Michigan, 1944, p. 38

260 Galatians 5:9

261 Note on Galatians 2:12: these certain men who "came from James" merely came from the Jerusalem church of which James was the pastor. They did not represent James.

262 Matthew 16:17-18

263 Acts 2:42

264 1 Corinthians 15:8-9

265 Butler, Trent C. Editor. Entry for 'Love Feast'. Holman Bible Dictionary. http://www.studylight.org/dictionaries/hbd/ view.cgi?n=3930. 1991.

266 Romans 7:6

267 Romans 7:8

268 G5485 (charis), Thayer's Greek Lexicon, website: http://www.blueletterbible.org/lang/Lexicon/Lexicon.cfm? strongs=G5485&t=KJV, accessed 6-5-14

269 Frederic Louis Godet, Commentary on First Corinthians, Kregek Publications, Grand Rapids Michigan, 1977, p. 270.

270 Galatians 1:6

271 James 5:16

272 Romans 6:14

273 1 Timothy 1:9

274 Galatians 2:18

275 "obey the truth" is omitted in the oldest manuscripts

276 Kenneth S. Wuest, Galatians, Wm. B. Eerdmans Publishing Company, Grand Rapids, Michigan, 1944, p. 88

277 Galatians 3:5, Blue Letter Bible (interlinear tab), website: http://www.blueletterbible.org/Bible.cfm?b=Gal&c=3&t=KJV&ss=1#s=t_conc_1094005, accessed 6-5-14

278 H5608 (caphar), Gesenius' Hebrew-Chaldee Lexicon, website: http://www.blueletterbible.org/lang/Lexicon/Lexicon.cfm? strongs=H5608&t=KJV, accessed 6-5-14

279 Galatians 3:16

280 Revelation 5:5

281 For further study, see The Real Meaning of the Zodiac, D. James Kennedy, Coral Ridge Ministries, 1989

282 Romans 6:1-5

283 2 Corinthians 4:13

284 Ven. Mahasi Sayadaw, "The Theory of Karma," Basic Buddhism, copyright 1996-2014, BDEA/BuddhaNet, website: http:// www.buddhanet.net/e-learning/karma.htm, accessed on 6-6-14

285 Galatians 3:15, Blue Letter Bible (interlinear tab), http://www.blueletterbible.org/Bible. cfm? b=Gal&c=3&t=KJV&ss=1#s=t_conc_1094015, accessed 6-9-14

286 Galatians 3:29

287 Romans 5:20

288 Romans 7:13

289 Words by William Cowper (1771), music: nineteenth-century meeting tune. Public domain.

290 1 Timothy 2:5

291 2 Corinthians 3:7

292 2 Corinthians 3:9

293 Kenneth S. Wuest, Galatians, Wm. B. Eerdmans Publishing Company, Grand Rapids, Michigan, 1944, p. 108. Wuest suggests that the word "Scripture" in Galatians 3:22 is referring to Psalm 143:2 or Deuteronomy 27:26 because both are referenced earlier in Galatians and both refer to condemnation under the law.

294 G3807 (paidagōgos), Thayer's Greek Lexicon, website: http://www.blueletterbible.org/ lang/Lexicon/Lexicon.cfm? strongs=G3807&t=KJV, accessed on 6-9-14

295 Kenneth S. Wuest, Galatians, Wm. B. Eerdmans Publishing Company, Grand Rapids, Michigan, 1944, p. 110

296 Daniel Johnson, "Prince Charles, the Longest Living Heir Apparent," The Telegraph, 11-11-13, website: http:// www.telegraph.co.uk/news/uknews/prince-charles/10436858/Graphic-Prince-Charles-the-longest-serving-heir-apparent.html, accessed 6-9-14

297 G5207 (huios), Thayer's Greek Lexicon, website: http://www.blueletterbible.org/lang/ Lexicon/Lexicon.cfm? strongs=G5207&t=KJV, accessed on 6-9-14

298 G3516 (nēpios), Thayer's Greek Lexicon, website: http://www.blueletterbible.org/lang/ Lexicon/Lexicon.cfm? strongs=G3516&t=KJV, accessed on 6-9-14

299 Kenneth S. Wuest, Galatians, Wm. B. Eerdmans Publishing Company, Grand Rapids, Michigan, 1944, p. 113

300 G4747 (stoicheion), Thayer's Greek Lexicon, website: http://www.blueletterbible.org/ lang/Lexicon/Lexicon.cfm? strongs=G4747&t=KJV, accessed, 6-9-14

301 John 1:17, NKJV

302 Kenneth S. Wuest, Galatians, Wm. B. Eerdmans Publishing Company, Grand Rapids, Michigan, 1944, p. 116

303 Mark 14:3

304 Adapted from "Identity, Acceptance, and Approval," Session 2, The Gospel of Grace video series, Rob Rufus

305 Acts 2:41

306 Romans 10:2-4

307 Genesis 14:18 and Psalm 110:4

308 Ten Commandments from Exodus 20:3-17, King James Version

309 1 John 4:19

310 Ephesians 4:32

311 John 13:34

312 Hebrews 12:20

313 2 Corinthians 3:7,9

314 Romans 8:2

315 G1097 (ginōskō), Thayer's Greek Lexicon, website: http://www.blueletterbible.org/lang/Lexicon/Lexicon.cfm? strongs=G1097&t=KJV, accessed on 6-10-14

316 Kenneth S. Wuest, Hebrews, Wm. B. Eerdmans Publishing Company, Grand Rapids, Michigan, 1947, p. 148

317 Daven Hiskey, "A Japanese Soldier Who Continued Fighting WWII 29 Years After the Japanese Surrendered, Because He Didn't Know", Today I Found Out, 2-9-10, website: http://www.todayifoundout.com/index.php/2010/02/a-japanese-soldier-who-continued-fighting-wwii-29-years-after-the-japanese-surrendered-because-he-didnt-know/, accessed 6-10-14

318 Hebrews 9:24

319 Exodus 40:12-15

320 Hebrews 9:1

321 Leviticus 16:8-10

322 Leviticus 16:21

323 Psalm 103:12

324 2 Corinthians 5:21

325 Isaiah 53:6

326 Isaiah 53:3, 12

327 Galatians 5:19-21

328 H3722 (kaphar), Gesenius' Hebrew-Chaldee Lexicon, website: http://www.blueletterbible.org/lang/Lexicon/Lexicon.cfm? strongs=H3722&t=KJV, accessed 6-10-14

329 Hebrews 10:2, Blue Letter Bible (interlinear tab), website: http://www.blueletterbible.org/Bible.cfm? b=Heb&c=10&t=KJV#s=t_conc_1143002, accessed on 6-19-14

330 G3953 (parrēsia), Thayer's Greek Lexicon, website: http://www.blueletterbible.org/lang/Lexicon/Lexicon.cfm? strongs=G3954&t=KJV, accessed 6-10-14

331 Definition of insufficient funds, Investopedia, website:http://www.investopedia.com/terms/i/insufficient_funds.asp, accessed on 6-11-14

332 1 Peter 1:10

333 2 Corinthians 5:16

334 Acts 10:28

335 Hebrews 12:2

336 G473 (anti), Thayer's Greek Lexicon, website: http://www.blueletterbible.org/lang/Lexicon/Lexicon.cfm?strongs=G473&t=KJV, accessed 6-19-14

337 Hebrews 13:5

338 G37 (hagiazō), Thayer's Greek Lexicon, website: http://www.blueletterbible.org/lang/Lexicon/Lexicon.cfm? strongs=G37&t=KJV, accessed 6-11-14

339 Hebrews 10:10, Blue Letter Bible (interlinear tab), website: http://www.blueletterbible.org/Bible.cfm? b=Heb&c=10&t=KJV&ss=1#s=t_conc_1143010, accessed 6-11-14

340 Hebrews 1:3, "Barnes Notes on the Bible", website: http://biblehub.com/nasb/hebrews/1-13.htm, accessed 6-11-14

341 James 4:7

342 Mark 5:8

343 Luke 13:12

344 G850 (aphesis), Thayer's Greek Lexicon, website: http://www.blueletterbible.org/lang/Lexicon/Lexicon.cfm? strongs=G859&t=KJV, accessed 6-11-14

345 2 Corinthians 10:5

346 Isaiah 54:9

347 Hebrews 13:5

348 John 14:6

349 G4190 (ponēros), Thayer's Greek Lexicon, website: http://www.blueletterbible.org/lang/Lexicon/Lexicon.cfm? strongs=G4190&t=KJV, accessed 6-11-14

350 Jude 3

351 G3670 (homologeō), Thayer's Greek Lexicon, website: http://www.blueletterbible.org/lang/Lexicon/Lexicon.cfm? strongs=G3670&t=KJV, accessed 5-19-14

352 From the time that Cain and Abel made the first sacrifice to God, Jews, including Noah and Abraham, made animal sacrifices to God in many places. When the Jews received the Ten Commandments on Mount Sinai, one of the new laws stipulated that Jews were no longer allowed to bring sacrifices to God just anywhere. They had to be made in the place where God's presence was (See Deuteronomy 12:13-14). In the desert, it was in the Tabernacle. Once King Solomon completed and dedicated in the Temple, animal sacrifices were offered only in the Temple. It would be a sin to offer sacrifices in any other place. Once the Temple was destroyed in 70 AD by the Romans Emperor Nero, no more animal sacrifices were offered. However, the book of Hebrews was written before Jerusalem's destruction.

353 G872 (aphoraō), Thayer's Greek Lexicon, website: http://www.blueletterbible.org/lang/Lexicon/Lexicon.cfm? strongs=G872&t=KJV, accessed 6-10-14

354 Hebrews 12:2, Blue Letter Bible (interlinear tab), website: http://www.blueletterbible.org/Bible.cfm? b=Heb&c=12&v=2&t=KJV#s=t_conc_1145002, accessed 6-10-14

355 Nehemiah 8:10

356 G3811 (paideuō), Thayer's Greek Lexicon, website: http://www.blueletterbible.org/lang/Lexicon/Lexicon.cfm? strongs=G3811&t=KJV, accessed 6-10-14

357 H5731 (Eden), Gesenius' Hebrew-Chaldee Lexicon, website: http://www.blueletterbible.org/lang/Lexicon/Lexicon.cfm? strongs=H5731&t=KJV, accessed 6-11-14

358 Genesis 2:15

359 H3427 (yashab), Gesenius' Hebrew-Chaldee Lexicon, website: http://www.blueletterbible.org/lang/Lexicon/Lexicon.cfm? strongs=H3427&t=KJV, accessed 6-11-14

360 Exodus 13:21

361 Exodus 17:1-7

362 H7508 (Rĕphiydiym), Gesenius' Hebrew-Chaldee Lexicon, website: http://www.blueletterbible.org/lang/Lexicon/Lexicon.cfm? strongs=H7508&t=KJV, accessed 6-11-14

363 H5999 (amal) and H6002 (Amalek), Bible Hub, website, http://biblehub.com/topical/a/amal.htm, accessed 6-11-14

364 Deuteronomy 25:17-19

365 H530 (emuwnah), Gesenius' Hebrew-Chaldee Lexicon, website: http://www.blueletterbible.org/lang/Lexicon/Lexicon.cfm? strongs=H530&t=KJV, accessed 6-11-14

366 Psalm 23:5

367 Deuteronomy 2:14 - "And the time we took to come from Kadesh Barnea until we crossed over the Valley of the Zered was thirty-eight years, until all the generation of the men of war was consumed from the midst of the camp, just as the Lord had sworn to them." After the spies were sent out, it took thirty-eight years for all of the men twenty and over to die in the desert.

368 Joshua 2:10

369 Deuteronomy 1:2

370 Numbers 14:29-30

371 Exodus 12:37

372 1 John 4:17

373 Vine, W.E. "sabbath" (sabbatismos), Vine's Expository Dictionary of New Testament Words, Minneapolis, MN, 1984. Print.

374 Ephesians 2:10

375 Romans 10:17

376 Mark 9:19

377 Romans 1:16

378 Matthew 13:31-32

379 Matthew 12:15

380 Mark 6:56

381 Romans 5:20

382 H7965 (shalowm), Gesenius' Hebrew-Chaldee Lexicon, website: http://www.blueletterbible.org/lang/Lexicon/Lexicon.cfm? strongs=H7965&t=KJV, accessed 6-12-14

383 Kenneth S. Wuest, Mark, Wm. B. Eerdmans Publishing Company, Grand Rapids, Michigan, 1950, p. 96

384 Kenneth S. Wuest, Mark, Wm. B. Eerdmans Publishing Company, Grand Rapids, Michigan, 1950, p. 98

385 Mark 11:22-24

386 Mark 5:1-20

387 Mark 5:15, 18

388 G3148 (mastix), Thayer's Greek Lexicon, website: http://www.blueletterbible.org/lang/Lexicon/Lexicon.cfm? strongs=G3148&t=KJV, accessed 6-12-14

389 G4982 (sozo), Thayer's Greek Lexicon, website: http://www.blueletterbible.org/lang/Lexicon/Lexicon.cfm? strongs=G4982&t=KJV, accessed 6-12-14

390 G1599 (hygiēs), Thayer's Greek Lexicon, website: http://www.blueletterbible.org/lang/Lexicon/Lexicon.cfm? strongs=G5199&t=KJV, accessed 6-12-14

391 G2948 (kyllos), Thayer's Greek Lexicon, website: http://www.blueletterbible.org/lang/Lexicon/Lexicon.cfm? strongs=G2948&t=KJV, accessed 6-12-14

392 G1519 (eis), Thayer's Greek Lexicon, website: http://www.blueletterbible.org/lang/Lexicon/Lexicon.cfm? strongs=G1519&t=KJV, accessed on 6-13-14

393 Kenneth S. Wuest, Mark, Wm. B. Eerdmans Publishing Company, Grand Rapids, Michigan, 1950, p. 113

394 G191 (akouō), Thayer's Greek Lexicon, website: http://www.blueletterbible.org/lang/Lexicon/Lexicon.cfm? strongs=G191&t=KJV, accessed on 7-17-14

395 G1510 (eimi), Thayer's Greek Lexicon, website: http://www.blueletterbible.org/lang/Lexicon/Lexicon.cfm? strongs=G1510&t=KJV, accessed 6-12-14

396 G4920 (syniēmi), Thayer's Greek Lexicon, website: http://www.blueletterbible.org/lang/Lexicon/Lexicon.cfm? strongs=G4920&t=KJV, accessed 6-24-14

397 Kenneth S. Wuest, Mark, Wm. B. Eerdmans Publishing Company, Grand Rapids, Michigan, 1950, p. 135

398 1 John 4:17

399 "Turn Your Eyes Upon Jesus," Helen H. Lemmel, 1922, Public Domain

ABOUT THE AUTHOR

Involved in ministry for decades, Tricia Gunn has always had a passion to see God's beloved children healed and delivered - physically, emotionally, and spiritually.

Tricia is a Bible study teacher, conference speaker, talk show host, and writer. Tricia has lead dozens of conferences and has touched countless lives through her teachings and writings. She is the wife of Mark and the mother of five wonderful children. Tricia and her family reside in Birmingham, Alabama. She is the founder of Parresia Ministries and host of A Real View talk show. Tricia is an ordained minister through Grace Church in Orlando, FL.

Visit her website for her latest teachings, announcements, and event schedule: www.ParresiaMinistries.com.

Made in the USA
Lexington, KY
30 November 2019